Baseball Between the Lies

Other Books by Bob Carroll

The Hidden Game of Football

The Cincinnati Reds Trivia Book

The Dodgers Trivia Book

The Boston Red Sox Trivia Book

The Whole Baseball Catalogue
(with John Thorn)

Baseball Between the Lies

The Hype, Hokum, and Humbug of America's Favorite Pastime

BOB CARROLL

A Perigee Book

New York

Perigee Books
are published by
The Berkley Publishing Group
200 Madison Avenue
New York, NY 10016

Library of Congress Cataloging-in-Publication Data

Carroll, Bob (Bob Newhardt)
Baseball between the lies : the hype, hokum, and humbug of
America's favorite pastime / Robert Carroll.
p.   cm.
ISBN 0-399-51857-6
1. Baseball—United States—History Miscellanea.   2. History—
Errors, inventions, etc.   I. Title.
GV863.A1C37   1994   94-2893 CIP
796.357'0973—dc20

Cover design by Lisa Amoroso

Printed in the United States of America
1   2   3   4   5   6   7   8   9   10

Contents

⚾ 1 ⚾

A Bad Case of Credulity: An Introduction

The baseball fan is a singularly trusting soul. He may be wise in the ways of the world, crafty in financial matters, prudent in affairs of the heart. He may wink at those who believe in Santa Claus or supply-side economics. He may even feel, deep down in his heart, that Shirley MacLaine is not clairvoyant. But deliver him a hunk of hokum in a plain, brown baseball wrapper, and he'll believe it. Whether it's an ancient historic whopper like Babe Ruth's called shot, or a new statistical sophistry like the game-winning RBI, or a timeless strategic humbug like the sacrifice bunt, baseball fans—at least several millions of them—will swallow the guff as easily as they bolt down a hot dog during a seventh-inning stretch.

Case in point. A couple of years ago while in a playful mood, I penned an outrageous piece of fiction for *Oldtyme Baseball News*, a publication directed toward a very knowledgeable clientele. At the time, I figured there couldn't be anyone over the age of ten who still believed that General Abner Doubleday had really invented baseball on the green up in Cooperstown. That story had been in the dumper since before Gaylord Perry learned to spit. So, facing an unforgiving deadline and feeling secure in the belief that *everyone* would get the joke, I sent off the following to the editor:

A newly discovered document suggests that contributions to American sport by the Doubleday family may have been far greater than is presently believed.

The document in question is a letter written to the Mills Commission [created by Albert Spalding in 1904 to investigate the true origin of baseball] by Hamilton J. Cresap in August of 1904. It was found only this year in an old trunk stored in the attic of Mrs. Louise Cresap Haines, Hamilton Cresap's great-granddaughter. Mrs. Haines resides in Credulous Hollow, New York, near Cooperstown. She happened on the trunk while looking for possible contributions she might make to the local old clothing drive conducted by the the Third Methodist Church.

The letter was addressed and sealed but never mailed. Mrs. Haines has investigated her ancestor's history through the family Bible and news clippings from the *Credulous Hollow Gazette*. She believed the letter was unmailed because Cresap met an untimely demise beneath the wheels of a Coopers Brew beer truck before he could consign his story to the post office. Handwritten on lined paper, the contents of the letter are here published for the first time.

August 17, 1904

Dear Mr. Mills & Gentlemen,

The last time I talked to my old friend A. Graves he told me he had communicated some information to you about our mutual acquaintance A. Doubleday and a certain day in 1839. Unfortunately, from his description, Mr. Graves seems to have got some of his facts wrong.

I well remember that April morning for it happened to be my sixteenth birthday. My uncle George Cresap gave me a new bat for the occasion. I named it "Herschel" and put it in a cage in my room. As it turned out, Herschel was not a very good pet. He slept all day and caused quite a ruckus at night. I finally released him to the more congenial confines of the Third Methodist Church belfry.

Later on the morning in question, a number of us boys turned out with ballbat and ball at our local green, intent upon a rousing game of One-Old-Cat. We were met there by A. Doubleday. However, this was not Abner but instead his first cousin Anser.

I can understand why Mr. Graves mis-remembered. No doubt all of us who knew him would like to forget Anser. He was a perverse individual, who gained pleasure by forcing others to his will. For a time he was known as "Bully" Doubleday. This was later shortened to "Bull."

Doubleday told us we were not going to play our usual game of One-Old-Cat but instead a new game that he'd thought up in his spare moments at the Cooperstown Iron Foundry where he worked. He ordered us all home to procure the necessary equipment.

When we returned we discovered that Bull had set four stones on the lawn, placed so as to form the corners of a rectangle. These, he instructed, were the boundaries around which we were to race. Then we all put on our roller skates and spent the morning playing Bull Doubleday's new game which he called "Roller Derby."

The last I heard of Anser Doubleday was that he had disgraced his family by showing the yellow streak at the Battle of Manassas. In fact, his cowardice was so pronounced that the affair has since been widely known as "The Battle of Bull's Run."

In hopes that this will clear up any unfortunate misunderstandings caused by my old friend Graves' faulty memory, I remain

> Your Obedient Servant,
> H. Cresap

Now understand, there was no lady, no great-grandfather, no letter, no Anser Doubleday, and no Credulous Hollow, New York. I'd made 'em all up on a day when my time might have been better spent raking leaves. When the little yarn was finally published, I hoped someone might get a chuckle out of it. Then I returned to writing a more serious piece on the South Uruguayan three-toed gecko.

I had just looked up how to spell gecko when my telephone rang. It was the *Oldtyme Baseball News* editor asking what he should do with "the letters."

"What letters?" I asked naively.

It turned out he was getting letters about the Doubleday story. Some letter writers still defended Abner as the Originator, but most were along the lines of "In light of this startling new evidence . . ."

"You mean they actually believed it?" I yelped. "It was all fake!"

"Well, I *thought* it was," the editor said, his voice awash in doubt, "but . . ."

Looking back, I should have known better. After all, there was the case of Sidd Finch, or, to give it the full-blown title it got when George Plimpton published it in book form in 1987, *The Curious Case of Sidd Finch*. Sidd was a Tibetan pitcher with a 168 m.p.h. fastball who began his career as an April Fool's joke in *Sports Illustrated*. Yet there were people who actually took him seriously. As I recall, the Mets supposedly held his rights; you gotta wonder if that helped season ticket sales in New York.

Years ago, some folks thought Frank Merriwell was straight biography. Maybe it's in our national character. Tell us a baseball story, no matter how absurd, and a lot of us are going to buy it. I guess in our hearts-of-hearts we want very much to believe there's no lying in baseball.

Of course, believing in the Easter Bunny is nice too. Just don't bet him to win, place, or show.

All that simmering baseball susceptibility presents a problem when one sets out to write about baseball's lies and legends. I probably won't have to go into hiding as the Salman Rushdie of the diamond set; after all, baseballers are *forgiving* fanatics. But where does one start? Which lie came first? Where does one end? What's the latest legend?

Earlier I mentioned my conviction that *everyone* knew the Abner Doubleday story was complete malarkey. I was quickly proven wrong. And since then, I listened to a respected play-by-play announcer not only credit Doubleday with baseball's invention but even add up the years since 1839 to see what anniversary should be celebrated. Remember, this was no casual fan who takes in a baseball game on the nights when a tractor pull isn't in town. This was a guy who daily presumes his knowledge of the game to exceed that of owners, managers, players, and umpires.

While many of the big legends date from the last century, a few have been foisted upon the public only recently. For the most part, the modern fan may not be quite so naive as was the fan of fifty years ago. Modern fans are more likely to place their faith in statistics or the "Book," that wondrous compendium of misinformation that managers have been using to excuse their bonehead maneuvers ever since Connie Mack had acne.

Why don't we start off with the primal legends, traverse whole generations of gullibility, and then grope our way through the smoke and mirrors of modern stats and strategy. All of which brings us back to Abner Doubleday again . . .

☾ 2 ☾

The Doubleday
Duplícíty

One night in 1889, about three hundred people got together at Delmonico's famous restaurant in New York to honor a batch of baseball players who had just returned from an around-the-world tour sponsored by Albert Goodwill Spalding, president of the National League baseball team we now call the Cubbies, and, not so incidentally, owner of America's largest sporting goods business. Albert goodwillingly figured if he could get the fellows along the Thames and the fellahin along the Nile playing baseball, he'd have some juicy new markets for his bats and balls. So he shipped away during the off-season with a couple dozen baseballers who showed off their diamond skills to thousands of natives who wondered just what the hell those Americans were doing. The triumphant return from Spalding's less-than-triumphant tour made a dandy excuse for steaks, whiskey, cigars, and speeches at Delmonico's. Eating, drinking, smoking, and orating in the crowd that night were such celebrities as Chauncey DePew, a famous speechmaker despite a surname that lent itself to amusing comment, Mark Twain, the author of novels far funnier than anything said that evening, Theodore Roosevelt, just getting started on a career that would land his phiz on Mt. Rushmore, and, unfortunately, Abraham Gilbert Mills.

A. G. Mills had been president of the National League for a couple of years in the mid-'80s. During his short time as prexy, he'd resolved a ton of disputes among N.L. clubs and between his league and other leagues. Naturally, they called him the "Bismarck of Baseball," which makes sense if you know anything about German history. Another of his triumphs was to get the reserve clause, with which teams kept the rights to a player's

11

services throughout his career, nailed firmly into every player contract, ensuring that his legacy would be a lot of litigation in the next century. With all that going for him, they had to invite him to the party. Besides, he was the emcee.

Lord knows what all A. G. said in his role as emcee that night. Perhaps, Carsonesque, he deadpanned some snappy patter about greenbacks and a few zingers about Custer. Or perhaps he played it straight, assuming that with enough whiskey the crowd would be as well done as the steaks. At any rate, toward the end of the evening, just before last call, Mills stood up before God and all those people and declared that "patriotism and research" had established once and for all time that the game of baseball was strictly and absolutely American in its origin. Mills may have been saturated with patriotism or whatever, but as far as research went, he knew about as much as a sea cow knows about dairies.

It didn't matter. The crowd was ready to believe and started hollering "No rounders! No rounders!" the way Al Pacino yelled "Attica!" in that dog movie. The New York *Clipper* reported that Mills' assertion "forever squelched" any claims that baseball had begun as the simple English game of rounders. This dedication to prognostication based on investigative journalism may explain why you can no longer buy a New York *Clipper* to peruse while munching your morning Danish, but it doesn't tell us why everybody was so ready to believe A. G. Mills' denunciation of rounders when Henry Chadwick said the story was a totally different caldron of seafood.

Father Knew Best

Henry Chadwick was born in England in 1824. He and the rest of the Chadwicks immigrated to Brooklyn, which is usually identified as part of the United States, in 1837. Young Henry grew up to be a serious sort of fellow who nevertheless carved out a career for himself writing about baseball, a subject most scriveners deemed too frivolous for the weighty work of shoving adjectives against nouns. Henry wasn't quite the first baseball writer, and, unless you're really hung up on nineteenth-century verbiage, he wasn't the best. But he was without doubt the most knowledgeable, ubiquitous, and influential baseball writer of his day. You could almost go so far as to say, as some have, that he was the first sportswriter. He wrote miles of newspaper columns about games and players and piles of books about seasons and rules. And those miles and piles got him tagged, unofficially of course, as "The Father of Baseball." He even invented the box score, although his rudimentary box was small potatoes compared to the tell-all, take-a-quarter-hour-to-read box scores you find in *USA TODAY* today.

From the mid-nineteenth century to the beginning of the twentieth, Chadwick was pretty much the last word on baseball. But he *would* keep saying one thing that rubbed a lot of people the wrong way. According to Henry, the game that was sweeping America and rapidly becoming our most accessible religious experience was actually descended from an old English game called "rounders," which, if you come to think of it, meant "The Father of Baseball" was denying his own paternity. Anyone who's ever played rounders knows that it is indeed played with a bat and ball and that the ball is pitched and batted and then the batter runs like hell around the bases. So Henry had a pretty good argument, because that *does* sound an awfully lot like baseball. You know the drill: "If it walks like a duck . . ."

But some people refused to be convinced. They were bound and determined to make this particular duck into an eagle. It wasn't so much what Chadwick said as WHEN he said it. Remember, in the latter part of the nineteenth century, the U.S. was just beginning to feel its oats. There it was, emerging as a world power for the first time, big and brawny and very much unsure of itself. When a nation's psyche hits that emerging state in its time line, a scary mixture of unbridled arrogance and bridled self-doubt often results in its setting out to prove that it's way ahead of everybody else in everything all the time and always has been. If you're old enough, you might remember back in the 1950s when the U.S.S.R. got to the point of being a superpower, we had Russians taking bows for inventing everything from the electric light to rock and roll. We laughed at the Russkies then, little remembering that we'd gone through our own jingoistic stage only about four score years before.

Another thing to remember about the late nineteenth century is that, as a people, we were none too fond of England at the time. Today, of course, we think of the English as our dear friends, having exchanged gifts like our army (twice) for their Beatles. But back then in the 1800s, we really didn't trust those guys. There were still old folks alive who could remember our second war with the Brits (the War of 1812), and then, during our Civil War, they'd gone and meddled around just enough to be a pain. And besides, they talked funny.

So the upshot was that when Henry Chadwick said Our National Pastime started out as an English game, a lot of true-blue sons of the red, white, and blue got very uptight. They quickly pointed out that rounders had *four* bases, which weren't really bases anyway but poles stuck in the ground. Moreover, in rounders, the runner ran around those poles *clockwise*, which was certainly unbaseballish. *And* he could be put out by plunking him with a thrown ball. That was positively un-American! Well, anyway, unhealthy.

The Commission

Things stayed impassed for a dozen years with the Spalding-Mills crowd inveighing against rounders and Chadwick defending the old English game. None of them were getting any younger, and Spalding must have begun to worry that Chadwick would outlive him and thereby get in the last word (which no doubt would be "rounders"). Ironically, one of Chadwick's duties was as editor of the annual *Spalding Base Ball Guide* published by you-know-who. In 1903, Chadwick included in the annual a long dissertation on the history of baseball going all the way back to its origin as the R-game. Spalding himself retaliated with a longer dissertation putting forth the irrefutable argument that baseball was entirely American in origin because he said so.

At last, Spalding caused a blue-ribbon commission to be set up to actually investigate instead of pontificate. That looked like a step forward until you noticed that the committee was stacked with National League president Nick Young, former N.L. president Morgan Bulkeley, and a couple of sporting goods magnates in George Wright and Al Reach, all of whom were already firmly in Spalding's All-American corner. The chairman was none other than old "No Rounders" Mills. It was like sending the mice to investigate the curious disappearance of the cheese.

To give them credit, the committee didn't do what you might expect—like announce their findings while on the way to their first meeting. They waited a couple of years before coming down four-square on the Spalding–America First side. Not only that, they actually pinpointed the time and place of baseball's invention as 1839 at Cooperstown, New York, and named its inventor as Civil War hero General Abner Doubleday. That certainly settled *that*!

The Mills Commission admitted to getting, oh, lots and lots of evidence and statements sent in from all over the country (including a letter from Henry Chadwick), but most of the stuff was later lost in a convenient fire—apparently the same kind of conflagration some companies develop just before audits. None of it really proved anything, the commission said. And fortunately, the one piece of absolute, pristine, take-THAT! rounders! evidence was still safe.

Baseball's smoking gun came in the form of a letter from one Abner Graves, a mining engineer from Denver, but originally a native of Cooperstown. Graves said he had actually been there on that day in 1839 when young Abner told them how to play, directed them where to stand, and even gave his creation a name—Base Ball.

Although much of the baseball establishment was willing to tie its history to the Book of Graves, a few uncomfortable questions were raised.

Like, how accurate could the old man's memory be after more than sixty years when few of us remember what we had for lunch yesterday?

Or, because Doubleday showed a bunch of kids how to play baseball, does that prove he invented it? Miss Ziegler taught us algebra but *she* didn't *invent* it.

Or, what was Doubleday doing at Cooperstown that spring when he was supposed to be at West Point? Did the army suspend the A.W.O.L. rules for baseball?

Or, how come Doubleday went his whole life (he died in 1893) and even wrote his memoirs and never mentioned to man or beast that he had thought up America's pastime? Did it slip his mind?

And, finally, the game that Graves described Doubleday as inventing had four bases and allowed "plunking." So, when you come right down to it, doesn't that sound more like rounders or one of its derivatives like "One Old Cat" than it does like baseball anyway?

On to Cooperstown

To anyone who looked into the thing with an open mind, the Graves scenario was obviously tapioca, but that didn't keep the Doubleday yarn from being accepted. It was, after all, a lot easier for pseudo-historians to credit baseball's beginning to a particular person in a particular time and place than to go into a boring, long-winded explanation about rounders. Furthermore, Doubleday was a legitimate hero—he fired the first Union gun at Fort Sumter—so why not add another feather to his cap? And he had that great, old-fashioned name that conjured up visions of lemonade on the porch swing, horse-drawn milk carts on Main Street, and kids playin' ball on the vacant lot next door. Wotthehell! If baseball wasn't invented by Doubleday, it *should* have been!

About thirty years after the Graves letter, an old, beat-up baseball was discovered in a Cooperstown trunk and immediately labeled THE Doubleday Baseball much like Crusaders used to identify every chunk of wood found in the Holy Land as part of the true cross. The baseball was put on display and, along with the Doubleday Legend, helped get the Baseball Hall of Fame located at Cooperstown.

Cooperstown, home of James Fenimore Cooper, who wrote *The Last of the Mohicans* and lots of other books no one's read in years, is a pretty little town in upstate New York. Having a Hall of Fame there lets the shopkeepers on the main drag sell stuff other than Cooper memorabilia and Mohican-on-a-Sticks. From a commercial standpoint, putting the Hall there worked out fine. But establishing a Hall of Fame anywhere also meant that there'd be a sort of research center which would in turn cause scholars and such ilk to start checking into the facts. If you put a research center for the study of coffee stains over your garage, you'd be knee-deep in coffee-stain experts within the week. It's a natural law: academia abhors a vacuum.

The paint was barely dry on the Hall of Fame's front door when in 1940 Robert W. Henderson published *Baseball: Notes and Materials on Its Origins*. Under that catchy title, Mr. Henderson poked so many holes in the Doubleday Legend, you could drain your pasta in it. In a little book of children's games that came out in London in 1829, ten years before and an ocean away from Doubleday's supposed invention, Henderson found the rules for rounders. He traced them to this side of the Atlantic where five years later (and still a half decade before Doubleday) they were republished as "Base Ball."

After that came the deluge. More and more references to pre-1839 baseball kept turning up in dusty manuscripts, some preceding Abner by as much as a hundred years. If there's one thing in this world you can absolutely lay the rent money on it's that Abner Doubleday did *not* invent baseball.

So how does the Baseball Hall of Fame handle all this anti-Doubleday stuff? In a recent program commemorating the latest enshrinees, three and a quarter pages are devoted to retelling the story of of the Mills Commission, the Graves letter, and the Doubleday Baseball. Then comes a paragraph that begins, "From time to time over the years, various critics have challenged the speculation on Doubleday." Three short sentences sum up the evidence against Doubleday, along with the grudging admission that "Many of these contradictory theories have been well-documented by their proponents."

Then the program dispenses with the whole subject as apparently beneath consideration: "Whatever may or may not be proved in the future concerning Baseball's true origin is in many respects irrelevant at this time. If Baseball was not actually first played here in Cooperstown by Doubleday in 1839, it undoubtedly originated about that time in a similar rural atmosphere."

But deeds speak louder than words, as my grandfather used to say loudly. After more than fifty years of elections, Abner Doubleday hasn't come close to getting a plaque in the Hall of Fame that honors the game they'd have you think he invented.

⚾ 3 ⚾

The Cartwright
Addendum

Enshrined in the Baseball Hall of Fame are most of the big baseball names from the past along with quite a number of people whose "fame" today doesn't extend much beyond the corners of their bronze plaques. If you ran across one of the maybe hundred baseball fans who can correctly identify every one of the more than two hundred Hall of Fame enshrinees, you wouldn't want to challenge him to a trivia contest. Nevertheless, former players like Bobby Wallace and Elmer Flick were famous in their day. Even executives like Will Harridge and umpires like Tom Connolly were no strangers to the sports page in their prime.

However, one enshrinee leads the league in obscurity. He is not only generally unknown today, he was even less famous a hundred and fifty years ago when he was supposedly doing the things that eventually got him named to the Hall of Fame. Let's have three cheers for Alexander Joy Cartwright, Jr.

Who?

All right, let's look at his plaque. The likeness shows an honest face ringed by longish hair and one of those neatly trimmed jawline beards that tend to make the wearer look like his muffler is too high. Could this be the first Amish Hall of Famer? No, according to the plaque, A. J. Cartwright, Jr., was the "Father of Modern Baseball."

Now wait a minute! Henry Chadwick was the "Father of Baseball," Harry Wright was the "Father of Professional Baseball," James Madison was the "Father of the Constitution," and Necessity was the "Mother of Invention." What's this "Modern Baseball" stuff?

A. J. Jr.'s plaque continues: "Set bases 90 feet apart. Established 9 innings as game and 9 players as team. Organized the Knickerbocker Baseball Club of N.Y. in 1845. Carried baseball to Pacific Coast and Hawaii in Pioneer Days." An HOF induction day program also gives him credit as the one who "provided for three outs per side, set an unalterable batting order, and eliminated throwing the ball at a runner to retire him." Whew! You've got to admit that anybody who did all that and still found time to trim his beard deserves a little recognition.

Which is exactly how the Hall of Fame electors felt back in 1938 when Bruce Cartwright, grandson of Alexander, shoved his grandfather's accomplishments under their noses. Bruce had had it up to here with all the huzzahs for Abner Doubleday and was out to get his ancestor named the real inventor of the game. The election committee stopped short of coming out and saying that Cartwright could have patented baseball, but they were only too happy to put Bruce's grandpa into the Hall of Fame. It was perfect. Not only could they do a good turn for old Alexander Cartwright's memory by identifying him as the inventor of everything except the infield fly rule, but they could also get in a dig at the Abner Doubleday myth by in effect proclaiming that the general had NOT invented any of those things.

But Did He?

The unfortunate fact, however, is that they went a bit overboard in passing out kudos to Cartwright. Some of the stuff he's credited with he didn't do. Some he didn't do alone. And some he didn't do first. Other than that, we have no quibble with him or his plaque.

Back in the 1840s (ah! it seems like only yesterday!), a lot of the young, up-and-coming business and professional men around New York City enjoyed going out after a hard day's work to play ball. After that, they'd retreat to an available tavern and celebrate the healthful benefits of hardy exercise. It was kind of like the guy today who plays a round of golf to work off the pounds and then has several rounds at the nineteenth hole to put them back on. Among their numbers were insurance clerks, bank clerks, doctors, lawyers, and anybody else who could take off work in the middle of the afternoon. There wasn't a ditch-digger among them. Young Alex Cartwright, a bank clerk and volunteer fireman, was one of the ringleaders. In 1845, some of these athletic celebrants, Cartwright included, decided to start a club. We can't know all of their motives, but one of them surely was that once they'd formed their little group they could keep lesser mortals out by the simple expedient of blackballing them. Apparently it had become annoying to have some *déclassé* fellow horn into a game and go four-for-four.

They called it the Knickerbocker Base Ball Club. The name was chosen not because they all wore knickerbockers (knickers for short), those dumb-looking trousers that are gathered below the knee; a Knickerbocker (with a capital K) is a descendant of one of the early Dutch settlers in New York. It was a status thing, like having an ancestor come over on the *Mayflower* or being a daughter of the American Revolution. Not that many, if any, of the young fellows organizing the Knickerbocker Base Ball Club could trace their ancestry back to the days of Peter Stuyvesant; but they *did* think they were something special. Today, Knickerbockers is best known to most of the country in its really shortened version as the name of a New York basketball team, the Knicks. And there are still quite a few Knickerbocker this's and that's scattered around New York City and State.

But back to 1845. Cartwright's Knickerbocker Club wasn't the first ball-playing club in the city. The New York Base Ball Club had already been around since at least 1839, according to Dr. Daniel L. Adams, another leading Knickerbocker. We needn't dwell on the coincidence of 1839 as being the same year Doubleday was supposedly inventing the game upstate, but you'd have to be a real Doubleday diehard to imagine he invented baseball in the spring and then hustled down to the Big Apple to talk a bunch of people into starting a club to play it. At any rate, the New York Base Ball Club played *something* they *called* "baseball." As a matter of fact, that's where Cartwright, Adams, and Company, who started with the New York, etc. got the idea to start a new club. Apparently, the New York Base Ball Club was too loose and disorganized for their taste. That sounds suspiciously like the N.Y.B.B.C. was letting just anybody in.

What the Knickerbockers, the New York Club, and anybody else were playing up to 1845 was apparently some version of rounders, but the interesting thing, to repeat, is that they *called* it "Base Ball." Once you name something, it's only a short step until you have it housebroken. Probably no two groups played exactly the same rules, each having its own variations on outs and strikes and what have you. And these could vary from week to week as somebody came up with a new "bright idea."

That all changed on September 23, 1845. Somebody—not Cartwright—actually wrote down the rules the Knickerbockers would play by. In compiling this list of do's and don'ts, the Knickerbockers no doubt considered all the various interpretations of rounders rules being played around the city and then voted on this and that. At this late date, there's no way to tell if any of the rules actually originated with the Knickerbockers themselves, much less whether our hero Cartwright was the first to bring anything to the floor except his own two feet.

The Knicks' Way

All told, there were twenty rules, many of which, like "No stump match shall be played on a regular day of exercise," we needn't concern ourselves about. The significant ones were these:

The distance from home to second base and from first to third base was set at forty-two paces. Most historians have agreed that by setting a "pace" at three feet, the bases—home-to-first, first-to-second, etc.—will end up just about ninety feet apart. However, more on that later.

Three outs ended a team's inning.

Three strikes (providing the third was caught) were an out.

Any ball hit outside first or third base was a foul. This is a lot more important than you might think at first. By establishing foul territory, the rules also established an area for spectators to stand and watch. Had foul territory been in play, as it is in cricket, spectators would have been forced to watch from much farther off, and under those circumstances, it's hard to imagine baseball becoming as popular as it did. It would be nice to think that the Knickerbockers, with remarkable foresight, reasoned all this out. Alas! the foul rule seems to have been dictated by the shape of the field they played on.

Runners were to be put out by tagging them with the ball. No more plunking! This was really crucial because in the long run it meant a harder ball (which could be hit farther) could be used. If they'd still been plunking in 1927, the Babe would never have come close to 60 homers. Again, though, it's doubtful that any of the Knickerbockers were thinking of the future; they were just good and tired of getting smacked by a baseball.

The fact that the rules were written down is of historical weight (although other rules were published earlier), but to credit the whole shebang to Alexander Cartwright is patently ridiculous. He was one of the

Knickerbockers' leading lights, but not the only one. Nowhere is there any proof that old Alex ever said anything like, "You know, fellows, I think three outs would make a smashing number for an inning." In fact, if anybody is to get the lion's share of credit, it could be Doc Adams, who was elected president of the club and served for years and years.

Furthermore, it's worth looking at what else is put on A. J. Cartwright's plate that was NOT in the rules. First of all, there's no mention of nine men on a side, and we know from various sources that they usually played with eight and sometimes with eleven. And, according to the Knicker-bocker rules, games weren't nine innings long; they played until one side scored 21 runs. (Thank God, no one kept ERAs in those days!)

The Pace of Change

The one thing that seems to be most tied to Alexander Cartwright is the ninety-foot distance between bases. Supposedly, he had the surveying skills to figure out the perfect distance. No less an authority than the late Lee Allen, for years the Hall of Fame's historian, has written: "When you consider that it takes a fast runner slightly longer than three seconds to run from home to first and the good fielder almost the same length of time to pick up the ball and throw to that base, it is a source of wonderment that Cartwright knew how far apart the bases ought to be. Had he picked a different distance, the game might have died out entirely."

Two things. First, according to one set of memoirs, it was a "Mr. Wadsworth" who showed up at a meeting with a diagram of the new field design. Second, the bases weren't ninety feet apart!

Remember, that ninety feet is based on the assumption of a three-foot pace for the forty-two paces *across* the diamond from home to second and from first to third. It turns out that the measurement of a "pace" in 1845 was a bit murky but most commonly set at *two and a half* feet. That would make the distance between bases just under seventy-five feet. (Well, no *wonder* they could play to 21 runs!)

So did old Alex Cartwright do ANY of the stuff his plaque says? Yes, he did indeed carry "baseball to [the] Pacific Coast and Hawaii in Pioneer Days." But that doesn't mean he was some sort of Johnny Baseballseed trekking westward while planting baseballs in every open field. In 1849, gold was discovered in California. All sorts of Easterners, including some baseball players, were infected with get-rich fever and took off for Sutter's Mill. Cartwright was one of them. Because he liked to play baseball, he showed others how to play, no doubt enjoying his role as the final arbiter of what came to be known as "The New York Game." Apparently, no one ever considered calling it "Cartwright's Game."

Meanwhile, back in the Big Apple, life and games went on. Eight years after Cartwright had headed west to seek his fortune, a rules committee headed by Doc Adams set teams at nine players to a side and games at nine innings.

One final note—an opinion really: Had the name "The New York Game" persisted, baseball would never have become really popular nationwide. Americans living between the coasts have a natural antipathy for anything labeled either "New York" or "Los Angeles." Few people in those cities understand this. They put any show of hostility from the heartland down to simple jealousy. Some of that may be involved, but the truth is Cincinnatians, Kansas Citians, Memphisites, and so on generally think of people from New York or Los Angeles as weird and their cities as strange outposts on the edge of reality. Interesting places to visit; you couldn't pay us to live there. Stick the name of one of those places on a product or activity and you're sure to meet resistance. More Pittsburghers eat kielbasas than New York strip steaks and none of them drink LA Beer.

⚾ 4 ⚾

The Cummings Con

The fourth most famous person named Cummings—after poet e.e., actor Robert, and actress Constance—was a pitcher named "Candy." Before you ask how a big, husky baseball player got tagged with a name better suited to a stripper, you should be apprised that "the candy" was slang for "the best" during the nineteenth century. So William Arthur Cummings probably liked being called "Candy," although whether he ever WAS "the candy" is a matter for debate. One thing is sure; he was never big or husky. In truth, he was a skinny little runt by modern standards, never weighing more than 120 pounds. His lack of size may have indirectly led to his doing the thing that made him famous—inventing the curveball.

The way the story is usually told, young Arthur (no one had any reason to call him by any confectionate nickname yet) was walking along a Brooklyn beach one day getting sand in his shoes and idly tossing clam shells into the ocean. He happened to notice that he could make the shells curve and, from that, learned to curve a baseball.

Well, as anyone who has ever thrown a clam shell and a curveball can tell you, that story is ridiculous. You arc a clam shell by throwing it straight and letting the shape of the shell take over. You curve a baseball by snapping your wrist when you let it go. If you snap your wrist while throwing a clam shell, it's going to go end-over-end—flut-flit-flat-flut-splash!

To give Arthur credit, that is not the story he told some forty-something years later when he was angling to be named the curve's inventor. The way he put it, he was *inspired* by his clam curves to see if he could learn to make a baseball do the same thing. That makes a wee bit more sense, but the

24

betting here is that when looking back to his boyhood for a place to begin his yarn, Candy (by then, of course, everybody called him Candy) decided the clam shell gimmick would be a good grabber. A more likely inspiration for inventing the curve was a flurry of line drives off enemy bats.

Whatever gave him the inspiration, Cummings admitted himself that he had no luck at first in curving a baseball. One of the reasons is that his beginning stabs were to put special gyrations into his windup. He somehow thought that if he did something weird *before* throwing the ball, the ball would do something equally weird *after* he threw it. He was straddling the problem and sooner or later he was bound to come up with the idea of doing something weird *when* he threw the ball.

In 1864 at age fifteen, he went off to boarding school in Fulton, New York, still curveless. His continued efforts to put a wrinkle in a pitch became, he said, "a standing joke."

Nevertheless, curve or not, he must have had some pitching ability, because after graduating, he found a spot as a hurler for the Brooklyn Star Juniors. According to one count, he won 37 out of 39 games. Whatever, his performance was good enough to get him an invitation to join the Excelsiors, a top Brooklyn amateur team in 1867. And it was while pitching for the Excelsiors that all his experimenting finally paid off.

Eureka!

The act of pitching a baseball in those days was quite different from our modern way. The pitcher stood in a marked rectangle, called the pitcher's box, the front edge of which was a mere forty-five feet from home plate. He could get a running start on his delivery, but he had to let fly before he stepped past that forty-five-foot barrier. Moreover, the rules said he had to "pitch" the ball—toss it underhand. Some pitchers then as now tried to get by with muscle, simply firing the ball in there as fast as they could, but the most successful fellows, then as now, were the pitchers who changed speeds and upset the batters' timing. Then, in a game against Harvard College, William Arthur (soon to be "Candy") Cummings tossed the curveball into the equation.

Obviously, he had been getting there with his experiments. It wasn't like he got up that morning and said to himself, "Gee, I wonder what I can try today." But conditions were ideal; there was a good wind blowing out from home plate—perfect for curving. Cummings delivered the ball with a snap of his wrist and the batter, he said, "missed it by a foot." The rest of the game continued in like manner with the Harvard team growing more and more frustrated. Cummings said he wanted to shout for joy but kept mum. One reason for holding his tongue may have been that it was illegal to snap one's wrist while delivering the baseball.

The rest, as they say, is history. By 1869, Cummings was being paid to pitch his curves. For a spate of seven or eight years, he was a top pitcher— if not "the candy" (the best), at least one of the "candiest."

Supposedly one day at the height of his powers, he snapped off a curve so hard he broke his wrist. This is a little hard to credit, considering he was pitching underhand, but maybe he had bones like the scarlet tanager. Or maybe he got cracked by a ball hit back through the box and the story got twisted. At any rate, they say he had to wear a special wrist guard after that.

Eventually, when he was still only twenty-eight, Cummings' curves stopped breaking and batters began knocking him all over the lot. Maybe the wind always blew in by then. While he was pitching badly for Cincinnati in 1877, a local newspaper called him "this evil." That's just flat-out nasty, and you've got to feel for the little guy. His National League record for 1876–77 is a so-so 21–22. But if you factor in four earlier seasons in the National Association, he gets up to 145–94. You could find at least a half dozen pitchers from the period with better records, but none of them invented the curveball.

Other Curvers

Of course, there have always been people around who said Candy Cummings didn't invent it either. One of them was Fred E. Goldsmith, who was a successful "slow-ball" pitcher for Chicago in the 1880s. Fred told everyone who'd listen that *he* was the first to throw a curve, and pointed to August 16, 1870, as the first time he exhibited his wrinkle publicly. Unfortunately for Fred, that was three years after Candy curved Harvard. Undaunted, Goldsmith stuck to his guns right up to his death in 1939, shortly after Cummings was named to the Hall of Fame. Some say Candy's enshrinement was responsible for Fred's death, but the best guess is that being eighty-three years old had more to do with it.

Henry Chadwick sometimes supported Cummings as the first curver, but then other times he wrote about seeing curveball pitchers in the 1850s. Perhaps old Henry was so embroiled in the rounders controversy he couldn't give curveballs his full attention.

For many years, a popular argument against Cummings' curves was that there was no such thing as a curveball. Some very bright people penned very learned articles proving that aerodynamically a baseball could not be made to curve. An optical illusion was the most common explanation, although a few held out for mass hysteria. Maybe swamp gas or weather balloons. Instead of just mindlessly shouting "Yes, I can!" pitchers would set up three poles in a row. Then they'd pitch from "inside" the first pole so that the ball would travel outside the second pole and then dip back inside the third pole. Today, with videotape, radar, and all that other stuff, we can prove absolutely that the ball does indeed curve, but there are still a few hardheads around who will tell you it doesn't. Well, there's also a flat-earth society out there and perhaps these two groups should get together.

Candy was given an official stamp of approval as the first curver in the 1890s when baseball established one of those commissions to look into the matter. Knowing now what we do about the accuracy of commissions' decisions, it's almost tempting to doubt Cummings' was number one just *because* the commission said he was. But, be that as it may, Candy wrote an article entitled "How I Pitched the First Curve" for *Baseball Magazine* in 1908. A lot of people read it, and that just about wrapped it up for him in the curveball derby. After that, Fred Goldsmith, Bobby Mathews, and all the other claimants could never be anything more than minority reports unless somebody comes up with a videotape, circa 1866.

The Big Question

The real irony in all this is that, except for the descendants of Cummings, Goldsmith, and a few other wannabes, who cares? All right, let's say Candy DID invent the curveball; it makes a nice footnote. Somebody else invented the screwball, the knuckleball, the spitball, the split-finger curve, and the Vulcan-deathgrip-downshoot. Some other guys invented the sacrifice, the hit-and-run, the stolen base, and on and on. How come none of those people—and most of them are known—have not been elected to the Hall of Fame? Is the curveball really of such overriding importance in the history of baseball that its inventor alone gets a plaque at Cooperstown?

If they really wanted to honor an early pitcher for being first at something, why not Big Jim Creighton? He really was "the candy." Creighton was a star batter and fielder by the time he was nineteen. According to some reports, he started the first triple play after making a fine catch in the outfield. Then in 1859 he took up pitching. Immediately, he changed the way baseball was played. In the next couple of years, the Creighton-led Brooklyn Excelsiors ranged up and down the East Coast beating the stuffing out of everybody they played. One day they gave an opponent eighteen players in the field and six outs per inning and still won 45–16. Try *that*, '27 Yankees!

What made Creighton so exceptional as a pitcher? First of all, he was fast. Up to then, pitchers more or less served up the ball like they were playing ring toss. Creighton was tall and rangy. He'd whip his long arm in a deep underhand motion and the ball would whoosh in like a cannon shot. Okay, call him the inventor of the fastball. Not satisfied with simply burning opponents away, Big Jim developed a devilish wrist snap that drove batters crazy. Contemporaries don't go quite so far as to say he threw curves, but the fact remains, he snapped and batters whiffed. And THEN, Creighton began changing speeds, adding still another "first" to his repertoire. Had he stuck around long enough, Big Jim would have no doubt invented every pitch known to man, built a better mousetrap, and cured the common cold.

Sad to say, Big Jim was killed by baseball in 1862. He swung hard at a pitch and something deep inside went pop. He was carried from the field and died a few days later at the age of twenty-one. His heartbroken teammates (and why not? they'd just lost their meal ticket) raised an unbelievably garish monument that still stands over his grave in a Brooklyn cemetery. This tower of granite has crossed bats, a base, a ball cap, a scorebook, and on top a stone baseball. Albert Spalding said it "would never be mistaken for anything else than the grave of a baseball player."

If all of Creighton's firsts (plus his monument) aren't enough to get him into the Hall of Fame ahead of Candy Cummings and his dinky little curve, try this. In 1860, the amateur Excelsiors got Jim away from the Niagaras by the never-fail maneuver of paying him—thus making him *the first professional baseball player*. It was done under the table, of course; they WERE amateurs.

⚾ 5 ⚾

The Cincinnati Subterfuge

Professor David Q. Voigt, in his admirable history *American Baseball: From the Gentleman's Sport to the Commissioner System*, said it this way: "Baseball's mythmakers seemingly have an unholy penchant for immaculate conceptions; no doubt they believe that if Venus could emerge full grown from a seashell, why not the game of baseball? While such logic saves its user the burden of thought, its repeated use in baseball leads one to suspect that the user has something against natural procreation and growth processes."

The average baseball fan may not be completely familiar with the details of Venus's birth (apparently a C-section on a mollusk), but he surely will get the gist of what the good professor is saying: things don't just all of a sudden materialize full-blown in real life *nor do they in baseball*. In this case, the particular object of the professor's ire happens to be the almost universally held belief that professional baseball began with the Cincinnati Red Stockings in 1869.

The Red Stockings make a good story. They played baseball, they were indeed paid in coin of the realm, and they were very successful, although perhaps a bit overrated by modern commenters. We'll get to them shortly, but first, let's all be grown-ups and agree that for all their virtues the fabulous Red Stockings were NOT the first baseball pros. In fact, by the time the Cincinnati nine got around to taking its first infield practice, a decade of play-for-pay had gone by.

29

Earning a Living

We've already pointed to Big Jim Creighton as one of the first, if not the
very first, to be paid for his ballplay. That was way back in 1859–60.
Within a year or two, most of the big-time teams were doling out wages to
a player or three. This is admittedly difficult to prove in the case of
individual players—the payments were made *sub rosa*—but it was an
open secret that money was being shelled out. Sometimes a player's
professionalism was neatly concealed behind an off-the-field job that
usually involved less effort than Darryl Strawberry expends combing his
hair (or playing right field, for that matter).

The reason for this secrecy goes back to the gentlemanly beginnings of
sport both here and abroad. Remember, baseball (and other sports) started
out as leisure activity for young men who had the time to play. The
Knickerbockers, for example, had to be able to knock off work by three
o'clock in the afternoon in order to make it for the first pitch. They
regarded themselves as being of a higher class than, say, a bricklayer, who
had to work until dark to get his quota of bricks laid for the day. The
Knicks were *gentlemen*, and that put them above earning their livings by
sweating. Unfortunately, knowing which fork to use doesn't mean you
can hit a fastball. The Knickerbockers were clobbered 21–1 in the first
game they played. Eventually, it became obvious that some people could
play this game and other people couldn't. The next logical step was to get
a few of the guys-who-can on your side so you wouldn't always have to
buy the first round at the post-game celebrations. Flattery or friendship
might bring another "gentleman" into your club, but if a good ballplayer
happened to come from the class that sweated, he had to be paid. Otherwise, he could hardly afford to spend his afternoons throwing a baseball
around a field with a bunch of guys who didn't have to worry about how to
pay the rent.

So, the professional ballplayer was born. To the Knickerbockers' credit
(or snobbism), they held out longer than most clubs before hiring anybody
(and even then, one of their earliest members resigned in a huff). Most
other clubs of any repute preferred to win games and jumped into the
payment thing. But, of course, no one wanted to admit that anyone on his
team was out there for anything but healthy competition and exercise.
Gentlemen all! More to the point, the National Association of Base Ball
Players, which could suspend players or clubs, was strictly a bastion of
amateurism. In fact, the N.A.B.B.P. was so determinedly amateur that it

didn't bother to put the A-word in its name; when it began there simply weren't any non-amateurs as far as the organization was concerned. And, thus, payments were made under the table.

If, in the earliest years, we can't say that exactly so-and-so was paid exactly such-and-such to play baseball, we still know that some of those so-and-so's were doing okay. One piece of circumstantial evidence is that teams began charging admission to their games. As early as 1863, according to Professor Voigt, "Porter's *Spirit of the Times* reported that many clubs were charging admission rates of as much as twenty-five cents." Obviously, the gentleman members of the clubs had grown weary of shelling out their own shekels to pay their ringers.

One of the most interesting reports dates to 1864 when the New York Mutuals, who played at the Union Grounds, and the Brooklyn Atlantics, who played at the Capitoline Grounds, each charged ten cents a head admission and then *divided the proceeds among the players*! If that's legitimate, and if all the players got a cut, it means that there were at least two all-professional teams six years before the Cincinnati Red Stockings scuffed their first ball.

For a long time, Al Reach was thought to have been the first paid player. We know now that he was further down in the pecking order, but he definitely received $25 a week from the Philadelphia Athletics to relocate to the City of Brotherly Love from Brooklyn in 1865. They called it "expenses." In a way, it's too bad he wasn't the first, because Al was just about the rarest thing to be found in baseball—a left-handed second baseman.

Be that as it may, Al Reach seems to have survived well enough to earn his keep and then gone on to start the sporting goods company that bears his name. But in 1866, a year after Reach was hired, the Philly Athletics got themselves into deep effluvium for paying players, and Al had nothing to do with it. The A's were accused of dishing twenty dollars a week to Dick McBride, Lipman Pike, and a third player named Dockney. That was worth a few headlines! Fortunately for the Philadelphians, the accuser failed to show at the National Association judiciary hearing, and the case ended up permanently tabled.

By the late 1860s, even most of the bigwigs in the National Association knew darn well that players were being paid all over the place. Nevertheless, teams continued to claim they were amateurs no matter how transparent their cover-ups. For example, in 1867, George Wright, maybe the best player in the country at that time, left the New York Gothams to play with the Washington Nationals. Supposedly, George went south to take a job with the government. According to the team's published roster, he was a clerk at 238 Pennsylvania Avenue. That was the address of a public park!

Meanwhile, Albert Spalding (yes, *that* Albert Spalding), a young pitcher from Rockford, Illinois, was offered $40 a week—a princely sum—to work for a Chicago grocery. Al told the grocers he didn't know a carrot from a leek. Not to worry; his real job was to pitch for the Chicago Excelsiors.

We Did It (And We're Glad!)

By the end of the '60s, the public had shown it was more than willing to pay to see a good ball game, so the National Association's power was just about nil. The only thing left was for some team to come right out and admit it was getting paid. And that's where Cincinnati comes in.

At the time Cincinnati's only real claim to national fame was the efficiency with which its many slaughterhouses butchered hogs. As a topic for civic boostering, this accomplishment had definite limitations. Especially around the dinner table. It seems, however, that there resided in "Porkopolis" a young lawyer-merchant with the prophetic name of Aaron B. Champion, who in his heart of hearts believed that a winning baseball team would bring honor, fame, and a ton of new business to town. The 1868 Red Stockings, led by Harry Wright and with four paid players, had done pretty well locally but was considered bush league compared to some of the strong eastern teams. Especially after the Philadelphia Athletics and Brooklyn Atlantics toured through and knocked their red stockings off. So in 1869, Champion decided to go whole hog (to use a local expression). He got the cash together and then set out to hire the best team money could buy.

At first, he ran into some problems. His original idea was to hire the nine top players in the country according to medals handed out the year before. Naturally, players began using Champion's offers as bargaining chips to gouge some extra dollars out of their old clubs. Champion was mad as hell, but there wasn't much he could do about it. Finally, he told Harry Wright to go out and get the players for him.

Harry Wright was a jeweler by trade but a few years earlier he'd given that up to come to Cincinnati to teach the members of the Red Stocking Club how to play cricket. Then, when local interest switched to baseball, Harry stayed on to mentor in that. At age thirty-five, his best years as a player were probably behind him, but folks in Cincy thought he knew everything there was to know about baseball. In the years to come, he proved that the locals' assessment was right on the button.

Harry kept about half the players from the '68 Red Stockings, including himself of course, and then filled in the gaps with all-stars he inveigled to join up. The foremost star he bagged was his younger brother George, a power-hitting shortstop of the first water. George didn't come cheap; in fact he demanded $200 more than Harry got.

The team Harry put together made no bones about their professionalism. Their salaries for the season came down to us thus:

George Wright	Shortstop	$1,400
Harry Wright	Center Field	1,200
Asa Brainard	Pitcher	1,100
Fred Waterman	Third Base	1,000
Douglas Allison	Catcher	800
Charles Gould	First Base	800
Andrew Leonard	Left Field	800
Calvin McVey	Right Field	800
Charles Sweasy	Second Base	800
Richard Hurley	Substitute	600

Years later, George Wright said he really got $2,000, but his memory may have been playing tricks or he might have intentionally boosted his take to more like what players were making by that time. Actually, at $1,400 he was well paid for that day and age; a skilled craftsman made a little over $800 for a year at the time, and a common laborer half that. The Red Stockings were craftsmen. Their contracts ran from March 15 through November 15.

The unique thing about the Red Stockings, remember, was not that they were paid but that they admitted—bragged about—getting paid. They were out of the closet! Of course, had they gone on from there to just an ordinary record, they'd barely be remembered today.

After a couple of warm-ups, the Red Stockings went east. Within a couple of weeks they were the most famous baseball team in the country, having handily knocked off the New York Mutuals, Brooklyn Atlantics, Philadelphia Athletics, and Washington Olympics, plus a host of lesser lights. Then they moved west, mowing down every team in their path, all the way to San Francisco. You can chalk up that coast-to-coast tour as another "first" in the Cincy column. All told for the year, they beat fifty-nine club teams and six all-star teams (often by horrific scores like 35–2).

They even made a profit. $1.39!

George Wright was their star of stars. Reportedly he hit 59 home runs in 52 games, but don't get too excited about that. The Red Stockings played a lot of small-town patsies on fields with no outfield fences. Whenever ol' George slapped one between the outfielders, he could circle the bases before the ball stopped rolling. George was probably more valuable for his fielding than for what he did with a bat.

The Red Stockings were the toast of the baseball world (and certainly of Cincinnati) for that winter. In 1870, they started out with another string of victories, but on June 14, they took on the Atlantics at the Capitoline Grounds. Fully nine thousand fans paid fifty cents each to watch. The game was tied 5–5 after nine, and the Atlantics were willing to call it a day. The Red Stockings insisted the game go on. Cincinnati scored a pair in the top of the eleventh inning, but the Atlantics came back to score three in the bottom half. The winning run scored when first baseman Charlie Gould let an easy grounder that Bill Buckner could have handled in his sleep go right between his legs.

Once the spell was broken, the Red Stockings lost a couple more. Fans stopped going gaga and attendances fell off. The team lost money, the backers backed out, and when the season ended, the fabulous Red Stockings were history.

Just how good were they really? Obviously they were the best around in 1869 when they defeated all the important clubs, but that actually involved only about a half dozen games. The rest of their fabulous record was compiled against lesser lights who never had a chance. With that kind of competition, the Red Stockings' victory string depended only on how many games they could schedule.

We can get some idea of how talent was distributed on the team by looking at how they performed in the first organized league, the National Association (1871–76). Harry Wright went to Boston where he managed N.A. pennant winners from 1872 through 1875. He played center field in all but the final year, when he was forty years old. Accompanying Harry was his brother George, who hit .353 over the five years of N.A. play. Also in Boston were Andy Leonard, with a .321 N.A. batting average, and Cal McVey, who thumped at .362. These four certainly continued to star. Doug Allison was never a great hitter, but he was regarded as an outstanding catcher for five years in the N.A. and five more in the National League after that.

On the down side, Fred Waterman hit .323 in 61 N.A. games over four seasons but never found steady work. Charlie Sweasy hit a miserable .188

in the N.A. and couldn't nail down a steady job either. Charlie Gould was a mere .251 hitter. Dick Hurley played two games in 1872 and got nary a hit. Shorn of the big bats of George Wright, McVey, and Leonard, Asa Brainard fell on hard times. His "career" mark in the National Association was 24–56.

Obviously the Red Stockings were not an all-star team, as some mythmakers would have you believe. What emerges is a picture of a good ballclub with a couple of real gems in the lineup and only a couple of clunkers. That was good enough in 1869, but never again.

◖ 6 ◗

Bad League–Good League

Once upon a time, there was a sort of baseball league (but not really) called the National Association and it was very, very bad. Teams dropped in and out at will. Schedules were a joke. Players went on the field drunk. When they sobered up, they jumped from team to team without warning. Everyone was under the thumb of gamblers. And a lot of games weren't played on the up and up. The public became so disgusted with all the bad things that it was very near to giving up on baseball altogether and turning to honest, civilized sports like boxing, horse racing, and bear-baiting.

Just when everything was at its worst and baseball seemed doomed, a real major league called the National League rode out of the West to restore honesty, stability, and sobriety. Steadfast teams followed strict schedules. Honest, abstemious players served their teams loyally. Gamblers were banished. And baseball lived happily ever after.

At least, that's the way they tell it around the National League.

The truth is a little different.

The National Association

The amateur National Association of Base Ball Players had become obsolete by the end of the 1860s if for no other reason than that most of the good players in the country were no longer amateurs. In 1870, the amateur

36

side of the group split off and soon disappeared into the mists, leaving baseball in the hands of the N.A. of Professional B.B.P. Once the amateurs faded completely, the professionals took to calling themselves simply the "National Association."

In the spring of 1871, the N.A.'s baseball clubs met in New York and laid down a set of rules for winning the national baseball championship: each member club was to play each other club in a best-of-five series, the club winning the most series to be declared the champion. This was a wonderful step forward even though it didn't work.

To compete for the national championship—in effect, to join the first league—clubs had to put up a $10 fee. (Eat your hearts out, Marlins and Rockies!) You'd think they would have had prospective members running out their ears, but only nine clubs started off the season: the Boston Red Stockings, Chicago White Stockings, Cleveland Forest Citys, Fort Wayne Kekiongas, New York Mutuals, Philadelphia Athletics, Rockford Forest Citys, Troy Haymakers, and Washington Olympics. The Brooklyn Eckfords (where did they get these names!) finally scraped together $10 in August when it was too late to count.

Boston's Red Stockings were Harry and George Wright, along with the cream of the former Cincinnati Red Stockings. Philadelphia had pitcher Tricky Dick McBride and a host of good hitters. But the best team from the git-go was Chicago. Then, just when it seemed the White Stockings would wrap up the first pennant, Mrs. O'Leary's cow kicked over a lantern (to cite a non-baseball legend), and Chicago burned down, taking the White Stockings' ball park, uniforms, bats, balls, water bucket, and pocket money with it. The team had to finish up on the road with borrowed uniforms, cadging meals as best they could.

As the White Stockings faded, Philadelphia and Boston came on. Boston had already won its series with Philly, so naturally the National Association committee voted that the championship would be decided by one big game between Philadelphia and Chicago. Harry Wright yelled foul, but the committee was packed with Philadelphians and that was that. As expected, the Athletics won the game and the first pennant.

Harry and Boston got their revenge by winning the next four pennants. His Red Stockings just kept getting stronger. By 1875, when Boston went 71–8, there was no semblance of a pennant race. In fact, any falloffs in baseball attendance might as easily be blamed on the Red Stockings' complete dominance as on any other factors.

Most of the charges laid against the National Association were true. Teams did indeed drop in and out precipitously, but that wasn't altogether a bad thing. If a crew like the 1875 Keokuk Westerns thought they could stand up against the big boys, they got a democratic chance to prove it. And, when they started the season by losing twelve of their first thirteen games, there wasn't much point in playing a fourteenth.

That ease of entrance and exit seems to be at the crux of the National League's contention that the National Association wasn't a true major league. One has to wonder how "major league" might be defined. If you and I could gather all (or nearly all) of the best ball clubs in the country together for a season, along with a competitive method to determine a champion, and if there was no other comparable organization around, would we have a major league on our hands? What's missing? A league logo and a TV contract?

Drunkenness and hippodroming (as not playing on the square was called) were present in the National Association, although probably not to the extent the National League insisted later. To hear the N.L. tell it, there wasn't an N.A. player who could pass a bottle or a bribe without salivating. But wait. The same National Association players who were boozy hippodromers in 1875 played in the supposed teetotaling, square-shooting National League of 1876. Did they all suddenly get religion? In truth, charges of hippodroming continued for the next fifty years until long after that quaint expression had gone out of style. Most of the charges were sour grapes from disappointed fans, but some turned out to be true. As for alcoholism, that's still a problem today, along with its equally insidious sidekick, drug addiction.

That National Association ballplayers were jumping from one team to another in search of more money, a practice called "revolving," was certainly true. Greedy players seldom showed any team loyalty when they could make bigger dollars playing for someone else. (Thank heaven, *those* days are past!) Doug Allison, the erstwhile Cincinnati Red Stocking catcher, played for seven different teams in seven seasons after leaving the Queen City. He was either revolving or had one hell of a case of wanderlust. Other players moved around more or less annually. But when the National League puts revolving in the debit column for the National Association, it's simply being hypocritical. First, because the N.L. couldn't figure how to stop jumpers from jumping for its own first few seasons. But, more important, because the National League was formed precisely so that its founder could get away with the biggest revolving score of all time.

Mr. Hulbert Builds His Dream Team

After the Chicago Fire took the wind out of the White Stockings, Chicago laid out of the National Association for a couple of seasons. When they returned in 1874, they found themselves one of the also-rans in the middle of the standings. That didn't sit well with William A. Hulbert, the beefy, self-made businessman who'd become club president in 1875. But if a middling won-lost record was bad, a middling profit was worse.

In looking over the situation, Hulbert decided the National Association's policy of letting just about any team in that would post its nominal fee was a blueprint for disaster. It forced big-city teams like his White Stockings to travel to little burgs and play before unprofitable, minuscule crowds. Hulbert decided the little fish had to get out of his pool.

Another thorn in Hulbert's fiscal side was revolving. To keep a player from jumping to another team or to get him to jump to your team necessitated dishing out more moolah than any bottom-line man like William A. liked to. He was willing to pay top dollar for a first-rate ballplayer, but the practice had a maddening trickle-down effect that ultimately caused ordinary and even sub-par players to receive more than they were worth. That really grated on Hulbert's banausic soul.

But Hulbert could complain until he was blue in the face. It wouldn't do him any good. The National Association was just what it said it was—an association of professional ballplayers. Everyone was an associate; no one was really in charge. With no central authority, the N.A. was run in effect by the ballplayers. Catch them making a rule against revolving!

Hulbert wasn't the only one complaining, of course. He was just the only one who figured out how to solve the problem. He launched a sneak attack on Boston.

Boston was loaded. In addition to the two Wrights (who never made a wrong), the Red Stockings fielded such worthies as Andy Leonard and Cal McVey from the old Cincinnati club. Deacon White, a terrific hitter, was a versatile catcher-third baseman-outfielder-whatever. Second baseman Ross Barnes was adept at taking advantage of the rules of the day with his "fair-fouls." At the time, any batted ball that landed fair and then skipped foul before reaching a base was still in play, and Barnes annually added a hundred or more points to his batting average with this little trick.

The best of the Red Stockings was their magnificent pitcher, young fireballer Albert Spalding. (Yes, again, *that* Spalding!) In five National Association seasons, A.G.S. had won 207 games and batted .320. He was coming off a season in which his record was an absurd 57–5. Had there been a Cy Young Award, they could have given it to him at midseason.

Hulbert decided that Boston had too many stars for any one club not from Illinois and began negotiating with Spalding and some of the boys before the 1875 season ended. As loose as the National Association was, it still had rules about revolving—or even agreeing to revolve—while a season was still in progress. "Don't worry, fellows," Hulbert told the players, "you men are bigger than the Association." Pretty soon word got out that Spalding, White, Barnes, and McVey were headed for the White Stockings the next year. Boston fans made the rest of the jumpers' season miserable by booing them unmercifully. (Can you really imagine yourself booing a pitcher going 57–5 for your team?) Albert was, after all, a midwestern boy who'd been a happy grocery clerk in Chicago, so he was probably just succumbing to the lure of returning home. Well, all those Chicago dollars *may* have helped convince him.

Having grabbed off half of the N.A.'s championship team, Hulbert moved on to Philadelphia, where he signed heavy hitter Adrian "Cap" Anson away from the Athletics. Then he skedaddled back to Chicago to chortle.

Mr. Hulbert Builds His Dream League

However, he couldn't sit around twiddling his thumbs for long. There was a strong chance that the eastern N.A. clubs, under the influence of Boston and Philadelphia, might retaliate for his raid by suspending the White Stockings. That would be extreme, but so was the provocation. And most of the votes were in the east—just another thing a midwesterner like Hulbert found annoying.

In December, Hulbert, along with the N.A. St. Louis club owner, called a meeting in Louisville with representatives of strong independent teams from that city and Cincinnati. His proposal was simple: ignore the National Association and start a new league. He had some of the best players under contract. If the N.A. went under, there'd be plenty of players around for the other clubs to grab for a song. By eliminating the Keokuks and other such minnows, teams should be able to schedule profitably. It was a brave new world!

With his four western clubs in place, Hulbert turned toward balancing his league with four teams from the east. But no little fish. He called Boston, Philadelphia, New York, and Hartford. You'd think the Red

Stockings would have turned him down flat, having just lost four of their best to his raiding, but Harry Wright was no admirer of the National Association, primarily on moral grounds. He was willing to listen to Hulbert, and if Boston fell in line, the other three could hardly stand aloof.

They all got together at the Central Hotel in New York City in February. A legend surrounding that meeting is that Hulbert locked the door, pocketed the key, and said no one could leave until they all agreed with him. This is patent nonsense, of course. Hulbert had a far better means to woo the others. All he had to do was say the secret word: money.

And thus, while many of its members didn't even know it was happening, the National Association was erased. In its place was the tight, eight-team National League, with control resting in the hands of the owners. Other clubs could apply, of course, but they could only come in if one of the originals left. And they had to be in cities of at least seventy-five thousand. And they had to post an admission fee of (gasp!) $100.

To placate the eastern clubs, who were still grumbling a bit, Hulbert had one of their owners, an affable politician named Bulkeley, installed as figurehead president of the new endeavor. No one was fooled. Hulbert was still in charge. Then they all went home to bad-mouth the National Association until the 1876 season could get underway. It was important, you see, that the fans understand this had all been done for the good of baseball.

Just for the record, Chicago won the first National League pennant by six games over St. Louis. Ross Barnes led the league in batting with .429. Anson hit .356; McVey .347; White .343; and Spalding .312. Spalding's pitching record was 46–12, with a 1.75 ERA. But the stats that gave Hulbert the most satisfaction were no doubt to be found in the White Stockings' ledger books.

⊗ 7 ⊗

Five for the *

I don't know if all of you remember Roger Maris' asterisk, but you should. It was such a wonderfully looney example of how *not* to mix public relations, hero-worship, and statistics.

For anybody who's mislaid the story somewhere in the hidden recesses of his cranium, I'll review: As the 1961 baseball season drew to a close, Yankee outfielder Maris was engaged in an all-out assault on baseball's most cherished record—Babe Ruth's 60 homers in a single season. And a large part of baseball's most fanatical fandom—maybe a majority—was rooting against him.

By all accounts, Roger Maris was a nice young man, an exceptional defensive outfielder, and a strong home run threat. But he was too much of a private person for the New York media to love, never exhibited bizarre behavior, was not known to have called his shot, didn't eat, drink, and make merry till dawn, and hadn't been accused of building Yankee Stadium. For all his virtues, Maris was no Babe Ruth. And, therefore, by the lights of many, he was unworthy of breaking the Babe's record. Baseball is the only sport where breaking a record is a question of morality as well as muscle. Searching desperately for a way to drop Roger a peg or two no matter how many homers he hit, a few purists argued that Maris had an unfair advantage in that the Yankees were scheduled for 162 games in '61 whereas Ruth's '27 Yankees had got by on 154.

So Baseball Commish Ford Frick, who never saw a fence he couldn't straddle, ruled Roger would have to sock his sixty homers within 154 games or forever have an asterisk beside his name in the record book. Rog then took the full season to get 61 home runs, if only to call Frick's bluff.

Well, everyone except Frick knew the asterisk was a bad idea because it managed to demean BOTH Maris and Ruth, so it's been long retired. But I remember thinking at the time, "Boy, when I get to be commissioner, you'll never see *me* messing with asterisks!"

I was wrong. Oh, I'm not commissioner. Not yet. But I am going to advocate, with heart and soul, the application of a few well-chosen asterisks to the record book. Before I explain why, let me show you what I think you should see when you open to the page that deals with pitching victories:

	Years	G	W–L	Pct
Cy Young	1890–1911	906	511–313	.620
Walter Johnson	1907–1927	802	416–279	.599
Christy Mathewson	1900–1916	636	373–188	.665
Grover Alexander	1911–1930	696	373–208	.642
Warren Spahn	1942–1965	750	363–245	.597
*Pud Galvin	1879–1892	697	361–310	.538
Kid Nichols	1890–1906	621	360–203	.639
*Tim Keefe	1880–1893	601	344–225	.605
Steve Carlton	1965–1988	741	329–244	.574
Eddie Plank	1901–1917	622	327–193	.629
*John Clarkson	1882–1894	531	326–127	.648
Don Sutton	1966–1988	774	324–256	.559
Phil Niekro	1964–1987	864	318–274	.537
Gaylord Perry	1962–1983	777	314–265	.542
Nolan Ryan	1966–1991	767	314–278	.530
Tom Seaver	1967–1986	656	311–205	.603
*Mickey Welch	1880–1892	564	311–207	.600
*Old Hoss Radbourn	1881–1891	528	308–191	.617
Lefty Grove	1925–1941	616	300–141	.680
Early Wynn	1939–1963	691	300–244	.551

Source: *The Baseball Encyclopedia*, 7th edition.

Aside from winning 300 games, what do all the asterisked pitchers have in common? Right, they all had most of their fling at flinging during the 1880s. And the reason I want them star-tagged is that what was called pitching in them days was clearly unlike what we call pitching today. It wasn't any extra eight games; the way they flung was so dissimilar that it can be qualified as a whole different ball game.

Actually, what I'd really like to see is those five guys—Pud Galvin,

Tim Keefe, John Clarkson, Mickey Welch, and Old Hoss Radbourn—taken out of the regular 300-game-winner list altogether and put into a special category of their own—"Pleistocene Pitchers" or something. As far as *I'm* concerned, when Nolan Ryan won his 300th, he was the fifteenth "real" pitcher to do it, not the twentieth. That's a bit extreme for most folks. After all, they say, the archaic five did really have "WP" after their names 300 or more times each. It's not like they spread typhoid. They shouldn't be quarantined. So I'll happily settle for an asterisk to show that what they achieved was done under less duress than what Early Wynn faced.

Don't get me wrong. I'm not advocating the Faded Five be bounced out of the Hall of Fame. They were the best at doing what they did when they did it. It's just that no one's had their particular advantages since. And I don't think it's fair to rank them with real pitchers.

The Ancients

Let me tell you just a little more about each of these guys before we go on.

Pud Galvin was a chubby right-hander and the first man to get 300 wins. The Big Mac lists him at 190 pounds, but he filled up on so many 1880s Big Macs that he usually weighed in at an eighth of a ton or more. You hear different stories, but I think "Pud" was short for "Pudding," which was what he most often resembled. One historian calls him the all-time greatest fat pitcher, but I'd rank him behind Bobo Newsom, Mickey Lolich, and Freddy Fitzsimmons. When he retired, Pud opened a bar in Pittsburgh. A trusting soul, he went broke while all his bartenders soon opened their own saloons.

Tim Keefe, the second 300-game winner, looked like what an 1880s ballplayer should look like—big handlebar mustache and all. His effectiveness when he pitched for the Giants was mainly due to good control and an ability to change speeds. He joined his brother-in-law, John Montgomery Ward, in fighting against salary caps, and small wonder—he was one of the most important cappees. They say he had a nervous breakdown once when he nearly killed a batter with a purpose pitch, but both he and the batter got over it.

John Clarkson was even more sensitive than Keefe. He needed more pats on his back during a season than Barry Bonds gives himself in a week. John wasn't worth a fig if his manager scolded him. But praise him and he'd pitch up a storm. He didn't mind embarrassing others, though.

The story goes that he once threw a lemon up to the plate to prove to an umpire that the park had grown too dark to continue the game. I guess it was funny at the time. The really funny thing is how shocked everyone was when Boston paid $10,000 for him in 1888. Today, the only pitcher you can get at that price is one to hold lemonade.

Mickey Welch was the Giants' second pitcher behind Tim Keefe for most of his career. He followed Keefe to three hundred wins and to the Hall of Fame. As a matter of fact, he's the one usually cited as an example of how three hundred wins automatically gets a pitcher into Cooperstown even if he hasn't got anything else going for him. They say he threw a screwball before those other Giants greats Mathewson and Hubbell. Actually, Matty called his a "fadeaway" and Mickey probably called his an "in-shoot," but it's the same pitch.

Hoss Radbourn got to the Hall of Fame for that 1884 season when he won 60 games (or 59, according to some revisionists), but he had enough other good seasons to climb over 300. Actually, he was called *"Old* Hoss" even though he was only thirty when he had his big year. Radbourn got the monicker because he was dependable like an "old horse."

The Way They Were

Maybe if these fellows had been born later, they'd still have become great pitchers. My quarrel is not with them but with the rules under which they starred. So let's look at 'em.

You probably remember that hurlers once had to pitch underhand, but that really doesn't affect our story here. In 1878, the ball had to be delivered from a point below the waist, but a lot of flingers cut that pretty fine. So, in 1883, they said anywhere below the shoulder was okay. Still, a smart pitcher could get around that by leaning over a little. In 1884, the rulemakers gave up and told the pitchers to throw any damn way they wanted to. Both Radbourn and Keefe continued to submarine it. I don't know about the others, but it doesn't matter. There have always been effective underhand pitchers like Eldon Auker, Ted Abernathy, Kent Tekulve, and Dan Quisenberry. When they say Gaylord Perry had "underhanded ways," they mean something else.

A series of rule changes that really made a difference related to balls and strikes. In the first place, all during the 1880s, the strike zone ran from the bottom of the knees to the tops of the shoulders. Until 1887, a batter could call for a "low" ball (waist to knees) or "high" ball (waist to shoulders), and that cut the zone in half, but it was no worse than what the umpires call today.

A bigger deal was how hard it was to walk anybody. Starting with 1879, here's how many bad pitches it took.

> 1879—9 balls.
> 1880—8 balls.
> 1881—7 balls.
> 1884—6 balls (in National League).
> 1886—7 balls.
> 1887—5 balls.
> 1889—4 balls at last!

You keep hearing how Keefe and others had such great control, but with those rules Rex Barney would have been a control artist. In 1879, you could go out for lunch during an intentional pass.

The other major rule aid for an 1880s pitcher was the distance to home plate. Up until 1881, they tossed from a box, the front end of which was only forty-five feet from home plate. We still say a pitcher gets "knocked out of the box," even though we haven't had a pitcher's box for a hundred years. When they changed the rule, they moved the pitcher's box back only five feet and there it stayed through the 1880s until 1893, when they finally went to a bar (or, pitcher's rubber) sixty feet, six inches from home plate. You can say the 1880s pitcher had to release the ball while he was in the box and the 1893 pitcher could step forward off that pitcher's bar, but the earlier guys still had at least a five-foot advantage. Can you imagine batting against Nolan Ryan or Roger Clemens if they were five feet closer? Holy Automatic Whifferooney, Batman!

From 1892 to 1893, the National League dropped from 6.47 K's per game to 4.25. And by 1893, all of our five 1880s 300-game winners were washed up. None of them could hack it at the modern distance.

Here's an odd fact I got from Pete Palmer, the statistician: today, a passed ball happens about once every five games. For most of the 1880s, games averaged about two PBs a game! Catchers not wearing gloves was the major reason, of course, but I'll bet the more acute angle at which the ball cruised up to the plate was a factor too. That's the thing about giving those pitchers a five-foot head start; they not only pitch faster but they also come at the batter from sharper angles.

My point, in case you forgot, is that those 1880s guys had extra help that makes their 300 wins less impressive than they would be today.

Forget the Rules

If you think I haven't made my case for asterisking those 1880s pitchers, let's skip the rules altogether and come at it from another direction—the one I think is most important of all.

In those days, when a pitcher started a game, he was expected to pitch the whole thing though the heavens fell. If Old Hoss had a bad day, he just kept chuckin' it in there and hoped his team would outslug the enemy. As a result, he almost always got a decision every time he started. Which means any number of 20–17 victories. And when a top pitcher was brought in to relieve, the game was usually on the line. Better than one-third of an 1880s ace's rare relief appearances yielded him a decision.

A modern starter—even an ace—will get no decision in about a quarter of his starts. Modern managers can't wait to bring in a fresh arm. This doesn't mean today's pitchers are wimps; it's just how they do things these days. And a modern ace's relief appearances are usually as a setup man early or late in his career. Meaning he seldom gets a decision there either.

On the following page are the figures for the top ten winners of the 1880s and the top ten winners of the past few years.

Taking just those top ten 1880s pitchers, they received credit for a decision in 96.2 percent of their starts on average and 40.9 percent of their relief appearances. The modern pitchers, on the other hand, received decisions in only 78.6 percent of their starts and a mere 17.8 percent of their relief jobs. And remember, Kaat and Niekro did a lot of relieving.

Does it make a difference?

Bet your booties!

Just for the fun of it, I sat down with Mr. Calculator and worked out what each of these two groups would have done, win-lose-wise, if each had the benefit of the other group's decision-percentages. In other words, suppose Don Sutton received a decision in 96.2 percent of his starts and 40.9 percent of his relief appearances, while Pud Galvin had to get by on 78.6 and 17.8. (I know, I *know* there are other factors! I said, "Just for the fun of it!" Pay attention!)

	G	W–L	Pct	Starting						Relief		
				GS	CG	Record	Pct	Dec	%Dec	Rel	Rec	%Dec
Galvin	697	361–310	.538	682	639	358–308	.538	666	97.7	15	3– 2	33.3
Keefe	601	344–225	.605	595	558	342–225	.601	569	95.6	6	2– 0	33.3
Clarkson	531	326–127	.648	518	485	325–173	.653	498	96.1	13	1– 4	38.5
Welch	564	311–207	.600	549	525	308–205	.600	513	93.4	15	3– 2	33.3
Radbourn	528	308–191	.617	503	489	300–186	.617	486	96.6	25	8– 5	52.0
Mullane	556	285–215	.570	505	469	270–210	.535	480	95.0	51	15– 5	39.2
McCormick	494	264–214	.552	488	466	261–214	.549	475	97.3	6	3– 0	50.0
Buffinton	414	231–151	.605	396	351	224–151	.597	375	94.7	18	7– 0	38.9
White	403	229–166	.580	401	394	229–165	.983	394	98.3	2	0– 1	50.0
Caruthers	340	218– 97	.692	310	298	207– 95	.685	302	97.4	30	11– 2	43.3

	G	W–L	Pct	Starting						Relief		
				GS	CG	Record	Pct	Dec	%Dec	Rel	Rec	%Dec
Carlton	741	329–244	.574	709	254	327–240	.577	567	80.0	32	2– 4	18.8
Sutton	774	324–256	.559	756	178	321–253	.559	574	75.9	18	3– 3	33.3
Niekro	864	318–274	.537	716	245	304–263	.536	567	79.2	148	14–11	16.9
Perry	777	314–265	.542	690	303	305–253	.547	558	80.9	87	9–12	24.1
Ryan	767	314–278	.530	733	220	309–278	.526	587	80.1	34	5– 0	14.7
Seaver	656	311–205	.603	647	231	310–203	.604	513	79.3	9	1– 2	33.3
John	760	288–231	.555	700	162	284–228	.555	512	73.1	60	4– 3	11.7
Jenkins	664	284–226	.557	594	267	279–218	.561	497	83.7	70	5– 8	18.6
Kaat	898	283–237	.544	625	180	259–218	.543	477	76.3	273	24–19	15.8
Blyleven	667	279–238	.540	661	241	279–236	.542	515	77.9	6	0– 2	33.3

Legend: G = Games pitched; W = Wins; L = Losses; Pct. = Percentage; GS = Games Started; CG = Complete Games; Starting Record: Win-Loss Record in Games Started; Dec = Number of Decisions in Starts; %Dec = Percentage of Decisions in Starts / in Relief; Rel = Relief Appearances; Relief Record = Win-Loss record in Relief.

Revised	W–L
Don Sutton	410–323
Phil Niekro	404–345
Steve Carlton	397–297
Jim Kaat	392–326
Nolan Ryan	388–331
Tommy John	384–309
Tom Seaver	376–249
Gaylord Perry	375–324
Bert Blyleven	343–295
Ferguson Jenkins	328–269
Pud Galvin	290–249
Tim Keefe	281–186
John Clarkson	266–142
Mickey Welch	260–173
Hoss Radbourn	246–152
Tony Mullane	218–188
Jim McCormick	212–173
Chas. Buffinton	191–123
Will White	183–132
Bob Caruthers	171– 75

Fun or not, I think that makes my point. Asterisk 'em!

⚾ 8 ⚾

Raising My Gonfalon Bubble

I can still remember the day more than forty years ago when I was idly thumbing through a friend's baseball magazine and came upon an article in which the author used his considerable knowledge and experience to pick an all-time team for the Chicago Cubs. What really startled me was the subtitle: "No Tinker, No Evers, No Chance!" This was pre–Mark Grace, pre–Ryne Sandberg, pre–Ernie Banks, pre- a lot of good ballplayers who have played for the Cubs in the interim. This was a time when the Cubs were resting comfortably at the bottom of the National League. The only thing I knew about their history was that they'd once won a whole slew of pennants because of Tinker, Evers, and Chance. And here was someone who wouldn't name them to his all-time Cubs team! Sacrilege!

In truth, I guess I did know one other thing about Cub history: the poem.

Baseball's Sad Lexicon

These are the saddest of possible words,
Tinker to Evers to Chance.
Trio of bear cubs, and fleeter than birds,
Tinker to Evers to Chance.
Thoughtlessly pricking our gonfalon bubble,
Making a Giant hit into a double—

Words that are weighty with nothing but trouble:
Tinker to Evers to Chance.

—FRANKLIN PIERCE ADAMS
New York *Globe*, July 10, 1908

As I recall, whoever it was that picked that all-time Cubs team pre-ferred Billy Jurges at shortstop and Rogers Hornsby at second. His choice of first baseman escapes me. Maybe Charley Grimm. The writer argued with statistics on his side; mere literature didn't stand a chance. But I guess I wasn't fully convinced; the memory of that article has stuck with me all these years.

Since then, I've even heard intelligent people proclaim that the trio of bear cubs were ONLY famous because of Adams' poem. Once, a radio talk show host leaned across his microphone and asked me if I didn't agree that Tinker, Evers, and Chance were the most undeserving of all the members of the Hall of Fame. I guess he didn't like my answer. He never invited me back on his program.

I still feel that the trio has been down-sized too easily. But proving it is not the easiest matter in the world. The statistics hurt.

Joe Tinker (1902–16) batted .263 for his career. Of all the shortstops in the Hall of Fame, only Rabbit Maranville (.258) and Luis Aparicio (.262) had lower career batting averages. Both had considerably longer careers and both were considered fielding "geniuses." Tinker was considered a very good fielder in his day, but I don't think the word "genius" ever was used. Or considered, for that matter.

Johnny Evers (1902–17) batted .270 for his career, which is 18 points lower than any other Hall of Fame second baseman except Joe Morgan, who brightened his stats with a ton of home runs, RBI, and runs scored. And, again, Evers was a good fielder but hardly legendary.

Frank Chance (1898–1914) had a career batting average of .297, which ranks higher than several first basemen in the Hall, but the ones below him were all big home-run hitters. Chance hit 20 over his whole career. Moreover, Chance only had six seasons in which he played in over 100 games. And, like the other two, his fielding was good but it wouldn't stop traffic.

Of course, in Adams' poem, they are portrayed as a great double play combination. Yet, in all their time together, only Tinker ever led the league at his position in turning twin-killings.

Such stats do not a Hall of Famer make!

We can make some allowances for the period in which they played—the dead ball era. Most batting averages were low. During the stretch from 1906 through 1910, when the Cubs won four pennants, only two National League second basemen batted .300 in a season—the Giants' Larry Doyle twice and Johnny Evers once. (And Doyle led the league's second basemen in errors three straight years.) Chance was one of the better-hitting first basemen at the time, but his major offensive contribution seems to have been stealing bases. As for Tinker, he usually outhit the rest of the league's shortstops with the glaring exception of Honus Wagner. Old Honus had started as a heavy-hitting outfielder, and though he'd switched to shortstop in 1901, he continued to hit like an outfielder.

It's not unreasonable to assume that all three Cubs would have raised their batting averages 15 or 20 points had they played twenty years later. Of course, you can say that about everybody from the era—even the heavy-hitting Honus.

Fielding is always hard to evaluate with statistics, particularly in the dead ball era. Batters tried to hit the ball on the ground to squeeze it through the infield; pitchers tried to get them to hit it in the air because that was a surer out. Because gloves were rudimentary, infields were rough, and scuffed, dirty balls were kept in play, errors were far more common than today. Ironically, just for that reason, sure-handed fielding and good range probably were more valuable then than today. Teams won with pitching, speed, and defense.

Perhaps instead of looking at T., E., and C.'s individual fielding stats, we should simply note that the Cubs led the N.L. in fielding in 1905, 1906, 1907, 1908, and 1910. They had other good fielders besides the trio in question, of course, but Tinker, Evers, and Chance handled more batted balls than anyone else on the team.

As we said, the Cubs did not lead the league in double plays during those years. Actually, there were surprisingly few double plays anywhere in those days. In 1908, the entire National League turned only 600; in 1958, the league made 1,287. One reason for the low number of DPs back then was the high number of stolen bases. Again, in 1908, the N.L. stole 1,372; in 1958, 388. Couple the stolen bases with the hit-and-run, which was almost automatic when a runner reached base, and there were not very many *opportunities* to turn a double play of the traditional tag-second-and-throw-to-first variety. There just weren't that many runners hugging first base when the ball was hit.

Moreover, to compound the problem for our legendary Cubbie trio,

Chicago had the best pitching in the league. Their pitchers were always among the leaders in fewest hits, fewest walks, and most strikeouts. The Cubs not only put few men on base, they also allowed fewer than average batted balls. For Tinker, Evers, and Chance to lead in DPs under such circumstances was nearly impossible. Significantly, the year that Tinker actually did lead in DPs was 1905, before all the pitchers hit their peaks.

With a little understanding, it's fairly easy to see that Tinker, Evers, and Chance were good players. But good isn't great. I still haven't proved their right to plaques at Cooperstown.

On the other hand, I don't think much proving is needed for Frank Chance. He'd belong in the Hall of Fame if he'd never played an inning. He won four pennants as a manager! Among twentieth-century managers who are eligible for the Hall, the only ones to win four pennants and not yet be enshrined are Billy Southworth, Earl Weaver, and Dick Williams. Southworth seems to be downrated because a couple of his pennants came during World War II, but Weaver and Williams are likely candidates who could go in any year.

Some have criticized Chance because he didn't build the team. That's true. He inherited a juggernaut built by Frank Selee, who retired in 1905 because of health reasons. But managers are not usually expected to do the building. In most cases, that's the job of the front office. Casey Stengel didn't "build" his Yankee teams; he just ran them wonderfully. And, after all, Chance wasn't called "The Master Builder"; he was called "The Peerless Leader."

Johnny Evers' claim to greatness has little to do with his statistics. In fact, of the three, he probably was third in actual ability. But Evers burned with a terrible desire to win. A frail man, he could exhaust himself by the end of a season, but in doing so, he kept his teammates fired up.

Johnny would do anything to win. He studied the rule book to find an edge. In 1908, he realized that a common practice among baserunners was illegal. At that time, when a runner was on first in the last of the ninth inning and another runner scored the winning run from third, the runner on first usually headed for the dugout instead of proceeding on to touch second. No one worried about it. The situation was fairly rare and no harm seemed to be done. But the rules clearly stated that play was not ended until that runner touched second. Johnny realized that if he could get the ball and touch second before a runner arrived, he'd have a force-out and the "winning" run would be disallowed.

In early September, the situation came up in a game the Cubs played at Philadelphia. But, when Johnny stood on second with the ball, umpire Hank O'Day chickened out and said he had not seen the play and maybe the runner had touched the base already. The Cubs still lost.

Evers was undaunted. Enraged, but undaunted. A couple of weeks later, when a crucial game with the Giants at the Polo Grounds went into the bottom of the ninth tied, he warned O'Day, who happened to be umpiring that game. Sure enough, the Giants put runners on first and third with two out. New York shortstop Al Bridwell singled and the runner came home from third to score the apparent winning run. But the runner on first, a youngster named Fred Merkle, headed for the club-house—just what about any other runner in baseball would have done at the time. Eventually, Johnny got the ball and O'Day had no choice but to call Merkle, the runner, out. The crowd on the field by then made continuing play impossible, and the game was declared a tie. When the season ended, the Cubs and Giants were in a dead heat for first; the tie was replayed, and the Cubs won.

Poor Merkle was castigated as a "bonehead" by thousands of New York fans who didn't know the rules either until Johnny Evers taught them. Players have batted or fielded their teams to pennants; Evers was one of the few who ever won one by being smarter than his opponents.

After the Cubs broke up, Johnny went to the Boston Braves in 1914. The fires still raged. The team was in last place as late as July 18, but with Evers leading the charge, the Braves roared to the front, won the pennant and then the World Series in a "miracle" finish. Evers was voted the N.L. Most Valuable Player although his statistics were no better or worse than what he'd compiled in Chicago. Obviously, the voters looked beyond the numbers.

Of the three bear cubs, Joe Tinker may have had the most ability. His batting average was lower than that of either Evers or Chance, but he hit with more power. He even led the team in home runs in 1908 with a grand total of six. His fielding statistics would seem to indicate that he was always among the league's top two or three shortstops in the field. He held down the key defensive spot for one of the great baseball aggregations, and that's something. He had several fine years after the Cubs stopped winning pennants. But was he more than just a very good shortstop? Was he a deserving Hall of Famer?

More than the other two, I think Tinker's Hall of Fame plaque is dependent upon his being a member of a famous trio on a famous team. Had he played for a lesser team, he would have been every bit as good, but he would probably have never come close to getting a vote for Cooperstown. In Joe's case, the poem wasn't just helpful, it was necessary. Hey, it's not the Hall of Statistics; it's the Hall of *Fame*!

If no one else will, I'm willing to admit Tinker, Evers, and Chance to the Hall of Fame.

But I'll admit something else. If I were picking an all-time Cubs team today, I'd have Ernie Banks on first, Ryne Sandberg on second, and Don Kessinger at short. No Tinker, no Evers, no Chance!

⚾ 9 ⚾

If It Ain't Broke— Fix It!

If you believe the history books, baseball faced its darkest moment in the wake of the Black Sox scandal. According to legend, the American public was of a mood to turn its back on baseball altogether once it learned the shocking news that eight Chicago White Sox stars had conspired to throw the 1919 World Series. Had Babe Ruth not come along to thrill ball fans back to the parks with a flock of majestic home runs, baseball would have died on the vine and our national game might have ended up being duck pins. At least that's how most historians tell it.

However, a look at the major league attendance figures for the period doesn't back up that scenario. In 1919, when teams played 140-game schedules, total attendance came in at 6,532,439, or 5,843 per game. It was the first postwar year, and the total was baseball's best since 1911. That October, the Black Sox lay down during the Series and let Cincinnati stomp all over them. Only a few people knew for sure the guys were in the tank, but hundreds had their suspicions that something was fishier than Friday night at Murphy's. Still, most fans were willing to accept the unexpected triumph of a fair Reds team over a great White Sox club as one of those David and Goliath upsets and let it go at that.

Nevertheless, the dark rumors continued into the next season. They weren't just whispered in back alleys either. You could find them on many sports pages. Yet, instead of staying home in disgust, baseball fans set a new all-time attendance mark in 1920 with 9,120,875, or 7,391 per game.

Much of that gain has been credited to Ruth's propensity for propelling the pill into purgatory, but the National League attendance rose even more than the American League's.

Just before the end of the '20 season, the story of the fix broke and all America learned that eight White Soxers couldn't be trusted with the family silver. If fans were about to reject baseball, it would show up in the 1921 attendance figures.

Well, there *was* a drop-off—a little over half a million to 8,607,312. But that was still the second-highest attendance in history. And it came at a time when the country was in a mild depression. As a matter of fact, most of the attendance drop could be found right where you'd expect it to be: among teams that were slipping toward the bottom of the standings. Cleveland and Brooklyn, the 1920 pennant winners, failed to repeat; Cincinnati was down to sixth; both the Red Sox and White Sox, shorn of their stars (though by different means), were on track to long residency in the A.L. cellar.

Of course, attendance figures don't tell us much about attitude. It's probable the guy in the bleachers was a lot more cynical in 1921 than he'd been in 1919. But he was still buying tickets. It would appear that those reports of baseball's near extinction circa 1921 have been exaggerated.

Once Upon a Time

One reason the American public may not have been quite so shocked at revelations of fixed games is that the Tainted Hose were not the first mugs to think of it. Right from the start, during the days of the old Knickerbockers, there had always been allegations of fixing. Most of such charges came from the disgruntled who bet on the losing side, but, like the man said, "Where there's smoke, somebody's smoking." The National Association (1871–75) was supposedly rife with fixing, as the National Leaguers tell it, although they were not exactly disinterested bystanders.

The National League was only in its second season—1877—when it was rocked by a fixing scandal. The Louisville Grays seemed on their way to a pennant that year when they began losing a lot of games they should have won. Then someone noticed that utility infielder Al Nichols was sending and receiving more telegrams than Ulysses S. Grant. The wires were intercepted and it was easily seen that a code word, "sash," was being used to tell gamblers when Louisville would lose. Unless you're into military uniforms, "sash" is not the easiest word to work into ordinary conversation. It turned out that three Louisville stars, pitcher Jim Devlin, outfielder George Hall, and shortstop Billy Craver, were doing the fixing with Nichols as the go-between. When confronted, all four confessed. William Hulbert, by then National League president, barred them for life. Supposedly, Devlin showed up at league meetings for years afterward dressed in rags and begging for reinstatement. He drank himself to death in 1883.

The year before, in 1882, an umpire of all people was banished for letting gamblers dictate his decisions. To this day, despite what you thought about that out call in last Tuesday's game, Bill Higham is the only major league umpire ever to have based his strike zone on how many dollars he had down.

Baseball got through the rest of the nineteenth century without another big fixing scandal, but there were always rumors and innuendoes every time some fan's team lost a game he thought they should have won. In the early part of the twentieth century several attempts were supposedly made to bribe players, but those didn't come to light until after the Black Sox were exposed.

The absolute master of the fix was first baseman Hal Chase, who showed up in the majors in 1905. Chase, once described as having a "corkscrew brain," was so good at his dishonesty that, even though everybody knew he was doing it, no one could ever prove it. He was a brilliant fielder, and that was where he did his cheating. At a key moment, he'd arrive just late enough or juggle a tricky hop enough or be forced to pull off the bag enough that a run would score. If you hadn't seen it before, you'd swear ol' Hal had just made a terrific try. Once in a while someone would accuse Chase of cheating, but the accuser always ended up with egg on his face because there was never any hard evidence. When New York Highlander manager George Stallings told the team owner what Chase was doing, the owner fired Stallings—and replaced him with Chase.

It was said that Hal doubled his salary with what he made on bets. It's a little late for an audit, and he was careful not to leave a paper trail. Eventually, Chase became a real embarrassment to baseball. Clubs began passing him around like a bad Christmas tie. No doubt each new employer thought, "Hal may have cut some corners before, but I'll see that he's on the square or else." Then, six months later, they'd trade him for whatever they could get just to be rid of him. Finally, in 1919, Chase was banned for life more on accumulated suspicion than for any proven dishonesty. Talk about locking the barn door! By then he was thirty-eight years old and nearing the end anyway. He was starting to strike out in the ninth with the bases loaded even when he didn't want to. Unrepentant, Hal retired to California and lived to a ripe old age. Word had it that he made $40,000 betting on the Reds in the 1919 World Series. Who said cheaters never win?

The Stained Stockings

The point has been raised that having someone like Hal Chase get away with his fixes for years may have encouraged other players (i.e., those in Chicago) to think they might do the same. If so, they should have checked their SAT scores first. Chase was evil but smart. The Black Sox were just dumb.

In the first place, they told at least three different groups of gamblers and God knows who else about their plans. They had such loose lips you'd almost expect one of them to jump into a cab and say, "Take me to Comiskey Park, where I'm presently engaged in throwing the World Series." They not only made it certain that the odds on the games would plummet and that the word would eventually get out to someone who counted, they also got themselves to the point where they didn't even know who was supposed to pay them off.

Moreover, by not getting the money up front, they never were paid what they'd been promised. In other words, they were such dumb cheaters they let themselves be cheated. That's not an excuse for throwing games—in for a dime, in for a dollar—but it does end up making them such *chintzy* crooks.

Then, because they weren't being paid what they expected, they tried to play some games on the square. It's likely that after the first two games there never was a time when all eight knew whether they were supposed to win or lose that afternoon. Had they played the season with the same intelligence they showed in the Series, they would have finished last.

Finally, they were stupidly obvious. Hal Chase could fix a game and come out looking like a hero. The Black Sox might as well have worn signs: pitcher Eddie Cicotte, one of the best-fielding moundsmen of his day, made critical errors, control artist Lefty Williams walked everybody but the umpire, outfielder Joe Jackson played out of position like a raw kid just up from Tacoma.

The amazing thing is not that they got caught but that it took a year before the world found out.

Faith Springs Eternal

The *really* amazing thing is that more than seventy years after the Black Sox were banned for life, some naive souls are still trying to get them reinstated in baseball's good graces. Buck Weaver and Joe Jackson are the subjects of most of the pleas, but a few parties would like a general whitewash. The arguments seem to be that they didn't do it, and anyway there were extenuating circumstances.

Let's look at some of those circumstances first.

White Sox owner Charles Comiskey was a real skinflint. There's just no other way to put it. He paid his players about half what players of equal ability and experience were getting at the time. Therefore, goes the argument, he *deserved* having his players cheat on him.

But wait a minute! That idea runs counter to what we see in real life. Is the cashier at your local Burger Burner entitled to rifle the cash register just because he's only getting minimum wage? If you get mugged at the end of your lane are you going to tell the cops, "Forget it, the bandit just wanted to move into a higher tax bracket"? So they weren't being paid what they were worth. Are you? Of course not. So, are you planning to take off for Brazil with the company treasury?

The real ugly part is that Ol' Man Comiskey wasn't the only one who got cheated. Also on the Black Sox' list were their honest teammates and all their fans. Throw in the Cincinnati Reds and their fans who will always wonder if they could have won on their own. Oh, yes, the short end of the stick also went to anybody who bet his lunch money on the Sox. And anybody who loved baseball. Or any other sport. Does that cover all the victims? There was a peasant in Manchuria who never heard of baseball; he wasn't hurt a bit. Let HIM lobby for the Black Sox.

A particular extenuating circumstance is often extended to Buck Weaver by the bleeding hearts. Good ol' Buck, it is said, refused to join in any fix. He knew about it. He sat in on the meetings. Maybe he even made a suggestion or two. But he was honest! Some would even give him points for NOT blowing the whistle on his crooked buddies. How Buck could give his all when he knew the Series was in the bag is beyond me, but at least it set him up to blackmail his friends after the fact. Apparently he didn't try, but a couple of years down the line if he needed some dough, well, who knows? That aside, there is a thing called "conspiracy" and it doesn't ask how much you made on the deal. By keeping his mouth shut, Buck was cheating everybody in sight except seven crooks. A real stand-up guy!

On any given day, you can get a goodly crowd together that favors letting Joe Jackson off the hook. Hey, goes the argument, the guy was such a great hitter he belongs in the Hall of Fame. Yes, he was indeed a terrific hitter. And since he didn't ever have to suffer any of those end-of-career bad seasons that pull other hitters' lifetime stats down, he still ranks third all-time with .356.

All together now, Jackson was a great hitter. Hal Chase was a great fielder. Benedict Arnold was a great general. Vidkun Quisling was a great—well, I'll have to look that one up. Just being good at something does not give a person *carte blanche* to be a crook. Bonnie Parker was a good shot. Nixon went to China.

The naysayers will tell you that Jackson and the boys were tried and acquitted in court. That's true, but it was in the same Cook County court that couldn't convict Capone of littering even though he kept discarding bodies on street corners. The reason the Black Sox were acquitted was that evidence mysteriously disappeared—evidence like Joe Jackson's confession. It's pretty well known that gambler Arnold Rothstein paid $10,000 to see that at least four confessions were torched. If Nixon had burned those pesky tapes, he'd still be President today.

The Jackson crowd trumpets that Shoeless Joe hit .375 and knocked out twelve hits in the Series. How could he have been cheating, they ask? The next sound you hear will be gales of laughter coming from Hal Chase. It ain't what you do, it's when you do it.

Ah, but Jackson wasn't smart enough to fake it, say his fans. They paint him as some sort of walking cipher who could hit, field, and throw but never think. Well, he was illiterate, but no one ever said he couldn't count. Like, up to five thousand, which is the number of dollars he found under his pillow, and up to twenty thousand, which is what he told the boys he wanted.

As a last resort, the Jackson defenders try to tear down the reputations of other members of the Hall of Fame to show that they weren't angels. Tris Speaker and Ty Cobb were accused of fixing a game by an embittered former teammate, but you couldn't convict a cat of having whiskers on the evidence he offered. Some of the mud sticks. Cobb was a racist and a psychopath. John McGraw was close to it. Babe Ruth was a glutton. Cap Anson was a racist. King Kelly and quite a few others were drunks. But nobody ever said it was the Hall of Pleasant Companions. They all tried to win. Which is what fans plunked down their ticket money to see.

As far as we know, after they were banned, Jackson, Weaver, and the rest led honest lives. That's a point in their favor. They were one-shot crooks instead of habitual criminals. That they were talented players and inept crooks just makes it all the sadder Judge Kenesaw Mountain Landis felt he had to suspend them until hell froze over. The judge had this crazy idea that letting them off with a warning just might tell the American baseball fan that his game couldn't be trusted any further than he could bunt a brick. Landis was suffering under the delusion that welcoming the fixers back with open arms could somehow encourage other players to decide who'd win the game during warm-ups. That crazy old man had the weird idea that baseball should be played with a little more honesty than a backroom crap game.

You can see he was a fanatic.

Me too. Put Joe Jackson in the Hall of Fame? If it ever happens, they're going to have to fumigate upstate New York all the way to Utica.

Five Great Things That Never Happened in a Major League Game

Picture this: out on the mound stands a magnificent pitcher. Inning after inning, he's made the opponents' bats seem like wet noodles. Swaggering, cocky, he has it all today; his fastball crackles, his curve bites, his control is such that he could peel an orange from sixty feet away. Now, as the opposition drags itself to the plate for its final humiliation, the pitcher turns and waves his outfielders off the field. And then his infielders are also sent to the bench. The crowd buzzes with excitement.

Smiling demonically, the great pitcher strikes out the first batter on three pitches. Three more pitches and the second batter is gone. And then—unbelievably—strike one, two, and three; the side is out!

"Unbelievable" is the word for it. This episode in pitching preeminence has been told many times. The only thing certain is that it never took place on a major league diamond.

The pitcher most often the hero of this tale is Rube Waddell, the fabulously talented screwball who pitched for Connie Mack and the Philadelphia Athletics in the first decade of this century. The original man with a million-dollar arm and ten-cent head, Waddell was a marvelously talented left-hander who would much rather have spent his time chasing after fire trucks, fishing off a pier, or sampling the wares of the nearest saloon than toiling on the mound. Before he joined Mr. Mack's Phila-delphia Athletics, he spent time with several other teams driving their managers crazy. One of his early teams was Pittsburgh where he roomed with Tommy Leach, the undersized third baseman famed for his ability to crank out three-base hits.

According to Leach, Waddell actually pulled the wave-in-the-outfielders stunt once in spring training while the Pirates were wending their way north. In those days, major league teams often paid their expenses by taking on the amateur and semi-pro ball clubs of towns along their route. It's perfectly possible that Waddell might be allowed to try such a thing in an exhibition game, especially one against the local yokels of some whistle-stop. Matching Waddell against some small-town stal-warts was like sending Godzilla against Bambi. It was a show.

But the difference between such an exhibition and a real major league game with something at stake is greater than the difference between the Grand Canyon and Steve Canyon. That any major league manager, much less a presumably intelligent one like the Pirates' Fred Clarke or the A's Connie Mack, would allow his outfielders to leave the field and thus risk turning a pop fly into a home run is inconceivable. And can you imagine the outfielders themselves putting their careers on the line for a nut like Waddell? In the wake of his short career and early death, many of the Rube's former teammates attested that he was a fine fellow, but not one of them ever said he had a brain.

Another pitcher sometimes credited with the *sans*-outfielders trick is Satchel Paige, a brighter bulb by far than Rube Waddell and an even better pitcher. Paige pitched in the Negro Leagues from the 1920s through the 1940s, but he probably tossed twice as many pitches in barnstorming ex-hibitions. To draw crowds to those affairs, Negro League teams often had to walk a high wire between professionalism and entertainment. Paige was the biggest draw and best-known player in black baseball, and he got that way with breathtaking examples of pitching prowess. That he sometimes called in his fielders in exhibitions would be as likely as tomorrow's sun-rise. But did he ever do it in a game that meant something? Probably not.

The Fence-Busting Catch

Many differences exist between what happens on the field in an exhibition and on the field in a real game. The same may be said, albeit by a lesser margin, between major and minor league baseball. Some of the most marvelous events that never happened in the bigs did indeed happen in the bushes. A couple of years ago, a minor league catcher tossed a peeled potato into the midst of play. It brought a chuckle from the press and a suspension for the player. Had it happened on a major league diamond with a major league pennant and who knows how many millions of dollars at risk, the potato man would have been drawn, quartered, and French-fried.

Another minor league incident of recent note saw an outfielder pursue a baseball into and *through* a fence. Someone captured the moment on videotape and it was subsequently shown and reshown on TV almost as often as Rodney King.

This brings to mind another old baseball wives' tale about a legendary catch made by Chicago outfielder Bill Lange in the 1890s. If Lange's name is not so well known today as that of Hugh Duffy, Ed Delahanty, Cap Anson, or some other pre-1900s sluggers, it can only be because his career ended abruptly after only seven glorious seasons. During that short span, he compiled a .330 career batting mark, with good power and outstanding speed. It was not a tragic injury that curtailed the "Cobb of the 1890s"; it was love. Lange wished to marry, but his bride's father refused to let his daughter wed a professional baseball player. Rather than give up his lady, Lange retired from the diamond. Baseball fans may derive some malicious consolation in learning the marriage eventually ended in divorce.

Lange was a terrific defensive outfielder who made numerous circus catches in center field for the Chicagos. One in particular captured the public's imagination—so much so that it was cited again and again through the first half of the twentieth century as one of the most exceptional happenings ever to occur on a baseball field.

The Colts, the name Chicago went by during the '90s, were playing in Washington, then a member of the National League, and had just taken a 6–5 lead in the top of the eleventh inning. Washington had two out and a man on base in the bottom of the eleventh when Kip Selbach of Washington smashed a drive deep to center field. Lange raced back, dived, grasped the ball, somersaulted, and then crashed into and *through* the wooden fence, disappearing completely. A moment later, he reappeared, still holding the ball high for the final out.

Small wonder that such a remarkable catch would be written about and wondered at for years thereafter. And small wonder that Arthur Ahrens, one of those SABR (Society for American Baseball Research) people who can't leave well enough alone, should decide to investigate. Arousing his curiosity was the universal omission of a date from any of the accounts. A Chicagoan, Mr. Ahrens did not let civic pride blind him to the truth as he meticulously researched newspaper accounts of every game played between the Colts and Washington during the period that Lange roamed center for Chicago.

It was reasonable to expect that such a dazzling catch would be noted in the headlines, but Ahrens couldn't find it even in the fine print. Many of Lange's defensive gems were chronicled in the dailies of the day, but none fit the precise circumstances of the legendary grab. And never was a "through-the-fence" catch mentioned.

However, he found one game that seems to be the germ of the legend. On August 31, 1896, Chicago and Washington went into the tenth inning of a scoreless game. In the top of the inning, Chicago first baseman George Decker was hit by a pitch that broke his arm. A hospital happened to be behind the right-field fence. Washington's Selbach used a ladder as a battering ram to knock a hole through the fence so Decker could be taken quickly for medical treatment. Then, in the bottom of the frame, Lange made a sensational, diving catch of a low liner to extend the game into the eleventh inning. Within a few years, the story elements of Selbach breaking through the fence and Lange's excellent catch became twisted into a wondrous play that never happened. And, for the record, Washington won the game 1–0 in the eleventh.

That Unassisted Triple Play

If Lange's catch-that-never-happened *had* happened, it would have still taken only second place in the outfield competition of amazing catches. Since 1878, a shaky first place has belonged to Paul Hines, who is sometimes credited with being the only major league outfielder to make an unassisted triple play. And who sometimes isn't.

An unassisted triple play is the second-rarest event in baseball. (The rarest is for a player to ask to renegotiate his contract at a lower figure.) In all of major league history, there have been only nine unassisted TPs. Well, *ten* if you count Paul Hines, which you can do only if you're able to suspend disbelief to the extent that you think *The Wizard of Oz* is a documentary.

On May 8, 1878, Boston visited the Providence Grays. Hines patrolled left field for the Grays. Jack Manning was on third and Ezra Sutton on second for Boston. Jack Burdock hit the ball just over the head of the

Providence shortstop for what looked like a certain safety, only to have Hines grab it off his shoetops. He then continued on the dead run to third, where he stepped on the base, and *then* he turned and threw to second baseman Charlie Sweasy.

Undoubtedly, a triple play had occurred. The question has always been how many putouts should be credited to Hines. Those arguing for three unassisted POs point to the next day's news story in the *Providence Journal* which stated that just before Hines' catch, "Manning and Sutton proceeded to the home plate." They argue that this means Sutton had rounded third and was thus out (along with Manning) when Hines stepped on that base. His throw to second base was simply for good measure, they say.

However, this is patent nonsense. Burdock's drive must have been of the humpbacked liner type because Sutton, an experienced player, would never have run hell-for-leather on a pop-up. Therefore, we are asked to believe that, in the length of time it takes a low line drive to reach a spot somewhere between the shortstop's and left fielder's normal positions, Sutton was able to run all the way past third base. More, he was sufficiently past that landmark that he was unable to return even that far in the time it took Hines to run to it from left field. Sutton would have had to be faster than Superman on his best day. And Hines would have had to have been faster yet.

But suppose the *Journal* reporter had written "Manning and Sutton proceeded *toward* the home plate." Any controversy ends. Manning was perhaps near home and running in the wrong direction when Hines made his catch. Hines, running in the right direction, was able to beat him to the bag. Sutton probably thought he had a good chance to get back safely to second base since Hines' attention was on third. But he also had to get himself turned around, and that was just enough time for Hines' throw to catch him at second.

A terrific play, yes. An unassisted triple play? Not on your life!

Tripling into a Triple Play

An even more famous triple play didn't happen in 1926. This was the oft-cited incident where Brooklyn's Babe Herman "tripled into a triple play." A simple review of what actually did occur will show that Herman neither tripled nor launched a three-outer.

The hero of the incident was no doubt baseball's second-most-famous Babe (after Ruth) and probably its second-most-famous Herman (after

Billy), but he was first among the Dodgers' fabled "Daffiness Boys" of the 1920s. He once hit as high as .393, but his critics complained that such a number more closely approximated his fielding average. Herman manfully defended his defensive prowess, particularly against the scurrilous accusations that fly balls oft bounced off his noggin. He had never been hit in the head by a fly, he insisted, adding that "hit in the shoulder don't count." As a baserunner, Babe also had his own unique style, as we shall see.

The incident for which he is most famous occurred on August 15, 1926, at Brooklyn's Ebbets Field with the Dodgers hosting the Boston Braves. The visitors led 1–0 as the game moved into the bottom of the seventh inning. Because he was bored and complained loudly about it, Brooklyn reserve catcher Mickey O'Neil was sent to the third base coaches' box at the inning's opening. He quickly found something to occupy his attention: Dodger Johnny Butler singled and then raced home to tie the score on Hank DeBerry's double. Brooklyn pitcher Dazzy Vance followed with another single as DeBerry moved to third. Chick Fewster walked to load the bases.

The Braves brought in a new pitcher, left-hander George Mogridge, who promptly induced Brooklyn's Merwin Jacobson to pop up for the first out of the inning. (If you are familiar with baseball rules, you are probably aware that a triple play after one out has been recorded in an inning is, to put it mildly, unlikely. Remember that point.)

Up to the plate stepped Babe Herman. Mogridge threw him a curve and Herman turned it into a fastball, blasting it high off the right-field wall. DeBerry trotted in easily from third to score the go-ahead run. Vance, coming from second and receiving ambiguous signs from third-base coach O'Neil, was a bit more cautious. Only when he was certain the ball had landed safely did he begin wending his way toward third base. Fewster, in the meantime, had no such doubts and fairly flew around second. Herman was also bold in his approach to baserunning. However, he seems to have been somewhat concerned with checking his shoelaces, for even though he ran all out, he kept his head down and his eyes averted.

Vance rounded third but had second thoughts. On the urging of O'Neil, he decided to return to the base. Fewster, nearing the bag, was astonished to see it already in use and pulled up a few feet shy of his goal. Herman, having galloped past second with the determination of Man O'War entering the stretch, steamed past Fewster and slid into third in a cloud of triumph and dust.

The Boston catcher, a clever fellow named Oscar Siemer, took one look at the crowd at third and quickly surmised that too many Dodgers were present. His solution was to begin tagging everyone in sight. His tag of Vance accomplished nothing, for Dazzy was entitled to the base under the rules. Nor did his tag of Herman advance the proceedings, for Babe had already made the second out of the inning when he passed Fewster on the base paths. They say he also tagged the umpire and his own third baseman, but that might only be embroidery to the story. However, all Siemer's tagging put the fear of God into Fewster, who lit out for some safer zone. He was finally chased down in right field, his tagging making the inning's third and final out.

In defense of the oft-maligned Babe Herman, the tripled-into-a-triple-play charge is a scandalous exaggeration; he only doubled into a double play. And, we must point out, in doing so, he drove in what eventually turned out to be the winning run.

Right About There

That plate company—you know the one: "We cannot guarantee that these plates will increase in value but similar plates have"—has a new TV offer, "The Called Shot." The plate in question has a fine painting of Babe Ruth completing what we can only assume is his home run swing. If you have an urge to eat your spinach off the Bambino's nose, I apologize for not getting the address or price for you. Frankly, I was reeling in astonishment that the platemakers chose to illustrate the end of a swing which, after all, looked pretty much the same 714 times. It was what came *before* the swing on that October day that makes it the stuff of legends.

Some things are easily agreed upon. The incident took place at Chicago's Wrigley Field on October 1, 1932, during the fifth inning of Game Three of the World Series. To that point, the Series had been distinguished mainly by unusually vicious verbal abuse pouring from each dugout. New York castigated the Cubs for voting only a fractional share of their Series money to Mark Koenig, a former Yankee called up by Chicago in August. Koenig had led the Cubs' pennant dash but stood to gain only a half share of the goodies. The Cubs fastened on the Yankee "millionaires" and their "fat" left fielder Ruth. Interspersed among such sneers as "cheapskate" and "fatso" were numerous less printable epithets centering on various ancestries and supposed moral turpitude of parents.

The Yankees won the first two contests, but Game Three was tied at 4–4 when Ruth, who had already hit a three-run homer in the first inning, came to bat with one out in the fifth. Cub veteran Charlie Root was on the mound to face him.

From there on, it gets a bit murky.

The count moved to 0-and-2, 1-and-2, 2-and-2, or 3-and-2—all four having been reported by eyewitnesses. Ruth himself favored 0-and-2, but the majority seems to tip the scales toward 2-and-2, with the strikes being called rather than swinging. However, there's no consensus to the order of strikes and balls that led to that number.

Everyone agrees that Ruth made some sort of gestures after the strikes and possibly after one of the balls. It's what those gestures were and what they signified that is at the core of baseball's most beloved legend.

The choices are:

1. Ruth held up a finger or two to the Cubs' dugout and to Root to indicate that he still had first two and then one strike left.
2. Ruth held up a particular finger to the Cubs' dugout and to Root as he exchanged more of the pleasantries that had already made the Series linguistically X-rated.
3. Ruth pointed to the center-field bleachers where he intended to hit one of Root's offerings.

Anyone familiar with Ruth's vocabulary would bet dollars to donuts that Number 2 is the proper choice. But the Associated Press and most observers opted for Choice Number 1 as better suited to the pages of family newspapers the next day. One headline read: "RUTH ENJOYS RAZZING CUBS / Raises His Fingers to Show Strike Count, Then Homers."

A couple of writers thought Ruth might have gestured vaguely toward the outfield, but Joe Williams, writing for the Scripps-Howard newspaper chain, saw something very specific. His column was headlined "RUTH CALLS SHOT." Ruth, he said, had pointed to the exact spot in center field where he forthwith hit his homer.

Williams, who admitted, "I always was a pushover for wonderful fairy tales," was one of the country's most widely read journalists. In discovering a magical intent behind Ruth's gesture and a mystical result to the Bamster's swing, Williams struck a nerve in a Depression-ridden nation that badly needed to believe in a hero. Within days, other respected sportswriters like Paul Gallico, Tom Meany, Bill Corum, and Fred Lieb were convinced they had seen the same marvel Williams had. Lieb quoted Lou Gehrig, who'd been in the on-deck circle and who followed Ruth's "shot" with a homer of his own: "What do you think of the nerve of that big monkey calling his shot and taking those two strikes and then hitting the ball exactly where he pointed?" On other occasions, Gehrig denied that Ruth had called anything printable.

The Cubs to a man disputed that any called shot had taken place. Of course, they were hardly neutral. On the other hand, Charlie Root was from the old school; he often noted that anyone actually attempting to call a shot on him would have worn the next pitch as an earring.

Most of the Yankees said most of the time that Ruth had done the deed. Over the years, so did the 350,000 fans who swore they were among the 49,986 in attendance. Probably some of them remembered Ruth holding up a blueprint of Wrigley Field with a big red X marked on it.

Ruth himself never quite said that he ever called it—at least not anywhere he was under oath. On several occasions, he confided to friends that the whole story was malarkey, but his hand wasn't on a Bible at those times either.

What it really comes down to with the "Called Shot"—or any of the other feats that never happened detailed here—is that scientific evidence and even common sense have no sway with a baseball fan who wants to believe. Faith can move mountains; it can even point to the bleachers.

⚾ 11 ⚾

The Most Overrated
Teams Ever

The other day I had some time to kill from my busy schedule because *Oprah* had a rerun, and I got to thinking about the legendary teams of the past. I had to admit that some of the most famous are overrated. I admitted this only to myself, of course. I'm a card-carrying member of OLDFARTS (Our Legendary Diamond Favorites Are Regularly Treasured and Sanctified) and I feared I might not be called for the next meeting if word of my blasphemy got out. But then I said to myself, "Self, if you don't reveal this here revelation to your readers, who are you going to tell? Those bald guys who come to the door with flowers?" I mean, you readers and me are the people who care—deeply—about baseball's history. Right? Hey, we understand each other.

No wonder we're reading about the Baseball That Was! We need a break from today. When we look at the front page of our daily newspaper, we've gotta be depressed. War, famine, disease, taxes. (Sigh!) And then we turn to the sports page and it's just as bad. Drugs, hypocrisy, selfishness, egotism. (Oh sigh!) Even the comic strips are depressing these days. Did you hear the Katzenjammer Kids just joined a street gang? Yesterday I did the crossword in my daily birdcage liner and 17 across was THEENDISNEAR. (Sigh! sigh! and double sigh!)

Ah, to meander untrammeled through the perfect baseball of yesteryear "when every player was a giant in his way"! How utopian it used to be! No drugs. Oh, sure, some players drank, but back then drunks were funny.

Remember? They never drove cars or got cirrhosis. They just hiccuped a lot. Most players weren't paid much in those days, which made them a lot easier to like when we were taking our pop bottles back to the A&P so we could eat on the day before payday. Oldtime players tell us they played *strictly* for the love of the game. I believe them. I write baseball books *strictly* because I enjoy banging my fingers on a keyboard.

But eventually we have to come back to earth and admit that we're remembering through a rose-tinted reverie. Some of the Greats weren't all that great. And some of the teams, like I said, were overrated. I'm going to run the five most overrated teams in history by you and tell you why I think they should be taken down a notch on our imaginary scale. For all but one, I'm going to consider them over a period of three or four seasons because a truly great team should be more than a one-shot deal. Four seasons can tell us if the team really had it or was only a juxtaposition of a lot of "career years." And I'll compare them with their less-celebrated betters of the same era.

Remember now, I'm not saying these teams weren't good—they just weren't as good as we remember them. Like your first pizza.

You can disagree if you want and even write nasty letters. Maybe you can convince me I'm wrong. But, please, just don't send me one of those SABRmetric formulas that are supposed to prove a point by doing something to statistics that would get you arrested in most states if you ever did it to a human being.

#5—Chicago White Sox, 1917–20

If you saw *Eight Men Out* or even the previews on TV, you were given the impression that this was the greatest team since Romeo and Juliet. But lovers these guys weren't. For all their talent, I have to believe that their loathing for each other took a few wins away each season, even when they were *trying* to come out on top. Talk about bad chemistry! Half this bunch wouldn't follow the other half up a dark alley. Not that personal animosity is a reason in itself to drop them in the dumper. We all know that Tinker and Evers didn't speak to each other; neither did Ruth and Gehrig.

And I'm trying not to down-rate them just because eight of them were crooks. It *does* strike me that a bunch of guys who put a few bucks ahead of winning, to say nothing of honor, honesty, respect, and loyalty, might have trouble finding the courage to come through in a really tight pennant race, but maybe I'm wrong there. Maybe the best and the brightest are all in Joliet. I've heard excuses made for the Sox' dishonesty because they were underpaid by Comiskey. What if I sent my publisher a note demanding more money or I'd start misspelling words?

To review: The Sox, when they were still unstained, took the 1917 pennant over a Red Sox team that had won in 1912, 1915, and 1916. And you'll remember the Philadelphia A's won pennants in 1910, 1911, 1913, and 1914. The Red Sox won again in 1918, a war year which we really can't consider because too many players were gone. The White Sox came back to win in 1919 and then went into the tank for the World Series.

So, for a period of ten years, all the American League pennants went to three teams. They were cut from the same cloth—speed, defense, and pitching. But I think the Red Sox and A's pennant winners were just a little better at it. If you disregard 1918, you'll find that the White Sox scored fewer runs in both '17 and '19 than any of the other pennant winners except the 1916 Red Sox. The Pale Hose had Joe Jackson, Eddie Collins, and Happy Felsch. They also had a couple of holes in their batting order named Ray Schalk and Swede Risberg.

Chicago had good pitching in Eddie Cicotte, Lefty Williams, and Red Faber. Dickie Kerr helped in 1919. But were these four better than Jack Coombs, Chief Bender, Eddie Plank, Cy Morgan, Bullet Joe Bush, Bob Shawkey, and Herb Pennock of the A's or Smokey Joe Wood, Hugh Bedient, Rube Foster, Babe Ruth, Ernie Shore, Carl Mays, and Dutch Leonard of the Red Sox? All of these weren't tip-top in any single season, but both Philadelphia and Boston had deep, DEEP pitching in their pennant years. Chicago had four starters (by 1919) and a lot of guys you never heard of.

Much of the White Sox mystique is based on what Might Have Been had eight of them not been booted out on their keisters. It's an article of faith that they'd have won the 1920 pennant. But would they have? On September 28, when the evil eight were suspended, the Sox were a half-game behind with three to play. Cleveland had six to play. The Sox lost two of three to the Browns while the Indians won four of six to clinch. If you want to award two more wins to the Sox (and remember, the Browns were a .500 ballclub in 1919) because they were shorthanded, you can just as easily scratch the season-closing loss the Indians took *after* they'd already clinched the pennant. But, even leaving the Indians at 4–2, the most the Sox could have done with three straight wins was tie Cleveland and toss the whole thing up in a playoff.

The Black Sox Faithful (now, *there's* an oxymoron!) also assume their team would have kept on winning into the 1920s had it stayed whole. Not likely. The game was already changing in 1920. By '21 the Yankees with Ruthian power were in. The aging, line-drive hitters of the Sox wouldn't have kept up, although they might have made it close once or twice. Hap Felsch, who hit 14 homers in 1920, and Joe Jackson, who hit 12, were the only Sox likely to get into double home run figures regularly. Of course, they all hit better in the Might-Have-Been.

Here's *my* Might-Have-Been: When Judge Landis clears them to play again, the eight sail away on a world cruise to celebrate. The ship sinks and they spend three weeks on a raft before they are rescued. They are all so moved by the experience that they go to Tibet and spend the rest of their lives as holy men.

I just got a note from my editor: "You ALWAYS misspell words. They pay ME the big bucks to fix your mistakes!"

#4—Boston Red Sox, 1948–51

People still wonder how such a powerful team avoided a slew of pennants during this period. What a lineup! Ted Williams, Bobby Doerr, Dom DiMaggio, Johnny Pesky, Vern Stephens, Billy Goodman, Al Zarilla, Walt Dropo, Birdie Tebbetts, Clyde Vollmer! The Sox led the American League in runs scored in every one of those years. In 1950 they plated 1,027, still the most by any team since World War II. The Sox hit for average and they hit for power, but they weren't a hit in the standings, finishing second twice and third twice.

Were they the best team ever to not win a pennant? No. They may have been the best collection of hitters not to win, but when you took the wood out of their hands they were nothing special. Defensively, the BoSox were the SlowSox, although Doerr and DiMaggio were fine fielders. Pesky was an okay shortstop but he was playing third base. If they'd flip-flopped him with Junior Stephens at short, they might have won in '48 and '49.

What the Red Sox really lacked was pitching. Mel Parnell was first-rate, but he was an underused rookie in '48. After that, he was overused because so many others couldn't hack it. Ellis Kinder had a big year as a starter in '49 and did some good relieving in the next two years. Joe Dobson had a couple of fair seasons. But overall, well—the team's ERAs for four years were 4.20, 3.97, 4.88, and 4.14. Not even the Sox Sockers could make up for that kind of pitching.

In other words, the Sox finished exactly where they deserved to finish.

In the meantime, the Yankees won world championships every year from 1949 through 1953. I never thought I'd say a Yankees team could be underrated and maybe it's only my imagination, but it seems like when people are lauding the great Yankees teams of the period, they focus on the 1955–58 and 1960–64 teams—the ones that sometimes lost a World Series. The 1949–53 bunch didn't have the impressive individual seasons that the later clubs could brag about. What they did have was MORE. They were possibly the deepest team ever. If everyone wasn't a superstar, they were at least two deep in certified major leaguers at every position. And they wallowed in pitching depth too. Cleveland had better starters (maybe) but the Yankees could trundle out eight or ten good pitchers every year.

Take the Yankees out of the A.L. from 1948 through 1951 and the BoSox hitters might have won a pennant or two. But bet on the National League in the World Series.

#3—Baltimore Orioles, 1894–97

The Orioles are the most glamorous team of the nineteenth century. They were so smart they invented "scientific" baseball. They were so tough they spit tobacco juice on broken bones and kept on playing. They were so good they just won and won.

At least that's the legend.

But the legend had some help. Ex-Orioles John McGraw, Wilbert Robinson, and Hughie Jennings managed in the majors long into the twentieth century. During rain delays they loved nothing more than to sit around and enthrall wide-eyed young newspaper reporters with tales of the old Orioles. No doubt about it, the Orioles had the best PR of any nineteenth-century team.

Not that the O's weren't smart, tough, and good. They won pennants in 1894–95–96. But the Boston Beaneaters won in 1891–92–93 and again in 1898–99 by being smarter, tougher, and better. That's a 5–3 advantage for the guys from Massachusetts.

In addition to McGraw, Robinson, and Jennings, the Orioles had a terrific outfield in Willie Keeler, Joe Kelley, and Steve Brodie. Second base was ordinary and the first baseman changed from year to year, with only old Dan Brouthers in 1894 being outstanding. During the 1890s, Boston always had the superior infield with first basemen Tommy Tucker and Fred Tenney, second baseman Bobby Lowe (of the four homers in one game), shortstop Herman Long (the best of the period), and third basemen

Billy Nash and Jimmy Collins (the future Hall of Famer). The outfielders—Hugh Duffy, Billy Hamilton, Chick Stahl, and Tommy McCarthy—were at least the Orioles' equals in most years. And catchers Charlie Bennett and Marty Bergen were better than Robinson defensively.

On the supposedly ironman Orioles, McGraw missed a third of the 1895 season and most of '96 through injuries and illness. On the Beaneaters, it took a railroad accident that cost him both legs to get Charlie Bennett out of there.

All the smart, "inside" baseball the Orioles were playing was also being played by the Beaneaters. Just who invented what is up for grabs.

But where Boston had it all over Baltimore was pitching. The Orioles seldom had two good pitchers to rub together. The Beaneaters had Jack Stivetts, Fred Klobedanz, Ted Lewis, Vic Willis, and John Clarkson in various seasons. But *all* the time they had automatic 30-game winner Kid Nichols. The O's never had a pitcher in any of their years to compare with him.

McGraw, Robinson, and Jennings succeeded in talking the O's into the glory spot for the nineteenth century, a niche that Boston deserved. Remember, McGraw managed the *New York* Giants, Robinson was across the river managing the *Brooklyn* Dodgers, and for a time Jennings coached for McGraw. That made them "hometown folks" to the New York writers. So if they said the Orioles were tops, they were going to be believed and quoted by the New York crowd. And, as anyone living in any other city in the U.S. could tell you, it's hard to be heard above the New York media.

#2—The Gashouse Gang, 1933–36

The Gashouse Gang was undoubtedly one of the most colorful aggregations ever to come down the pike. They were so famous—still so famous actually—that to mention that we're talking about the St. Louis Cardinals of the mid-1930s seems like we're talking down to any baseball fan. But let's not confuse color with ability. The Gang was good. The Cubs and Giants of the period were better. As a matter of fact, the Cardinals themselves won four pennants and two World Series in the pre-Gashouse era from 1926 through 1931. The Gashouse Gang, which can be dated from 1933 when Joe Medwick and Leo Durocher became regulars and Pepper Martin started third-basing full-time, won only one pennant (and World Series)—in 1934. In approximately the same period, the Giants won pennants in 1933, 1936, and 1937 and the Cubs won in 1932, 1935, and 1938. In the '33 through '37 period, the Giants played .600 ball, the Gang .586, and the Cubs .585. Yet all people talk about is the Gashouse Gang!

St. Louis had a great pitcher in Dizzy Dean; the Giants had Carl Hubbell—not as quotable but an even better pitcher. The Cardinals had Joe Medwick in the outfield; New York had an equally powerful hitter in Mel Ott. The Gang had Ripper Collins on first base; Gotham had Bill Terry, the National League's last .400 hitter. Durocher at shortstop? I'll take the Giants' Dick Bartell, who could hit as well as field. And Travis Jackson at third outhit and outfielded Pepper Martin, too. Add outfielder Jo-Jo Moore and catcher Gus Mancuso to the Giants to make up for the Cards' fading Fordham Flash Frankie Frisch fielding at second.

After you got past Diz and his brother Paul (who had two 19-win seasons before his arm died), the Gang's pitching was catch-as-catch-can. The Giants backed King Carl Hubbell with Prince Hal Schumacher, Fat Freddie Fitzsimmons, Tarzan Roy Parmelee, Gunboat Harry Gumbert, and Slick Clyde Castleman. Even in 1934 when St. Louis won, New York's team ERA of 3.19 was better than the Cards' 3.69. And the Giants' pitchers out-nicknamed the Cardinals too.

The Giants didn't sing or play ukeleles like the Gang's Hillbilly Band. Some of them even spoke grammatically, which wasn't nearly as "fun-quotable" as those outrageous things Diz used to say. On the field, the Giants were a better team, but if you wanted to make a movie, you'd do it about the Cardinals. In fact, they did in 1952. It's called *The Pride of St. Louis*, with Dan Dailey as Diz and Richard Crenna as Paul. Unless you're a big Dan Dailey fan, I wouldn't advise you to stay up for the Late Show.

#1—The '27 Yankees

"Overrated? The '27 Yanks? The Bombers? The Window Breakers? Why, the '27 Yankees were one of the greatest teams of all time."

I've got no quarrel with that last statement. So long as it starts with *"one of the."* What I object to is the knee-jerk reaction that automatically puts this team at the very top of every "greatest" list. One of the top half dozen maybe, but The Greatest? I don't think so.

They had terrific hitting: Ruth socked 60 home runs, Gehrig batted in 175, Bob Meusel and Tony Lazzeri each topped 100 RBI, and leadoff man Colonel Combs hit .356. The team scored 975 runs. But would it surprise you to know that ten other teams in history have scored more? The '27 Yanks were NOT the greatest offensive juggernaut of all time. Curiously, the '31 Yankees scored the most runs ever—1,067—and they didn't even win the pennant!

When we look at pitching, we find the '27 staff was strong and deep, with Waite Hoyt, Herb Pennock, Urb Shocker (in his last good year), Wilcy Moore (in his only good year), Dutch Ruether, and George Pipgras. Strong and deep, but could you honestly call this one of the greatest staffs ever put together? Could it have finished first with only average hitting behind it? Could Columbus have got here in a rowboat?

And even that marvelous lineup had some holes. Shortstop Mark Koenig was a journeyman at best. So were the catchers, Pat Collins and Johnny Grabowski. Joe Dugan at third base was washed up and soon retired. Take the four Big Boppers and the Colonel out of the lineup and this team would finish fifth in the American Association.

Another weak spot was the bench. Thank heaven everyone stayed healthy. The Yankees always said that outfield subs Ben Paschal and Cedric Durst could have starred for other teams. I think General Manager Ed Barrow was angling to make a trade, because when those two were given a chance they didn't make anything of it. The reserve infielders were so weak that Dugan and Koenig got to play.

The A's of 1929–31 had more balance, depth, and pitching. You can make a good argument that they were stronger than the '27 Yankees, but don't worry about it. They'd both finish behind the 1936 Yanks. *That* team had five guys with over 100 RBI—Gehrig and Lazzeri at their peaks, Joe DiMaggio, George Selkirk, and Bill Dickey. Moreover, Crosetti and Rolfe had it all over Koenig and Dugan as fielders and each scored over 100 runs. The team's 1,065 runs is the second-best ever. The team ERA of 4.17 doesn't look so hot until you realize it led the league. A lotta runs scored that year! Still, I'd match Red Ruffing, Lefty Gomez, Bump Hadley, Monte Pearson, Johnny Broaca, Pat Malone, and Johnny Murphy against the '27 staff.

But there's another reason I'm leery of hanging "The Greatest" tag on the '27 team. Or even the '36 club. How can a team be the greatest ever when it never had to face a significant number of the best players in America? Guys like Satchel Paige, Josh Gibson, Buck Leonard, Cool Papa Bell, and on and on. In my book (which admittedly isn't a best-seller) there can't be a pre–Jackie Robinson "best ever." Anything monochrome is overrated.

Next?

One thing I notice in going back through my arguments. Part of my reasons for downgrading each of the five comes down to pitching. But I don't think I'm the one at fault. Too often in looking at teams from the past, people look at the starting lineups, read the batting averages, and make a choice. If they look at a team's pitching at all, they seldom get beyond won-lost records. All I've done is note that these "great" teams had to spend half their time getting the other guys out. The Black Sox and '27 Yankees had good pitching, but contemporary teams just as powerful had better. The Cards were pitching thin. The Orioles even thinner. The Red Sox anorectic.

Another thing I note is that I went back at least forty years for the teams to downgrade. That's because I was looking for clubs whose bloated reputations have persevered through time.

Of course, there are some more modern candidates for my list of overrated teams. Just give me the perspective of a couple more years. Right now I'm warming up a spot for the Mets of the 1980s.

⚾ 12 ⚾

Baa! Baa! Red Sox

The only certain thing about baseball is that sooner or later it will break your heart. It's no coincidence that the most famous fictional baseball player is remembered for striking out in the clutch for the Mudville nine. Everybody loves a winner, but they'd rather moan about a loser. At the end of each season, after the MVPs, Gold Gloves, and Cy Youngs get their obligatory due, fans clear the decks and get down to the real nitty-gritty—assigning blame. Baseball's signature animal isn't a sacred cow, it's the goat.

Every franchise that's been around for any length of time has its legendary goats. You can always find a hitter who didn't, a pitcher who shouldn't have, or a fielder who couldn't. Yet it seems that they appear more often in Boston. Or maybe they just whine louder there.

It is hitters who are comparatively rare candidates for goatdom. Perhaps that's because fans realize that even the best of bashers will make two outs for every hit. If the natural order of things is to make an out, it's difficult to focus on any single pop-up with the bases loaded and say it "cost the season." To be named Goat of the Year, a hitter must flub through a whole series of key at bats.

That Pesky Goat

Surprisingly, it was Ted Williams who managed to qualify as a candidate for the Supreme Order of Goatery in 1946. Throughout his long career, Williams was the Rolls-Royce of hitters nearly every time he strode to the

81

plate. If he wasn't the very best basher of baseballs of all time (and many think he was), he so resembled the best you couldn't tell them apart without a dental check. In 1946, Ted came back from World War II to have a typical Williams year: he batted .342 with 38 homers, 142 runs scored, and 123 RBI. With Williams as the wind beneath their wings, the Red Sox swept into the World Series against the St. Louis Cardinals.

And then the unthinkable happened. For a period of seven games— exactly how many it took the Cards to win the Series—Ted Williams behaved like an ordinary hitter. In 25 at bats, he produced only five puny singles. Only twice did he score runs, and only once did he drive one home. It was as sorry a performance as Williams ever had in his life, and with the hindsight of history, it becomes doubly sad because Williams never appeared in another World Series to make up for his 1946 flop.

The only bright spot, if it could be termed that, for Williams Worshipers was that their hero finished a distant second in the Goat of the Games Sweepstakes that year. Primary public disapproval fell instead on the Red Sox shortstop, who deserved it not at all.

John Paveskovich did everybody in the press box a big favor by playing under the name of Johnny Pesky. It was an inspired choice, for not only was Johnny a reliable shortstop, he was a "pesky" hitter who usually finished his season batting around .300. In '46, he'd led the American League with 208 base hits. But in Game Seven of the World Series that fall, he achieved Immortal Goatdom by doing exactly what he was supposed to do.

To set the scene, the Red Sox had just tied up the seventh and deciding game at 3–3 by scoring twice in the top of the eighth inning. Dom DiMaggio, the BoSox' nimble center fielder, pulled a muscle while doubling in the two runs and was replaced by the considerably less nimble Leon Culberson. In to pitch the bottom of the eighth for the Red Sox came reliever Bob Klinger, making his first appearance of the Series.

Right off, the Cardinals' Enos Slaughter singled to center, but when Whitey Kurowski attempted to sacrifice, he popped out to Klinger instead. Del Rice flied harmlessly to left. It looked like Klinger might get through the inning okay, but then Slaughter took off for second base. Harry Walker, the Cards' left fielder, served a soft liner into left center. By the time Culberson tracked down the rolling ball, Slaughter was rolling toward third base. He ran through a stop sign by coach Mike Gonzales and slid across the plate with Pesky's relay throw from left center ten feet up the third-base line. When the Red Sox failed to score in the ninth, the

Cardinals were champs and Johnny Pesky was branded a chump for holding the ball in the outfield while Slaughter raced home.

The question is simply this: when he whirled with the baseball, was Pesky suddenly turned to stone in wonder at Slaughter's audacious baserunning? His back was to the infield as Slaughter rounded the bases. BoSox second baseman Bobby Doerr yelled to Pesky to throw home, but there was no way Johnny could hear with more than thirty-six thousand Cardinals fans screaming their lungs out. Pesky said later that he had in mind making a tag on Walker at second.

Film of the play reveals nothing more than a smooth turn and throw by the BoSox shortstop. If there ever was a hesitation, someone clipped out a couple of frames. Pesky's peg was less than perfect, but, had it been perfect, it still would have arrived too late to catch Slaughter. Of the news stories filed immediately after the game, only one makes much of Johnny's alleged hesitation. A couple stories, deep in the galleys, give guarded mention of some possible slowness; most ignore the idea altogether. But that would have left the world with no one to blame. Within a few days after the Series ended, sportswriters all over the country had united in electing Pesky the goat.

Remember, there was no videotape. Film of the Series was not available until weeks afterward. If one of the great minds in the press box discerned a hesitation—and insisted on it loud enough—you can rest assured that his compadres (who were no doubt watching Slaughter run) would soon remember seeing the same hesitation. And once it was chiseled on newsprint, it became the truth.

Buck Up, Billy Buck

However, when Boston fans think Goat, the name Pesky is not likely to spring first to their lips. Far more likely are they to grit their molars and moan "Buckner."

In defense of Bill Buckner, it should be pointed out that without his 102 RBI during the 1986 season, the Red Sox could never have found themselves in the totally unexpected position they were in on the evening of October 25 of that year—namely, ahead three games to two over the favored New York Mets in the World Series. And more specifically, one out away from a tenth-inning, 5–3 victory that would give Boston its first Series winner since 1918.

At that point, New York's Gary Carter singled. Then Kevin Mitchell did the same. Boston pitcher Calvin Schiraldi got two strikes on Ray Knight before the Met looped a third straight single to score Carter from second. With the margin down to one run, Bob Stanley replaced Schiraldi on the mound. Mookie Wilson came to the plate. Stanley worked the count to 2–1 and then Wilson fouled off three straight. One more strike!

No!

Stanley uncorked a wild pitch allowing Mitchell to streak home with the tying run. Knight took second. Wilson stayed alive on the next two pitches by fouling them off. Finally, he trickled a little bouncer down the first-base line and Buckner moved in front of it. Red Sox fans exhaled. Maybe their heroes could score again in the eleve—! Unbelievably, the ball bounced between Buckner's hightop shoes and out into right field! Ray Knight raced home with the winning run.

On any bad-to-worse scale of Goat-Making Activities, mental errors rank worse than physical errors. Buckner's error was physical, and though it cost the Red Sox the game, it was a contest their pitchers had already gone a long way to surrender. Moreover, it occurred in Game Six. No one had passed a law that the Red Sox couldn't come back and win Game Seven to render Buckner's miscue academic.

They didn't, of course. And Red Sox fans voted Bill Buckner into the Goat Hall of Fame on the first ballot.

When the Shoe Was on the Other Foot

Once upon a time, things were very different in Boston. Instead of being victims, the Red Sox capitalized on the mistakes of other teams' goats. It started even before they were the Red Sox.

In 1903, the team—then called the "Pilgrims"—won its first American League pennant. For postseason pleasure, a series of games were fixed up between the Pilgrims and the National League–winning Pittsburgh Pirates—the first modern World Series. Surprisingly, the upstart American Leaguers won, mainly because illness and injuries reduced the Pittsburgh pitching staff to a single healthy arm. However, a definite trace of *eau de la goat* was sniffed on the bat of the Pirates' greatest player. Honus Wagner, the unmatched Pittsburgh shortstop, was able to muster a mere .222 with only one extra-base hit for the whole Series.

In the way of Goatdom, Wagner's second-rate stats were no more than a Kid. The real thing showed up the next year to help Boston repeat as champs. The American League competition that year came from New York. Since this was 1904 and the Red Sox were still the Pilgrims, it's worth noting that the New Yorkers weren't the Yankees yet either; they were the Highlanders. But even though both teams played under assumed names, the 1904 pennant race ended as so many future races would, with a Boston–New York shootout. Everything was up for grabs on October 10 when they met for a doubleheader at New York's Hilltop Park.

Although they had to take both games for the pennant, the Highlanders had one big advantage—pitcher Happy Jack Chesbro, one of the earliest and greatest spitball pitchers. Apparently what kept Jack happy was winning baseball games, because, after winning twenty-plus several times in the National League, he was persuaded to jump to the American League in 1903 where he continued to spit and win. Come to think of it, the prosperity his New York contract brought him no doubt added to his joy. At any rate, everything that went before his 1904 season was prologue. At age thirty, Smilin' Jack had a season unmatched in this century.

He started 51 games and completed 48 of them. What with relieving a few times, his total innings pitched of 455 was just about a third of the innings thrown by the entire Highlander staff. And, despite the overload, he finished with a 1.82 ERA. When he went to the mound for New York in the first game of that crucial October 10 doubleheader, his record stood at a ridiculous 41–11. You'd almost expect the Pilgrims to concede the opener and go straight to game two.

They didn't, of course, and as it turned out, the game was no "gimme." New York took a 2–0 lead in the fifth, but Chesbro was betrayed by his defense in the seventh when a throwing error by the Highlander second baseman allowed Boston to tie. It stayed that way to the top of the ninth. Boston catcher Lou Criger led off with a single. A sacrifice moved him to second and a ground out sent him to third. On the mound, Happy Jack remained unperturbed as he wet the baseball for his next pitch. He was serene as he wound up. He may have been smiling as he let it go.

And, had New York catcher Red Kleinow been on top of a ladder, he just might have got his hands on the ball.

Criger raced home on the wild pitch. When New York failed to score in the bottom of the ninth, Boston had the pennant. And, probably just to underline the damage done by Happy Jack's sky-high toss, the Highlanders won the by-then meaningless second game of the double dip. Saner heads might note that had it not been for Happy Jack, the 1904 Highlanders would have struggled to get to the first division, but to most

New Yorkers Chesbro was forever branded the goat who threw away the pennant.

Interestingly, the good stuff Chesbro did before his wild pitch is probably why there was no World Series in 1904. The 1903 Boston-Pittsburgh affair had been popular and fans were looking forward to a second set of October games the next year. Throughout most of the season, it looked like the American League representative would be the Highlanders. That, however, was unacceptable to John T. Brush and John J. McGraw, the owner and manager respectively of the National League's pennant-bound New York Giants. Brush and McGraw hated the American League for many reasons, but most of all they hated having a rival American League team in New York. The thought of meeting the Highlanders in a World Series practically set both men to foaming at the mouth. Even should the Giants beat the Highlanders unmercifully, merely stepping on the same field with them would legitimize the American Leaguers' claim to a place in the New York sports scene. Had another team from another city been running away with the A.L. pennant, Brush and McGraw might have sung a different tune; a Series was likely to be a moneymaker. But, as soon as it began to look like the Chesbro-led Highlanders might actually win the flag, Brush and McGraw began making rude noises about how they weren't going to play in any dumb old World Series with their Giants, boy! There wasn't any rule that said they had to play, so that was that. By the time Boston finished first, Brush and McGraw had said no so many times they couldn't change their minds just because the Highlander crisis had passed.

But, in the parlance of the day, Boston "owed one" to the Giants. Eight years later, with the help of one of the all-time goats, Beantown got even.

The All-Time Muff

The 1912 World Series matched two of the best teams either the Giants or the Red Sox ever put on a field. The Giants, still managed by McGraw, had a whippet-fast track team that stole 319 bases on the season, but its strength was in the pitching of Christy Mathewson, Rube Marquard, and Jeff Tesreau. New York won 103 games to finish ten in front of second-place Pittsburgh. Boston, by now the Red Sox, took 105 wins and outdistanced its league competition by 14 games. The Sox had their great pitcher in twenty-two-year-old Smokey Joe Wood. The Smokester was an astounding 34–5 during what turned out to be his one near-perfect season before a sore arm felled him in 1913. Another source of pride in Boston was the outfield of Duffy Lewis, Tris Speaker, and Harry Hooper, still reckoned one of the best trios of flychasers ever put in one garden.

As befitted the meeting of two super teams, the World Series went to its seventh game—and beyond! At the close of nine innings in the final game, the Giants and Red Sox were tied 1–1. The visiting Giants batted against Wood in the top of the tenth. Smokey Joe got one out before New York left fielder Red Murray touched him for a ground-rule double. First baseman Fred Merkle followed with a hit to center. Speaker charged the bounding ball, but for once in his brilliant career, bobbled it. Murray scored the go-ahead run. Wood settled down to get the next two batters, but the horse was out of the barn. Had the goat election been held immediately after the top of the tenth inning, the peerless Speaker would have won.

Boston's task looked hopeless. Mathewson, practically a National Monument, was on the mound for New York. In nine innings the Sox had produced only one measly run against him all day. Moreover, in his last previous appearance against them he'd also held Boston to a single run. Here, they had but one last-gasp inning to produce a Series-saving run! Fat chance!

Clyde Engle batted for Wood. He lifted a high lazy fly toward right center which the sure-handed Giants center fielder Fred Snodgrass settled comfortably under. Can of corn! The ball plopped into Snodgrass's glove. And plopped right back out! Engle was all the way to second before Snodgrass could say "oops!"

Of course, everyone knew that Mathewson was a rock who would never be swayed by miscues behind him. The way he slammed his glove against his leg just then was just his way of saying he'd try harder. Curious, though, how he grooved the next pitch to Harry Hooper, who sent it rocketing deep into center field for what surely would be a game-tying hit. Except for Snodgrass. Off with the crack of the bat and running flat out, Fred somehow got close enough to the hurtling horsehide to re-ee-each out. And grab it!

With that, Matty should have been home free, but somehow, the greatest control artist of his time walked weak-hitting Steve Yerkes on four pitches. And up stepped Tris Speaker, still number one on the goat list. He virtually cemented his goatdom by lifting a little two-bit foul along the first base line. First baseman Fred Merkle could have caught it easily but he backed off when he heard Mathewson yell. Matty could have grabbed it with no sweat, but he was too busy yelling for catcher Chief Meyers to take it. And Meyers was the only one of the three closest Giants who . . . couldn't . . . quite . . . get . . . to . . . the . . . ball!

Given a new life, Goat Speaker promptly shed his horns by smacking Matty's pitch into right. When the dust cleared, Engle was home with the tying run, Yerkes was on third, and Speaker was at second. In desperation, Mathewson walked Duffy Lewis to set up a double play. And then he served a pitch high enough that Larry Gradner was able to knock it deep into right field to bring home the winning run.

To any fair-minded goat-voter, the leading candidate had to be Mathewson, who blew higher than John McGraw's cholesterol count during that fateful tenth inning. But baseball's opinion-makers, the press, couldn't bring themselves to find fault with their Matty. So, desperate to place the blame elsewhere, they settled on poor Fred Snodgrass, who missed the easy outfield catch, and enshrined him as one of the all-time goats. McGraw, who knew better, didn't criticize Matty either. But he gave Snodgrass a raise for the next season.

What Have You Done Wrong Lately?

In Red Sox Land, they've long since forgotten about Chesbro and Snodgrass. A few still grumble about Pesky or Denny Galehouse, the hapless starting pitcher of the ill-fated 1948 playoff against Cleveland. But for the most part, the mid-century goats have been supplanted by Buckner, and Mike Torrez, who served the infamous Bucky Dent home run in 1978.

Every season, nearly every lost game, has its mini-goat, of course. Those darned players are always doing silly things like bobbling a baseball or popping up to the shortstop to turn a sure win into a 14–5 loss. (Ah, if only those clowns on the field would play as well as we in the stands know WE could if given the chance!) But to achieve goat immortality, one has to be blamed for something really big. When will the next major goat appear at Fenway? Why, the next time the Red Sox lose a pennant or World Series.

You can count on it.

◖ 13 ◗

Catching Hell

Of all the jobs performed on a baseball field the hardest is singing "The Star-Spangled Banner." America's National Anguish has defeated nearly everyone from Robert Goulet to Roseanne Arnold. The words are strange and awkward to modern ears. (Quick now, is it "broad stripes and bright stars" or "bright stripes and broad stars"? And can you ever be sure if it's the rockets or the ramparts that have the "red glare"?) And then there's the range! It takes a bass on his knees to get down to "Oh-ho say" at the start and a soprano on tiptoes to hit "la-and of the *free*" at the end. Probably the majors expanded to Montreal and Toronto just so they could get a decent song before the game. If they'd thought about it, they could have brought in Paris and got "La Marseillaise."

Catchers don't have to sing, but their chores certainly rank second in degree of difficulty. During a typical game, a typical catcher does enough deep knee bends to cripple a typical centipede. He throws the ball more times than any pitcher, blocks the plate against a speeding locomotive, hikes to the mound five times, races after half a dozen foul balls, catches up to 170 pitches, and supposedly sizes up every situation so he can call for just the right pitch. You'd think in this enlightened age they'd have catchers automated by now.

Anyway, with all that on a catcher's plate, it seems like the poor guy should be exempt from ever being cast in the role of goat. Let a backstop blow a ten-run lead in the ninth all by himself and a fair world would pat him on the head and say, "That's okay, Hoss. You're a catcher."

Alas! this is anything but a fair world. If you think back through baseball's saddest days, you'll find that catchers get blamed for an awful lot of them. Even the great ones have not been immune. '

The Schnozz Takes a Snooze

Consider the case of Ernie Lombardi. Ernie was a wonderful catcher for Cincinnati during the 1930s. He was hulking and tough and had a pair of hands so big he could play "Button, Button" with a grapefruit. Of even greater size was Ernie's famous nose, which started in the middle of his face and ended somewhere near Cleveland. Had he been Pinocchio, you wouldn't have believed a word he said. Although there was no truth to the rumor that Lombardi needed the first fold-out baseball card, his storied proboscis earned him the nickname "Schnozz."

The other thing that separated Lombardi from the run-of-the-mill catchers in the league was that he could hit. In fact, he was one of the most powerful smashers of baseballs the game had ever seen. Twice he led the National League in hitting, which is one more time than all the other catchers in history combined. He didn't knock out a lot of home runs, but his line drives whistled through the infield like howitzer shots. It was just as well, for big Ernie was painfully slow of foot, and infielders routinely played him back on the outfield grass figuring they could still toss him out at first even if their throws had to be relayed.

Ernie was not only a great catcher, he was also an *interesting* catcher, the kind a sportswriter could write a fun column about on a day when rain washed out the game. ("After huddling under Ernie's nose for two hours to stay dry, the Reds left the field. Lombardi is expected to reach the dressing room by noon Friday.") You'd think that the boys in the press box would have shown a little compassion for the big guy in his one big hour of need, but instead they came after him with typewriters blazing.

It happened during the 1939 World Series. After years of nestling at the bottom of the National League, Cincinnati went out and won a pennant. No small part in the Reds' success story was played by their big-handed, big-nosed catcher. It was a pleasant season along the bank of the Ohio right up to the World Series. In that endeavor, however, Cincinnati was doomed from the start. The New York Yankees had made the Series sort of an end-of-season celebration ever since 1936, habitually treating the National League participants as no more than batting practice before the important business of opening the champagne. Growing impatient (or perhaps thirsty), they'd wrapped up their 1938 exercise in four games. And most folks agreed the '39 club was better. The Reds had about as much chance as Johnstown had against the Flood. If such a matchup were scheduled today, you'd probably get humanitarian appeals to desist from all over the world.

But give the Reds credit. They showed up, played hard, and lost the first game. And the second. And the third. Looking for one little ray of sunshine, Cincinnati took a 4–2 lead into the top of the ninth in Game Four only to give up two runs as a result of their shortstop's error.

The tenth inning opened with everybody knowing the axe was about to fall. The only question was how. Joe DiMaggio came to the plate with New York runners on first and third and answered the question with a sharp single to right to drive in what would be the winning run. Had the game been played in New York, it would have ended right there and saved Ernie Lombardi a lot of agony, but because it was the *top* of the tenth, play continued. Outfielder Ival Goodman was slow getting to the ball, and this gave Yankee runner Charlie Keller the idea of continuing on from third base to home. The burly Keller and the baseball arrived at Point Lombardi at the same moment and Ernie dropped the ball as Keller dropped him. The impression has long been that Charlie's shoulder collided with Ernie's head, rendering him momentarily unconscious. It seems more likely, however, that the real damage was done when Charlie's knee collided with another part of Ernie's anatomy and rendered him momentarily an able soprano. And while Lombardi lay supine, DiMaggio completed his circuit of the bases to score another run.

Perhaps the press-box boys had grown tired of describing the Yankees' annual victories and were looking for something new. At any rate, they chose not to notice that no other Red had stepped forward to cover the plate after Keller creamed the catcher, or that both extra runs were just that—extra, as in unneeded. Instead, they fixated on the "Snooze of the Schnozz" with alliterative glee to make Ernie somehow a goat.

Assault and Pepper

When there's a chance to hand out horns, baseball is no respecter of—well, of anything. Mickey Cochrane still ranks at the top of the all-time catchers' list with some folks. During his heydey, he was definitely regarded as number *uno*. Yet even he was enshrined in the Goat Hall of Fame after the 1931 World Series in which the St. Louis Cardinals topped the Philadelphia Athletics in seven games. Post-Series comments would lead you to believe that the Cardinals and their center fielder Pepper Martin in particular fashioned the victory by stealing everything but Cochrane's glove. "The Wild Hoss of the Osage," as Martin was tagged, rode roughshod over the *crème de la catchers*. Cochrane, it was alleged, had lost his "oomph" when he lost a fortune in the stock market.

The stolen base was going out of style in 1931. Cochrane's A's swiped a mere 27 all season. The combined totals for the rest of the American League show an average of about one steal taking place per game, with, surprisingly, the Yankees leading all with 138. The National League averaged only about three steals for every four games. Therefore, when the Cardinals swiped eight bases (five by Pepper Martin) in the seven-game series, they were going a bit beyond the norm.

However, more important than the Cardinals' total is the question of how much good it did them. Perhaps the steals gave the Redbirds a psychological lift, but as a measurable contribution to victory, they might just as well have not happened.

In Game One, Martin and Chick Hafey executed a neat double steal in the sixth inning, but it led to no runs, and the Cardinals lost, 6–2. Martin stole third in the third inning of Game Two and then came home on a sacrifice fly. But the next batter singled, so Pepper could have scored from second without the risk. In the seventh inning, he stole second, moved to third on a ground out, and scored on a squeeze bunt for an insurance run in the 2–0 victory.

The Cardinals stole no bases in winning Game Three 5–2. Martin and Frankie Frisch each had steals that led to naught in Game Four's 2–0 loss. George Watkins' stolen base in Game Five produced nothing although St. Louis won 5–1. There were no steals when the Cardinals lost Game Six, 4–1.

The Cards took the Series with a 4–2 win in Game Seven. Their second run was indirectly the result of a steal. In the opening inning, with one run already in and Watkins on third, Martin walked and stole second. Ernie Orsatti struck out on a low pitch which Cochrane blocked. Cochrane picked it up and threw to Jimmie Foxx at first to retire Orsatti (something he would not have had to do had Martin still been perched on the base). Watkins dashed in from third and scored when Foxx threw low to the plate.

Cochrane was universally named the Goat of the Series, and he did fail to throw anyone out in seven chances (counting the double steal in the first game as only one). Nevertheless, the truth is that the Cardinals would have won had they never stolen a base. All that running netted them one insurance run in Game Two and an indirect extra run in the finale.

Gowdy Steps in It

A few years earlier, another hero catcher made a strong bid for Goatdom, but he got lost in a crowd of candidates. The 1924 World Series went all the way to the last of the twelfth inning of Game Seven before Washington (Washington?) defeated the New York Giants in one of the strangest scenarios ever played out on a baseball diamond.

Before getting to the details of that fateful final half-inning, it should be noted that it was only necessary because of a curious happening in the eighth. Trailing 3–1, Washington loaded the bases with two outs. Player-manager Bucky Harris bounced an easy grounder down to New York third baseman Fred Lindstrom, who must have smiled inwardly at the ease with which the third out was about to be accomplished. But the perverse baseball, instead of bouncing on the seemingly limitless expanse of silk-smooth infield soil, chose instead to come down hard on what may have been the only pebble in Griffith Stadium and then ricochet high over Lindstrom's glove to score two runs.

Cut to the last of the twelfth. The inning began quietly with Ralph Miller grounding out to second. Up to bat came Washington catcher Muddy Ruel, who promptly raised an inoffensive pop-up foul. New York catcher Hank Gowdy had been a hero for the "Miracle" Boston Braves of 1914 and a hero three years later as the first major leaguer to volunteer for military service in World War I. He could hardly expect any raves for catching such a simple pop-up, something he'd done countless times before. Casually, he tossed away his mask. Too casually! The next second he stepped on it. Meanwhile, the ball descended. Gowdy shook the mask from his foot and resighted the rapidly falling baseball. A quick step brought him beneath it but also once more over the top of his mask, which affixed itself to his foot like a small but determined puppy. And before he could give either his mask or the baseball his full attention, the ball fell to earth. Ruel returned to the batter's box and doubled.

You might think that had Ruel gone on to score the winning run (which he in fact did), Gowdy would have earned a singular niche in the Hall of Goats. As it turned out, he could only share the honor.

Walter Johnson, Washington's magnificent pitcher, grounded to Giants shortstop Travis Jackson, a fielder so reliable they called him "Stone-wall." On this occasion, "Stonehands" was more like it, as Jackson fumbled to allow Johnson first base while Ruel held second. Pitcher Jack Bentley was no doubt muttering incoherencies; the inning should have been over.

Up stepped Earl McNeely, hitless on the day. He swung mightily and produced a dinky grounder to third. One that looked very like the pebble-hitting grounder of a few innings earlier. Very MUCH like! Especially when this one also met a pebble—could it have been the same pebble?—and soared past the crestfallen Lindstrom. Ruel dashed in from second and the Series was history.

Despite the clucking over Gowdy's attempt to stamp out his mask, he could hardly be blamed more than Jackson or Lindstrom (who allowed the litter at his position). One thing, no one doubted who the MVP was—that pesky pebble!

Robby's Rock

Pebbles make heroes; rocks make goats. Detroit fans never forgave catcher Aaron Robinson for his rock of 1950. Of course, they were somewhat predisposed against Aaron anyway. He had committed the unpardonable sin of coming to Detroit in a trade that cost the Tigers left-hander Billy Pierce, and as Pierce became one of the American League's better pitchers, Robby remained unforgivably one of its more ordinary catchers.

Nevertheless, Detroit made a gallant try for the brass ring in 1950, playing musical chairs with the Yankees for first place all summer long. By late September, they were in Cleveland with every game a "must-win," while the Yankees were hosting Boston. But while New York was pummeling the BoSox, the Tigers dropped two straight to the fourth-place Indians. The third and final game went beyond "must-win" for the Tigers; it was "win-or-else."

Many of the thirty-five thousand in Municipal Stadium had come over from Detroit to watch their Tigers' last gasp. There was a lot of gasping that day; even though the contest was played in daylight, the lights had to be turned on because the area was blanketed by a dark haze caused by forest fires in Canada. Ted Gray pitched for the Tigers, Bob Lemon for the Indians, and both were in top form. After nine innings the game remained tied 1–1.

Lemon disposed of the Tigers in the top of the tenth and then led off the bottom of the inning with a triple. Detroit's back was to the wall. The next two batters were walked intentionally to set up a force at any base. Larry Doby popped up to first baseman Don Kolloway for the first out. The Tigers saw a glimmer of hope: a double play would bring them safely out of the inning.

The next batter seemed tailor-made for just that scenario. Cleveland first sacker Luke Easter was a hard-hitting, oh-so-slow runner. And, like a gift from heaven, Easter bounced the ball down the first-base line toward the sure-handed Kolloway. The Detroit first baseman was a thing of beauty as he tucked in the baseball, stepped on first to retire Easter, and threw smoothly—perfectly—to Robinson at home plate. Lemon was chugging in from third base but still a first down away from home—the proverbial dead duck.

Robinson took Kolloway's throw, stepped neatly on the plate, and walked away while Lemon slid unmolested across the plate. Incredibly, Robinson had not seen Kolloway tag first and thus take off the force play.

The Tigers finished the season three games behind the Yankees, but Detroit fans knew in their hearts that, had Robinson tagged Lemon, the Bengals would have won not only that game but all the rest until a pennant flew in Motown. It was all Robinson's fault.

The Big One

Of all the catchers who've caught hell for the errors of their ways, none is more famous or infamous than Mickey Owen. And perhaps none has stood up better to the heat. Although Brooklyn Dodgers fans would never believe it, Owen's oops made no change in the ultimate outcome of the affair he was embroiled in—the Yankees were going to win the 1941 World Series no matter what Mickey did, short of hitting a grand slam every time he batted. The only difference caused by his infamous passed ball was in how many games it would take the Bombers to dispose of the Dodgers.

To remind you of the situation, New York had already won two of the first three games of that particular fall classic. The Dodgers were a good team, but an examination of the Yankees lineup that sported such names as Joe DiMaggio, Charlie Keller, Tommy Henrich, Red Rolfe, Phil Rizzuto, Joe Gordon, and Bill Dickey shows that the Yankees were an even stronger aggregation.

Furthermore, Fate and its fickle finger favored the Yankees. In Game Three, Brooklyn's portly right-hander Fred Fitzsimmons had stood New

York on its ear with a four-hit shutout through six and two-thirds innings, only to have Fate step in and show who was boss. The final out of the Yankees' seventh was a line drive by pitcher Marius Russo that caromed off Fitzsimmons' knee and into shortstop Pee Wee Reese's waiting glove. Fitzsimmons' knee was sufficiently injured to force his withdrawal— actually, they had to carry him off the field—and in the eighth inning the Yankees proceeded to beat Brooklyn reliever Hugh Casey like a rented mule. That turnaround should have told the Dodgers faithful that victory was not in the cards.

The next day, the Dodgers led 4–3 with two out in the ninth inning of Game Four, and, had Mickey held on to Tommy Henrich's third strike, the Series would have been evened. But anyone who dreamed the Yankees and Fate would have let the Dodgers win another one, much less two more, was surely visiting from the moon or a native of Brooklyn. As we all know, Mickey did not hold that third strike, allowing Henrich to run safely to first. But Owen didn't throw the pitches which followed and which resulted in three hits, two walks, and four runs.

Nor did he do anything dishonorable the next day when New York wrapped it all up with a 3–1 win. Face it, the Yanks were going to win this one come Helen Highwater or any of her sisters.

The really unusual thing about Owen's passed ball was that he was such a reliable catcher before and after. Earlier that season, he'd set a new National League record for accepting chances without a miscue. That this paragon among backstops should suddenly mishandle a third strike at this key moment has led many who were there, including shortstop Reese, to suggest that Casey may have put something wetter than his sweaty fingers on the baseball in making the pitch.

Casey has been dead for forty years, but Owen has always manfully taken all the blame on his own shoulders. He somehow forgot what signal he had flashed to Casey, he insists, and in effect crossed himself up. It could have happened that way. We've all forgotten things in the heat of the moment—though not usually anything so basic as how many fingers are on one's right hand.

The truth, however, is that reasons flutter away when discussing those odd plays that brand some players forever as goats. Mickey Owen caught thousands of difficult pitches over his long career, Mickey Cochrane cut down numerous speedy runners, Aaron Robinson tagged many runners out at the plate, and on and on. But, for a goat, there comes that one awful moment—always a crucial moment—when something he has done countless times just doesn't get done. Call it Fate.

⚾ 14 ⚾

The Curse

When a one-legged, no-tied hustler named Bill Veeck (as in "wreck") bought the Cleveland Indians in 1946, he acquired a team that had slogged through nearly a half century of American League seasons with modest but less than outstanding success. The Indians could usually be found lurking comfortably in the final season standings between third and fifth. The only pennant had been accomplished more than a quarter century before, and Indian fans had grown rather indifferent to the seemingly endless cycle of good-but-not-good-enough teams.

Along with the right to sign his name to the team paychecks, Veeck received the best shortstop in baseball and an innovative manager who hadn't shown he could win. Unfortunately for Veeck, the shortstop and the manager were the same person—Lou Boudreau.

Boudreau wore the five o'clock shadow of a "before" guy in a Gillette commercial and the longest eyelashes in the league, but as a shortstop, he had few natural gifts. He was slow afoot and his arm ranked only middling. It didn't matter. He was a genius at positioning himself just where some enemy batter was about to bounce the ball, and he nearly never fumbled what he could reach or made a dugout flinch with a throw. Moreover, his odd batting stance—hunched over, leaning back, and peering across his left shoulder like a kid watching for a cop—produced base hits on a regular basis.

The Trade That Was Not and What It Wrought

Veeck would have been happy to keep Lou-the-Shortstop had not Lou-the-Manager been part of the package. Alas, there seemed only one way out: both Lous had to go. Veeck girded his sport shirt around his chest and determined to boot Boudreau off to the St. Louis Browns, the A.L.'s Siberia, in exchange for Vern Stephens, a husky chap who defied all the canons of Shortstopdom by hitting home runs in large doses.

But when the good people of Cleveland heard of the fearful fate about to befall their Lou, they raised such a clamor—such a nasty stink actually—that Veeck fretted they might boycott his ballpark in numbers humongous. If there was one thing Bill Veeck did better than anyone who ever owned a baseball team, it was please the folks who bought the tickets. Therefore, after considering all the ramifications, he announced to the world that Lou Boudreau would once again play shortstop AND manage for the Cleveland Indians in 1948.

And THAT was the "First Trade"—the one that wasn't made.

What followed in '48 was totally unexpected. The Indians won the pennant and the World Series.

Calla-bunga, Kimo-sabe!

Up until mid-season, Philadelphia vied for first place with Cleveland. The A's faded in August, but by then New York and Boston came on. The Yankees had been champs in 1947 and still had Joe DiMaggio, Tommy Henrich, Vic Raschi, and Eddie Lopat, plus a young star in Yogi Berra. The Red Sox, with a lineup of sluggers led by Ted Williams, Bobby Doerr, and Vern Stephens (the homer-hitting shortstop from the Browns), started slowly and lolled in seventh place on Memorial Day. But then they got hot in June, and rose like an air bubble in a tube of water. On September 24, all three—the Indians, Red Sox, and Yankees—were tied at 91–56.

The Indians edged in front and led the Sox by a game on the morning of the final day, a Sunday. But Detroit's Hal Newhouser beat the Indians' Bob Feller while Boston topped the Yankees, 10–5, at Fenway Park. The regular season had ended in a Cleveland-Boston tie.

The historic one-game playoff was scheduled for the next day at Boston. For pitchers the Red Sox started thirty-six-year-old Denny Galehouse and Boudreau started rookie pitcher Gene Bearden. Youth was served, and Boudreau served two home runs over the left-field wall to make Cleveland the A.L. champs, 8–3.

The World Series pitting Cleveland against the Boston Braves is mostly remembered for the controversial call on a pickoff play at second base in the opener. Braves runner Phil Masi was ruled safe by umpire Jim Stewart, and a few minutes later Masi scored the only run against Feller in a 1–0 Boston win. The Indians won four of the next five in handy fashion to become World Champions.

Actually, it was a pretty good team. Catcher Jim Hegan couldn't hit a lick but he might have been the best defensive backstop ever put on this earth. Larry Doby, the American League's first black player, helped prove the stupidity of Jim Crow by playing a neat center field and hitting .301. Left fielder Dale Mitchell could slap out .300 as regularly as most men change their socks. Bob Feller, the pitcher *extraordinaire*, struggled for a while but came on strong at the end. Bob Lemon realized once and for all he was a major league pitcher instead of a minor league third baseman and won 20 games. The roster had any number of spear carriers with strong arms or legs or bats.

What put the '48 Indians over the top was the play of one rookie and three veterans, all of them having career years. Lefty Gene Bearden was a war hero with a metal plate in his head, another in his leg, and a knuckleball that danced through the league like an iron butterfly through warm butter. Down the stretch, he was the Tribe's most consistent flinger. He won his 20th game in the end-of-season playoff at Fenway Park that gave the Indians the pennant.

Second baseman Joe "Flash" Gordon clobbered 32 home runs, batted in 124, and fielded his position with the flair that earned him his nickname. Third baseman Ken Keltner, best known as the glove that stopped DiMaggio's hitting streak, dusted off his bat for 31 homers and 119 RBI.

But it was Boudreau himself who took the dual role of Mr. Irreplaceable and Mr. Irresistible. His raw figures: .355, 18 homers, 116 runs, 106 RBI. His rah-rah leadership can't be quantified. Suffice it to say that every time his team needed a lift Lou was there with his bat, glove, or some off-the-wall strategy that worked. They named him Most Valuable Player, but Most Valuable Entity would have been more like it.

The great season even inspired, if that's the word, a movie. Some night on the Late Show you can watch *The Kid from Cleveland* with all those Indian stars and George Brent. That is, if Veeck didn't find and burn every copy as he threatened to do. Anyway, it wasn't the worst film *Brent* ever made.

After the World Series win over the Boston Braves, Veeck totaled up his 2,260,627 home attendance, noted it was an all-time record up to then, and congratulated himself on avoiding the worst trade since those other Indians swapped Manhattan for $24 in trinkets. Meanwhile, all those Indians fans looked forward to more pennants.

That's not exactly what they got, but the next decade was the high point of Cleveland's baseball history as far as sustained excitement. It was as though the non-trade of Boudreau had somehow become a pact with Indians fans: the ballclub may not always win, but it will give you your money's worth of entertainment and heroes galore.

The Between Years

The thing about career years is that they don't just keep happening. In 1949, Boudreau, Gordon, and Keltner got old. Bearden ran into Casey Stengel, the new Yankees manager. Casey had managed in the Pacific Coast League when Bearden was there. He knew Gene couldn't get his knuckler over three times in seven pitches, and he counseled New York batters to wait for Bearden's fat fastball. Once word got around, Gene was through.

Cleveland finished third in '49 and fourth in '50. Veeck moved on to St. Louis and midgets. Boudreau moved on to Boston and the Wall. Others just moved. Still, these were good times because the hope was there. After all, a team with Doby, Mitchell, and a hot young home-run hitter like Al Rosen would score runs. And a pitching staff with Lemon, Feller, Early Wynn, and Mike Garcia was not to be sneezed at.

In 1951, Hank Greenberg was in charge of hiring and firing. He brought in Al Lopez as manager, and the Señor produced a near-miss second place, staying alive until September 28. Señor Al did it with pitching and power. The Tribe led the league in ERA and tied the Yankees in homers. What they couldn't do was field. The jokers put it this way: "Second baseman Bobby Avila can't go to his left; shortstop Ray Boone can't go to his right; first baseman Luke Easter can't go left or right; and third baseman Al Rosen can't handle anything hit at him."

There was enough truth in that to keep the Indians from a pennant again in 1952. Feller slipped badly to 9–13, but Lemon and Garcia each won 22 and Wynn won 23. The Tribe chased the hated Yankees all the way, but on September 15, New York beat Garcia before 73,609 disappointed fans at Municipal Stadium in the key game of the season.

In 1953, Boone moved to Detroit, hitting a ton at third base. However, he wasn't missed because Rosen hit two tons at third for Cleveland. Rosen was awesome with 43 homers, 145 RBI, and a .336 batting average. He won MVP, but Lopez's Indians still couldn't get past Stengel's Yankees. The Indians finished eight and a half games behind New York and seemed to be losing ground.

The problem in '53 was pitching. Almost everybody who checks into those years looks at the Indians' starters and genuflects. But look farther. The top reliever, Bob Hooper, had 7 saves and a 4.02 ERA. The staff totaled 15 saves to the Yankees' 39.

Lopez knew that whenever he looked to the bullpen, he was likely to find less talent than what he already had on the mound. So he stayed with his starters—often one batter too long.

The Big Year

After three seconds in a row, the Indians were elected King of the American League in 1954. They won 111 games, one more than the '27 Yankees and more than any A.L. team has done since with more games to do it in. From mid-July on, Cleveland was in cruise, slowly widening their lead over the Yankees. To top it off, Stengel's team won 103 games— more than they'd won in any of their five straight pennant years. How sweet it was!

A lot of the usual Tribe suspects were back—Rosen, Doby, Avila, George Strickland, Hegan, Feller, Lemon, Wynn, and Garcia. Mitchell was on the bench with Al Smith in left. Sometimes Art Houtteman started while Dave Philley patrolled right field and Vic Wertz played first base; but, for the most part, this was the same team that hadn't been quite good enough for three years.

The success of the Indians lay within the bullpen. Disaster lurked there in '53; they went platinum in '54. Head honchos were rookie right-hander Ray Narleski, 3–3 with 13 saves, who threw a fastball that made strong men weep, rookie left-hander Don Mossi, 6–1 with 7 saves, who threw curves as big as his ears, and sore-armed, supposedly washed-up Hal Newhouser, 7–2 with 7 saves. "This was back when the manager would tell his starters to tough it out," Lemon explains, " 'cause he didn't have anything better down in the bullpen. So having an accomplished bullpen like we did was something new. I don't think we could have done it without Mossi and Narleski. They were the key. We went as long as we could, then let Mossi and Narleski take over."

Safe from having to face that one last batter with tiring arms, Lemon, Wynn, and Garcia all posted ERAs under 3.00 while winning 65 games. Yogi Berra was MVP in '54, but Doby, Avila, Lemon, and Wynn finished in the top six in votes. Rosen, fighting a hand injury all season, didn't duplicate his 1953 numbers, but his leadership was invaluable. Lopez told of a time when Rosen had been smacked in the face by a ground ball (well, we never *said* he was a gloveman!) and both eyes had swelled shut. He came to the park at ten in the morning and spent the day on the trainer's table applying ice packs until he could open his eyes. He played that night.

"And, by God, got four hits," Lopez insisted.

It was a glorious year. At least until the end. In the World Series against the New York Giants, Willie Mays made a catch, Dusty Rhodes hit a couple of pop-fly homers, and the bubble burst in four straight.

In Decline

According to some, the decline started right there with Mays' catch of Vic Wertz's drive. Or at least, with the World Series loss. It WAS frustrating. The Indians spent three years chasing the Yankees, and then when they caught 'em and tromped 'em, they turn around and get squashed by the New York *Giants*! Most Clevelanders had forgotten there was a second team in New York.

But the decline wasn't precipitous. Lopez had them back in their familiar second-place role in 1955 despite Feller's age and Garcia's sudden ineffectiveness. Part of the slack was picked up by a young lefty named Herb Score, whose fastball, everyone predicted, would one day crumble Feller's strikeout records.

In 1956, Wynn, Lemon, and Score each won 20, and a bright new slugger appeared in the person of Rocky Colavito. However, Garcia continued his poor performance, Narleski hurt his arm, and Rosen retired after the season. The Indians were second again, but closer to third than to first.

The 1957 season was just awful. Tired of second-place finishes, the owners let Lopez go (to Chicago, where he finished second) and brought in minor league manager Kerby Farrell. Poor Kerby couldn't have picked a worse time to get his first and, as it turned out, only major league managing shot. Age caught up to Lemon, Avila, and Hegan, but, worst of all, the Yankees' Gil McDougald caught up with Score's fastball and lined it right back into Score's face. The twenty-four-year-old lefty was out for the year after five starts, and many wondered if he'd ever be the same again. Alas! the answer was that he wouldn't.

Desperate for starters, Farrell raped his bullpen by turning Mossi and Narleski into starting pitchers. They came through okay, but *après* them *le déluge*. Cleveland spun down to sixth.

Farrell was let go and Bobby Bragan was brought in. Then, after a floundering start in '58, Joe Gordon was named manager in midseason. The old Flash got the Tribe turned around, using a lineup that had Colavito for home runs, thirty-six-year-old Minnie Minoso for style, and seven other guys for ballast. The pitching was handled by twenty different flingers, including—for three hitless innings—Colavito. Somehow Gordon got the Tribe back into the first division by half a game, and hope flared for 1959.

The good news in '59 was that the Indians beat the Yankees; the bad news was that they didn't beat the White Sox. Second place again.

Yet it was an enjoyable team. Colavito had become the most popular player in Cleveland since World War II. Maybe since Nap Lajoie. Well, what's not to like about a handsome kid who leads the league with 42 home runs? Attendance wasn't what it had been for Bill Veeck, but it was pretty good. And Rocky put a lot of fannies into stadium seats.

He had help. Minoso hit 21 homers. Shortstop Woodie Held hit 29. (Shortstop?) Tito Francona started the season on the bench, but when Gordon turned him loose, he hit .363 with 20 taters. The pitching was so-so, but Cal McLish won 19 games and rookie Jim Perry showed promise. The club had a lot of young bats and arms. With any luck, it could win a pennant or two and contend for years.

The Second Trade

But then came Frank Lane. "Frantic Frankie," as the newspapers called him, had made his reputation as General Manager of the White Sox in the early 1950s with a couple of terrific trades. Among other swindles, he got Nellie Fox from Philadelphia and Billy Pierce from Detroit for something like a bag of salted peanuts each. Unfortunately, his early success deluded him into thinking that the purpose of running a baseball team was to move bodies around the league instead of around bases.

When Lane replaced Greenberg as Indians G.M. after the '57 season, the Tribe was down, so his body-shuffling act made some sense and raised few eyebrows. Then, in '59, the team was a contender and Lane made only a few moves, none major. How that must have galled!

As the 1960 season approached, Lane readied himself for his masterstroke—his Trade-of-Trades. On Easter Sunday, April 17, it happened. Colavito and his 42 home runs and 111 RBIs were sent to Detroit for Harvey Kuenn and his 150 singles.

It wasn't just that Colavito was getting better and Kuenn was on the downslide. It wasn't just that Rocky could win games that Harvey couldn't. Sure, in a baseball sense, it was a dumb deal, but that wasn't the worst of it. This was Rocky! Cleveland's Mr. Baseball! Lane had taken the cake AND the icing. He'd committed the unforgivable sin: he'd broken faith with both the team and the fans. "Trader" Lane had become "Traitor" Lane.

The Good Times were over. The "Second Trade" ended them.

The Indians reeled down to fourth in 1960, fifth in '61, and so on for more than thirty years. No team—not even the Cubs—has been so consistently disappointing. When the pitching has been decent, the hitters have hibernated. When the bats woke up, no one could throw strikes. Good players were hurt, even died.

Municipal Stadium has echoed in emptiness for three decades. Fans don't trust this ballclub. They're afraid to. They believe that any player who finds his way into their hearts will either turn out to be a flash in the pan like Joe Charboneau or shipped off like Colavito, Jim Perry, or Joe Carter. Don't get close to this team; it will break your heart.

Some want to trace the curse back to the last century when a real Indian, Lou Sockalexis, played the Cleveland outfield before he drank himself out of the league, but that ignores the first sixty years of franchise history: Nap Lajoie, Tris Speaker, Mel Harder, Joey Sewell . . . Most of all, it leaves unexplained those wonderful '50s when pennant talk was sincere every spring.

No. The curse began with the Colavito trade. That was when Cleveland fans and players said, "To hell with it!"

At last, after thirty years, the Indians *seem* to be on the right track. They've got some good, young players and a new ballpark on the way. Maybe . . . Well, we'll see.

⚾ 15 ⚾

Bums and Bombers: The Greatest Series of Series

Mickey Owen, Don Larsen, Al Gionfriddo, Billy Martin, and Sandy Amoros! Hodges, Page, Newcombe, Henrich, Black, Raschi! Jackie, Di-Mag, Duke, The Mick, Preacher! If *World Series* doesn't leap immediately to your mind, you must be a lacrosse fan. And not just any old Series either, but a clutch of special games played more than thirty-five years ago that were so memorable that for many they are emblematic of ALL the World Series, and by extension, of baseball itself.

No TV-trumpeted Final Four or shamelessly hyped Super Bowl can compare with baseball's World Series for sustained suspense and nostalgic thrills. Each fall, the Series keeps America on the edge of its collective seat for a minimum of four games and provides plays and situations to be reviewed, savored, and argued over around hot stoves for decades. In Bert Randolph Sugar's enjoyable *Baseball's 50 Greatest Games* (Exeter Books, 1986), more than a third of the contests detailed were played in a World Series, and, while many fans might disagree on the makeup of the final fifty, the percentage of Series games would likely be the same on nearly everyone's list.

Your personal favorite Series may depend on which team you root for. Pittsburghers revere 1960. Clevelanders look back to 1948. Cubs fans need elephant memories indeed. But high on any longtime fan's list would be some of the seven Series pitting the New York Yankees against the Brooklyn Dodgers between 1941 and 1956. These titanic meetings went beyond parochial loyalties. The combatants were each, in their own way, "America's Team."

Remember, this was before expansion. There were only sixteen major league teams. And for much of that period, they played in only eleven U.S. cities. Most of America had to choose its major league loyalties for reasons other than geographic proximity.

It was easiest to be a Yankee fan. Everybody loves a winner. The Bombers had come to the fore in the 1920s, paced by the world's most popular sports personality, Babe Ruth. By the start of the 1940s, the Yankees had won eleven of the last twenty American League pennants and their last seven World Series. Before the Yankees-Dodgers meetings ended in 1956, the pinstripers would enhance that record quite a bit.

A by-product of victory was familiarity. Those sometime fans in the hinterlands—those who only followed baseball avidly when the Series rolled around—had heard Yankee names year in and year out. They might think Greenberg was a city in North Carolina, but they knew Charlie Keller from Helen. It's always easier to care about players whose names strike familiar chords. The Yankees were the "team" of those who rooted for habitual success, constant professionalism, and high profiles.

The Brooklyn Dodgers were a harder sell, yet across the country they were perhaps even more popular than the Yankees. Some of you may remember that during the 1940s and 1950s, Brooklyn itself held a special place in Americana. Any contestant introduced on a radio quiz show needed only to say he hailed from Brookyn to receive a round of applause from the audience. Every war movie had its soldier from Brooklyn (usually played by William Bendix). Kids in the Midwest practiced speaking with their versions of a Brooklyn accent.

The touchstone of Brooklyn-mania was the Dodgers—"Dem Bums," as they were affectionately termed. They were the country's beloved underdogs. They'd never won a World Series. For twenty years, from 1921 through 1940, they went pennantless. Sixth-place was their usual home. Moreover, every baseball fan had a stock of tales to tell about the "Daffiness Boys," that collection of curious characters who'd performed for Uncle Robbie in the late '20s. "Tripling into a triple play" was the favorite.

Curiously, the underdog image continued into the 1950s when Brooklyn had become the scourge of the National League and arguably superior in talent to the American League's Yankees. With the Dodgers, fans could root for an underdog who usually won—a kind of baseball Nirvana.

Small wonder that each World Series between these two "America's Teams" produced moments that will live forever in baseball's history.

1941: Mickey's Miss

The 1941 Dodgers were perhaps the best team ever to represent Brooklyn up to that time. A nice mixture of potent veterans, like Joe Medwick and Billy Herman, and youngsters, like Pete Reiser and Pee Wee Reese. But they faced a Yankees team that had won World Series from 1936 through 1939, missed a year, and come back for blood. The Yankees outfield of Charlie Keller, Joe DiMaggio, and Tommy Henrich still makes many lists of the greatest patrol trio ever.

The teams split the first two games at Yankee Stadium and then adjourned to Ebbets Field for legendary doings. Game Three saw Fat Freddie Fitzsimmons, the aging right-hander, throw a masterpiece at the Yankees. Inning after inning, he mowed down pinstripe batters until he'd negotiated six and two-thirds frames with a mere four hits and zero runs allowed. Yankee pitcher Marius Russo became the third out of the seventh on a fly to Dodger shortstop Pee Wee Reese with an assist by Fitzsimmons. The reason for the scoring oddity was that Russo smashed a bullet off Fat Freddie's knee, and though Reese caught it before it landed for the out, Fitzsimmons was done for the day. When he was helped from the mound, the Dodgers' chances went with him.

In the bottom of the seventh, Reiser doubled for the Dodgers. Medwick struck out but catcher Bill Dickey dropped the ball and had to throw him out. In light of later events, it's worth remembering that Dickey drop. Had he failed to retire Medwick the Dodgers would have had two on, no outs, and who knows what might have transpired? As it was, Brooklyn went out without a score. In the eighth, the Yankees jumped all over reliever Hugh Casey. The Yankees had a win and the Bums had a might-have-been.

But the next day, the undaunted Dodgers had the win that would have again tied the Series in their grasp—okay, bad choice of words. But what else can you say when a team leads 4–3 in the ninth, gets two quick outs, and then the third batter strikes out? That's money in the bank, right?

Wrong. Casey had been shutting out the Yanks since he relieved in the fifth. Up until he seemingly had the third out in the ninth, he'd been touched for only two paltry singles. The third strike that the unlucky Mr. Casey threw past Tommy Henrich's bat was a thing of beauty, breaking down and away. Far down and far away. Does the word "spitter" ring a bell?

While umpire Larry Goetz raised his arm in the traditional strike three signal, the pitch skittered past Dodger catcher Mickey Owen like a flat stone on smooth water and went all the way to the backstop. By the time the frantic Owen retrieved it, Henrich was on first. Casey, who'd started toward the dugout when Henrich swung and missed, returned to the mound badly shaken.

The next few moments are the saddest in Dodgers history. DiMaggio singled to left. Keller doubled, scoring Henrich and DiMaggio. Dickey walked. Joe Gordon doubled to score both runners. The Yankees prevailed, 7–4.

The shattered Dodgers tried hard the next day, but the Yankees took the Series with a 3–1 win.

1947: Jackie, Cookie, and Al

The Yankees and Dodgers didn't go World Seriesing again until after World War II. Their 1947 battle is one of the most memorable of all not because it went seven games before New York triumphed, but because of one historical first, one hit, and one catch. Actually, it was a pretty sloppy Series, with the Yankees making four recorded errors and the Dodgers eight.

The historical first was accomplished in the top half of the first inning when Jackie Robinson stepped up to the plate as the second batter. For the first time, a black man appeared in a Series after forty-three lily-white "classics." He walked. Of course, by then, Jackie had just about completed a Rookie-of-the-Year season as the Dodgers' first baseman, so there were probably some among the new Series record crowd of 73,365 who thought, "Here's a good ballplayer," rather than the then-prevailing "Here's a good *Negro* ballplayer." Who says there's no progress?

The Yankees won two games before Brooklyn outslugged them 9–8 in Game Three. New York sent Bill Bevens to the mound for Game Four. Bill hadn't had much of a season—7–13 with a pennant winner—but he gained immortality in his first Series start. He entered the last of the ninth inning leading 2–1, having allowed nary a hit.

Not to say it was pretty. He'd walked eight and even allowed a run in the fifth on two walks, a sacrifice, and a fielder's choice. Still, no one had ever pitched a no-no in a Series game. Could he do it?

In the ninth, Bevens induced Dodger catcher Bruce Edwards to fly out to deep center. One away, but then he walked Carl Furillo. Spider Jorgensen fouled out to George McQuinn at first base. Two down, but little Al Gionfriddo went in to run for Furillo and the injured Pete Reiser pinch-batted for Hugh Casey. Yankees manager Bucky Harris reasoned that Pistol Pete was the only available Brooklyn batter who might homer to win the game. When Gionfriddo stole second and Bevens ran the count on Reiser to 3–1, Harris waved the Dodger batter to first. The intentional pass was the tenth free ride by Bevens. Speedy Eddie Miksis ran for the limping Reiser. Little Eddie Stanky was up next, but Dodger skipper Burt Shotten sent up veteran Cookie Lavagetto instead. Cookie was near the end of a fair career and had played in only 41 games that year, but he had perhaps a tad more punch than Stanky.

Bevens slipped over a strike on Lavagetto, but when he tried for a second, Cookie lined the pitch off the right-field wall. By the time Tommy Henrich ran it down and returned it to the infield, Gionfriddo and Miksis were across the plate for the win and Cookie was safe at second with the only Brooklyn hit of the day.

The Yankees took Game Five on Spec Shea's four-hitter, but the Dodgers came back to even things in Game Six. Gionfriddo, who'd scored the tying run against Bevens, had his big moment in the sixth inning. The Dodgers led 8–5, but the Yanks put two aboard with two out. DiMaggio jolted an orbit-shot to left. Back went Gionfriddo toward the 415-foot gate in front of the Dodgers bullpen. At the proverbial last second, he made a twisting, one-handed catch that brought down the house.

For the record, Game Six was the last major league game of Gionfriddo's career. Lavagetto's last game came the next day. He played three innings of the Dodgers' Series-ending loss.

1949: Old Reliable

The 1949 Yankees-Dodgers Series was perhaps the least remarkable of the Bombers-Bums duels, but it didn't start out that way. Rookie Don Newcombe was terrific through the first eight innings of Game One, scattering four New York hits. But Allie Reynolds was even stingier for the Yankees—only two hits through the top of the ninth. Tommy Henrich led off the bottom of the ninth for the Yanks. Newk missed on his first two pitches and then made the third one too good. Old Reliable pulled it into Yankee Stadium's lower right-field stands for a terrific 1–0 win. No one knew it at the time, but the game marked the beginning of Newcombe's World Series misery: 0–4 in five career starts.

The next day, Preacher Roe evened the Series with a 1–0 whitewashing of his own. When the Series shifted to Ebbets Field, the Dodgers got to the ninth inning of Game Three tied 1–1 before the roof fell in. New York scored three in the final inning and then took Games Four and Five to wrap up Casey Stengel's first World Championship.

1952: Billy the Kid Rides to the Rescue

The Dodgers were the class of the N.L. in 1950 and 1951 but somehow contrived to lose out at the finish line first to the Phillies' Whiz Kids and then to Bobby Thomson's "shot heard 'round the world." In 1952, they were back in the World Series where they belonged. In the meantime, with Series wins in '50 and '51, Stengel's Yankees were in position to win four straight, a feat accomplished only once before—by the 1936–39 Yankees.

The two best teams in baseball traded wins through the first five games, leaving Brooklyn ahead three games to two with two shots left at Ebbets Field. The Yanks tied up the Series in Game Six on a terrific relief job by Allie Reynolds.

New York took a 4–2 lead into the seventh inning of the final game, and it looked good when reliable Vic Raschi was brought in at the start of the frame. But for once, Raschi didn't have it. He walked Carl Furillo. Then, after Rocky Nelson popped to shortstop, Billy Cox singled to right. When Raschi walked Pee Wee Reese to load the bases, Stengel had seen enough. He brought in journeyman lefty Bob Kuzava to face left-hand-hitting Duke Snider, who already had four home runs and eight RBI for the Series.

Kuzava got Snider on a pop to third, bringing up right-hand-hitting Jackie Robinson with the bases still loaded and two outs. Stengel had a couple of right-handers available, including Johnny Sain, but he stuck with Kuzava. The Perfessor looked like a genius—well, maybe he WAS a genius—when Robinson skied a pop-up toward first base.

But what was this? First baseman Joe Collins lost the ball in the sun and stood there in a trance. Kuzava, equally agog, was no help. As the ball arced down, two Dodger runners nipped across the plate and Reese rounded third with the potential winning run. The ball was falling half-way between first and the mound.

Suddenly a skinny blur flashed in from second base. Billy Martin took the ball off his shoelaces and the inning ended.

Kuzava sailed through the eighth and ninth to make the Dodger faithful once more "wait 'til next year."

1953: Billy the Kid, Act II

The law of averages said Stengel's Yankees couldn't win five straight World Series. No one ever had. Of course, that same law said they couldn't be IN five straight World Series. No one had ever done that either. But there they were.

In retrospect, this Series seems like an inevitability. The Yankees were going to make history and the Dodgers couldn't stop them. It mattered not that the Bums' lineup of Junior Gilliam, Reese, Robinson, Campanella, Hodges, Snider, Furillo, and Cox may have been the best ever assembled. It didn't even matter that Carl Erskine (that's "Oiskin" in Brooklynese) set a new Series record when he struck out fourteen Yankees in Game Three. Nothing could help. The Yankees were fated to win.

They did it in six games, with Billy Martin the hitting star. Billy Martin?

Billy went through Dodger pitchers like they were marshmallow sales-men: Game One, 3-for-4 with 3 RBI; Game Two, a home run; Game Three, 1-for-3 with a run scored; Game Four, 2-for-4 and another run; Game Five, 2-for-5 and another homer; and Game Six, 2-for-5 and two more RBI. His 12 hits set the record for a six-game series and included a double, two triples, and two home runs. He batted .500 and had a Ruthian .958 slugging percentage. And his eight RBI led all batters. Not bad for a guy who punched out a mediocre .257 on the season!

The only bright spot for the Dodgers was Gil Hodges' .364 batting average. He'd gone through the whole 1952 Series without a hit.

1955: Next Year Is Here

Not again! After a year off, the Dodgers won another pennant in 1955, only to look up and see the Yankees facing them once more. Five times since 1941 the Bums had come up empty against the Bombers. Throw in the 1916 loss to the Red Sox and the 1920 loss to the Indians and Brooklyn was oh-for-seven in World Series. It hardly seemed worth draping the red-white-and-blue bunting on the fence.

Sure enough, the Yankees won the opening game 6–5 and Game Two 4–2. No team had ever come back from an 0–2 start. And there was a mismatch for Game Three in 9–10 lefty Johnny Podres against the Yankees' 17-game winner Bob Turley. Snowballs in hell are quoted better odds than the Dodgers were getting.

Podres took the mound on his twenty-third birthday and gave himself and the Dodgers a present—a seven-hit, 8–3 win. Chalk one up for the underdogs. The next day, Brooklyn evened the Series as Campy, Gil, and Duke homered. And the day after THAT, Snider hit two more home runs and the Dodgers won their third straight. Holy Hilda and her Cowbell! Was it possible that this time . . . ?

The smart guys knew the Yankees were only toying with the Dodgers. Whitey Ford was money in the bank for Game Six, giving Brooklyn a paltry run, while Dodger starter Karl Spooner didn't get out of the first inning.

With the Series tied at three games apiece, Stengel came with tough Tommy Byrne, the lefty who'd limited Brooklyn to five hits in Game Two. In the Brooklyn dugout, manager Walter Alston looked at his options. He'd used six different starters in six games and only Game Five starter Roger Craig and birthday boy Podres had ERAs under 9.00. He handed the ball to Johnny.

With 62,465 bulging Yankee Stadium, Gil Hodges drove in a Dodger run in the fourth inning and another in the sixth. Meanwhile, Podres got that far without letting a Yankee sully the plate. But in the bottom of the sixth, Billy Martin led off with a walk and Gil McDougald followed with a bunt single. Up came Yogi Berra, a good bet to power the ball out to the stadium's friendly right-field stands. Instead, he took the next-worst scenario and sliced one down the left-field foul line. The runners took off with joy in their hearts and wings on their feet.

Left fielder Sandy Amoros had been inserted in that inning for defensive purposes, but get real! Sixty-two thousand, four hundred and sixty-five fans, forty-nine ballplayers, two managers and their coaches, and assorted ushers, announcers, and vendors all knew he had no chance for Berra's slice. He'd be lucky to hold Yogi to a double, and both runners scoring was a given.

Only no one told Amoros. So, blissfully unaware that he was making an impossible catch, he motored over to the line, caught the ball, and then threw neatly to double McDougald off first.

Podres wasn't out of the woods. He got into a two-on jam in the eighth and then got back out of it. In the ninth, he retired Bill Skowron on a bounce-out, Bob Cerv on a fly. And then, in the fifty-fifth year of the twentieth century, Elston Howard grounded out, Reese to Hodges, and the Dodgers were—Holy Moly Mary Marvel!—World Champions!!!

1956: Perfecto

That 1956 would be Brooklyn's final appearance in a World Series couldn't have been predicted by anyone whose surname didn't begin with an Oh and then rhyme with "Valley." For a while, it looked like the Bums might even win again, but the seven games unfolded as a mirror image of 1955: Brooklyn won two, New York came back to win three, the Dodgers stemmed the tide temporarily with fine pitching in Game Six, but the Yankees took the finale.

Berra had ten RBI. He and Mickey Mantle each hit three homers. Don Drysdale, who'd do better on the other coast, pitched two innings and gave up the same number of runs. Clem Labine didn't give up an earned run in 12 innings.

All of this pales in relation to what happened in Game Five. Don Larsen, an unassuming 11–5 for the season, pitched the best game EVER thrown in a World Series, bar none. In '47 Bevens came close to a no-hitter, and there had been up to then two other one-hitters, but Larsen's masterpiece was in another dimension. A perfect game!

If you looked at the Yankees staff and gave odds on a perfecto, you'd start with Whitey. Then there was Bob Turley, with his bullet fastball, or 18-game winner Johnny Kucks or maybe bulldog Tom Sturdivant. But Larsen? The guy who'd gone 3–21 with the Orioles only two years before? The wild man who couldn't find the plate when he was shelled in the second inning of Game Two? That Larsen?

Yep.

Working with a no-windup delivery, Larsen was never in trouble, which is, of course, always true in a perfect game. More to the point, he didn't need any miraculous catches to save his bacon. The closest any Dodger came to a hit was a Hodges drive in the fifth that Mantle ran down. A nice catch, but no Amoros.

When the twenty-seventh Brooklyn batter, pinch-hitter Dale Mitchell, took a called third strike on Larsen's ninety-seventh pitch, Berra leaped from behind the plate and climbed tall Don's frame like a kid shinnying up a tree.

For the record, Larsen never pitched another perfect game or no-hitter and never again won more than ten games in any season. But for that moment, he was Cy Young.

Never Again

The series of Yankees-Dodgers Series had more than their share of records, unbelievables, never-befores, and never-agains. But everything that happened in them was multiplied tenfold by the way the nation viewed the participants—the yin and yang of "America's Team."

You'll never see the like again. No team is likely ever to achieve the dominance the Yankees had in them days. And the Bombers are going to take a while to recover from their self-destructive image-tarnishing of the past couple of decades.

The Bums ain't the same either. Once the Dodgers left Brooklyn for the West, they lost their special place in America's heart. Of course, they gained millions and millions of dollars, but are they REALLY happy?

Get serious!

⚾ 16 ⚾

The Best o' the Bucs

I don't know how it is in your neck of the woods, but out here in western Pennsylvania we can always work up a lather arguing over which Pirate team was the best ever. I think this became a really big pastime in the mid-1980s when the Pirates were so bad the only thing local fans could say about them was that at least they weren't the Mets.

The top candidates for Premier Pirate Pack are the teams from 1960, 1971, and 1979; all won World Series. The 1960 Buccaneers have a lot of backers left around—folks who still rank Mazeroski's World Series–winning homer as the apex of their lifetimes of baseball-watching. The 1979 Pirates made a good showing—there are Bucco fans who'll tell you Willie Stargell that year was the most inspirational presence in Pittsburgh since Billy Sunday toured through on the Chautauqua circuit. Probably the most popular choice for Best o' Bucs is the 1971 club with Roberto Clemente in right field—Clemente is so revered around Pittsburgh, you could sell Baghdad War Bonds if you put his picture on them.

Local fans feel pretty strongly about their choices for the best Pirate team. I've heard discussions so earnest they resulted in stitches.

Well, now, in my never-ending pursuit of Truth (not to mention Justice and the American Way), I decided to settle this disagreement once and for all, and to do it in the way that every red-blooded baseball fan finds immutable Reality—with statistics. Baseball fans think you can prove anything with statistics. Ask a baseball fan about his honeymoon and he'll give you percentages. Sometimes it's embarrassing.

115

The System

Finding numbers to crunch is no problem these days, what with the Big Mac, the Neft-Cohen encyclopedia, various *Sporting News* publications, and a veritable plethora of other record books available. But I decided to use *Total Baseball* because it has some particular numbers that lend themselves to this kind of quest. And also because I know one of the editors, statistician Pete Palmer, and figured I could phone him for advice (like: "Pete, am I gonna look like a complete idiot on this?").

In the section of the book called "The Annual Record," where team stats are given, you can find for each team FW, PW, and BW: standing for "Fielding Wins," "Pitching Wins," and "Batting Wins." The idea of, say, a "Batting Win" is to take how many runs a team's total batting record should produce during a season, given the accomplishments of the opposition, and then divide it by the number of runs necessary to produce a win in that season. The number of runs necessary for a win can change from season to season depending on a number of variables, and you use the run total the team *should have gotten* rather than what it *did get* because all kinds of factors can affect the actual total.

The FWs, PWs, and BWs are given in relation to an average team. For example, in a 162-game season an average team will win 81 games. So, if a team has a 1.0 in Fielding Wins and all other "Ws" are average, that team fielded well enough to win 82 games. If it was −2.0 in Pitching Wins, the team's hurlers were only good enough to produce 79 wins.

So, if I add up all a team's FWs, PWs, and BWs, I'll get a total (TW) that will tell me just how strong that team was, at least in relation to the baseball played at the time. So the Pirate team with the highest TW is *relatively* the best Pirate team ever.

I should point out that for many seasons there's an SBW, for Stolen Base Wins, in *Total Baseball*, but since it's not always there—the National League didn't always keep Caught Stealing records—I decided the best bet was to ignore it. I've gotten along for years ignoring things I didn't know the answers to, so why stop now?

Before going on, I decided to call Pete Palmer and ask him about my great idea. I was a tad nervous because *Total Baseball* doesn't list any such stat as "TW." You have to understand that Pete speaks fluent "statisticianese." For a half hour, he spoke eloquently about square roots, delta numbers, ratios, normalizing for home park advantage, and other numerical stuff. It would have been really enlightening if I'd had any idea what the hell he was talking about. But somewhere in his lecture, I distinctly heard him say, "That might work."

The Answer I Didn't Like

Now convinced I was onto something big, I sat down and added up all the FWs, PWs, and BWs for every Pirate team from 1887 through 1990. I won't give you the whole list, but on the page that follows are the best.

A side benefit of the system was that it identified the *worst* Pirate team ever. I'd expected it to be the 1952 team that Joe Garagiola always makes jokes about. Well, that bunch was pretty awful—a 42–112 record and 54.5 games out of first place—and the system gave them a *minus* 26.7 TW.

But bad as they were, they weren't the worst. The 1890 Pirates (actually, they were called the "Alleghenys" then) went 23–113 and 66.5 games behind. The system put them at minus 45.2, which means they'd have trouble beating the Little Sisters of the Poor on a day when Sister Mary Catherine has her fastball.

I was glad to know about that 1890 club. Still, to be honest, I found the "best team" TWs kind of depressing. According to my wonderful system, five of the six best Pirate teams played before World War I. It's a real downer to hear that the best of *anything* happened long before I was born. In fact, it's unacceptable. No matter what the numbers say, my heart refuses to believe that Pershing could out-general Schwartzkopf, that Bernhardt could out-act Streep, that Caruso could out-sing Pavarotti, or that the 1902 Pirates played better baseball than the heroes I grew up watching.

Oh, sure! The 1902 team *did* finish first by 27.5 games. And, right, it *was* the middle of three straight pennant winners. And yes, it had Honus Wagner, Fred Clarke, Claude Ritchey, Jack Chesbro, Ginger Beaumont, Tommy Leach, and Deacon Phillippe. But those were just *names*! I actually *saw* Dick Groat, Vernon Law, Willie Stargell, Bob Friend, Dave Parker, Bill Mazeroski, Steve Blass, and Manny Sanguillen. Hell, I saw *Clem Koshorek*! That *had* to count for something!

Hmmm. What do politicians do when the facts don't fit their answers? Simple. They say that the facts don't mean what everybody thinks they mean because the situation is different.

Now wait a minute. I think I'm onto something here. Everybody knows

ALL-TIME TOP TWENTY PIRATE TEAMS

No	Year	Fin	W–L	Pct	GB	R	OR	FW	PW	BW	TW
1	1902	1	103–36	.741	-	*775	*440	3.4	6.3	*15.4	26.5
2	1909a	1	110–42	.724	-	*699	447	*3.4	11.0	5.8	20.2
3	1901	1	90–49	.647	-	776	*534	1.2	9.1	8.8	19.1
4	1972b	1E	96–59	.619	-	691	*512	–0.0	8.7	9.2	17.9
5	1893	2	81–48	.628	5	970	*766	2.1	4.9	*10.6	17.6
6	1912	2	93–58	.616	10	751	*585	*6.0	5.8	5.4	17.2
7	1971c	1E	97–65	.599	-	*788	599	0.0	1.3	*13.3	14.6
8	1975d	1E	92–69	.571	-	712	565	–0.2	*8.9	5.1	14.2
9	1906	3	93–60	.608	23.5	623	470	2.2	7.7	3.6	13.5
10	1966	3	92–70	.568	3	759	641	0.4	0.8	*12.2	13.4
11	1925e	1	95–58	.621	-	*912	715	–0.9	8.2	*5.8	13.1
12	1990f	1E	95–67	.586	-	733	619	–0.4	3.6	*9.4	12.7
13	1935	4	86–67	.562	13.5	743	647	0.0	*10.0	2.4	12.4
14t	1903g	1	91–49	.650	-	*793	613	1.6	4.1	*6.5	12.2
14t	1908	2t	98–56	.636	1	585	469	1.9	2.8	7.5	12.2
16t	1927h	1	94–60	.610	-	*817	659	0.6	6.7	4.6	11.9
16t	1979i	1E	98–64	.605	-	*775	643	0.4	7.9	3.6	11.9
18	1960j	1	95–59	.617	-	*734	*593	0.7	4.1	6.9	11.7
19	1911	3	85–69	.552	14.5	744	557	*2.1	8.7	0.2	10.9
20	1965	3	90–72	.556	7	675	580	–0.1	*8.6	2.4	10.9

* = Led league

a = Won 1909 World Series from Detroit, 4–3
b = Lost 1972 LCS to Cincinnati, 2–3
c = Won 1971 LCS from San Fran., 3–1; World Series from Balt., 4–3
d = Lost 1975 LCS to Cincinnati, 0–3
e = Won 1925 World Series from Washington, 4–3

f = Lost 1990 LCS to Cincinnati, 2–4
g = Lost 1903 World Series, 3–5
h = Lost 1927 World Series to New York, 0–4
i = Won 1979 LCS from Cin., 3–0; World Series from Baltimore, 4–3
j = Won 1960 World Series from New York, 4–3

that baseball played before the advent of Babe Ruth and the lively ball was totally different from baseball played afterward. So different, in fact, that comparing a pre-1920 team with a post-1920 team is almost like comparing Apples and IBMs. It just doesn't compute. For all I know, there might even be something in that pre-1920 style of ball that automatically gives it a couple of extra PWs or FWs.

There was nothing wrong with my system that a little creative selectivity won't fix. Just skip the years before 1920 because they were so different. No lively ball. No artificial turf. No night games. Hardly any relief pitchers. No black players. No expansion teams. No three-dollar hot dogs.

Hold it! I didn't want to go too far or I'd end up with only the 1991 team to rank. I stopped at no lively ball.

So I decided simply to limit my survey to only post-1920 teams. This ensured that all the eligible teams were playing roughly the same kind of baseball.

So counting just the post-1920 Bucs, I came up with the list on the next page.

This is more like it! I was surprised to see the fourth-place 1935 Pirates ranked ahead of *both* the 1979 and 1960 Bucs, but I could live with it. After all, they had Pie Traynor, Arky Vaughan, and the Waners. I never saw any of them play, but Pie Traynor used to do ads for a furnace company on local TV. The sainted 1971 Clemente-led World Series winners finished second. And—surprise!—the best Pirate team ever, according to my system, was the 1972 club that lost in the LCS.

Actually, as surprises go, this one is only middling. In those heated Pittsburgh discussions I mentioned earlier, there's almost always someone who'll bring up the '72 Pirates.

The Best

They don't exactly jump off the page at you, but all things considered, manager Bill Virdon's 1972 Buccos very well may have been the best just like their TW rating says. For one thing, they had more depth than a bathysphere. Everybody important was back from the 1971 team and they all had good years.

The infield had Stargell (.293, 33 HR, 112 RBI) on first, backed by Big Bob Robertson, who hit 12 homers playing part-time. Second baseman Dave Cash (.282) often gave way to Rennie Stennett (.283), and Mazeroski was still around for experience. Shortstop Gene Alley (.248)

TOP TEN MODERN-ERA (1920–1990) PIRATE TEAMS

No	Year	Fin	W–L	Pct	GB	R	OR	FW	PW	BW	TW
1	1972	1E	96–59	.619	–	691	*512	0.0	8.7	9.2	17.9
2	1971	1E	97–65	.599	–	*788	599	0.0	1.3	*13.3	14.6
3	1975	1E	92–69	.571	–	712	565	–0.2	*8.9	5.1	14.2
4	1966	3	92–70	.568	3	759	641	0.4	0.8	*12.2	13.4
5	1925	1	95–58	.621	–	*912	715	–0.9	8.2	*5.8	13.1
6	1990	1E	95–67	.586	–	733	619	–0.4	3.6	*9.4	12.7
7	1935	4	86–67	.562	13.5	743	647	0.0	*10.0	2.4	12.4
8t	1927	1	94–60	.610	–	*817	659	0.6	6.7	4.6	11.9
8t	1979	1E	98–64	.605	–	*775	643	0.4	7.9	3.6	11.9
10	1960	1	95–59	.617	–	*734	*593	0.7	4.1	6.9	11.7

* = Led league

was a terrific fielder, and his sub, Jackie Hernandez, was okay though he couldn't hit a lick. Third baseman Richie Hebner (.300, 19 HR, 72 RBI) was only so-so with a glove, but sub Jose Pagan was all right and a tough pinch-hitter.

The outfield had Vic Davalillo (.318) in left, Al Oliver (.312) in center, and Clemente (.312) in right. How many teams can put three .300 hitters in the pasture? And Gene Clines off the bench hit .334!

Catcher Manny Sanguillen hit .298 and *his* sub, present Pirate batting coach Milt May, hit .281. No wonder they called this team "The Lumber Company."

The pitching was surprisingly good. The team's 2.81 ERA was only .03 above league-leader Los Angeles. The regular starters were all right-handers: Steve Blass (19–8), Dock Ellis (15–7), Nellie Briles (14–11), and Bob Moose (13–10). Blass ranked among the aces in the league with his 2.48 ERA. Bruce Kison was 9–7 as a sometimes starter. The bullpen, led by Dave Giusti, lefty Ramon Hernandez, and Bob Miller, saved 48 games.

A Dream Season and a Nightmare

The 1972 Eastern Division race had all the suspense of Bambi vs. Godzilla. The Pirates cruised through the season, winning the division by 11 games over the Cubs. First place was well in hand by late June, and after that it was just a matter of counting to the end. Pirate fans were also counting Clemente's hits. His last of the season was his 3,000th. A double.

In the then five-game LCS, the Pirates lined up against Cincinnati, which had won in the West almost as easily as the Buccos had blitzed the East. Today, of course, we know that "The Big Red Machine" was one of the half dozen best baseball teams ever, but in 1972 they were just the guys who'd lost the 1970 World Series, a mistake Pittsburgh hadn't made in '71.

Pittsburgh took the opening game behind Blass, 5–1, but the next day Bob Moose couldn't get out of the first inning and the Reds won 5–3. Briles, Kison, and Giusti held Cincy in check for a 3–2 win in Game Three to put the Pirates back in front. With the Reds one loss away from elimination, Ross Grimsley two-hit the Bucs to send the LCS to a fifth and final game.

Blass was back for Pittsburgh in Game Five, and he led 3–2 when Ramon Hernandez relieved him with one out in the eighth. Ramon retired the two batters he faced, leaving the Pirates only one teeny inning away from the pennant. But Hernandez was a left-hander, and right-handed hitters Johnny Bench, Tony Perez, and Dennis Menke were due up for the Reds in the ninth. Manager Virdon went to his bullpen for Dave Giusti, the man who'd been his stopper all year.

Giusti promptly showed his versatility by doing his Ralph Branca imitation. When Bench's home run landed, the score was tied 3–3. Perez and Menke singled, convincing Virdon that this wasn't Giusti's day. In came Bob Moose.

Moose got Cesar Geronimo on a fly so deep to right that even iron-armed Clemente couldn't keep George Foster, running for Perez, from moving to third. Darrel Chaney popped up for the second out, leaving Foster still at third. Sparky Anderson sent up Hal McRae to pinch-hit for Clay Carroll. Moose eyed him. Maybe McRae looked bigger than he was. Maybe Moose forgot how far it was to Manny Sanguillen's glove.

Maybe it was fate.

Moose fired the ball into the dirt in front of the plate. Sanguillen watched it skip away. And Foster raced home with the pennant for the Reds.

All in all, 1972 was quite an up-and-down year in Pittsburgh. It was, for instance, the last season for basketball's Pittsburgh Condors. But long-suffering football fans were thrilled that December when Franco Harris caught a ricochet pass to win the Steelers' first-ever playoff game. And, insofar as Moose's wild pitch was a Pirate tragedy, it paled by comparison with Clemente's death in a plane crash on December 31.

Maybe all that makes it a little hard to remember the '72 Pirates, but some fans—a few anyway—will tell you they came *that* close!

And the stats are on their side.

⚾ 17 ⚾

All "A's" in Pitching

As everybody knows, Connie Mack said pitching was 70 percent of baseball. Or was it 75? Or 80? Anyhow, a LOT! Whatever the percentage, it applies to all teams—no pitchee, no winnee.

But maybe it applies a little more to the Athletics, the white-elephant team old Connie started in Philadelphia (The City of Brotherly Love) back in 1901 when he was young Connie, and which now plays its baseball on the opposite coast in Oakland (The City of Shot-and-a-Beer Love). Those A's have had four dynasties in their near-ninety years. The common thread is great pitching.

The word "dynasty" has been tossed around loosely in recent years—ask any Mets fan—but a reasonable definition is at least three pennants in five years. By that standard, New York has been piggish—(1920–28, 1936–44, 1947–64, and 1976–78)—but the American League has had singleton reigns in Detroit (1907–09), Boston (1915–18), and Baltimore (1969–71), as well as the four Athletics dynasties. All of those pennant winners flaunted pitching, hitting, and fielding in more than acceptable amounts, but when you think of the other teams, it's usually the hitters who come to mind first—Ty Cobb, Tris Speaker, the Robinsons, Ruth, DiMaggio, Mantle. What do you remember most about the A's champs? Plank, Bender, Grove, Earnshaw, Hunter, Blue, Stewart, and the Eck. It's like the ghost of old Connie is hovering around this team, chortling, "See, what did I tell you!"

The Yankees' Don Mattingly pegged the '89 A's right when he said, "Take their pitching away and they ain't no better than anybody else . . .

it's their pitching that sets them apart from the rest of us." That can be said (and probably said more grammatically) about all the A's great teams.

Almost a Dynasty

Mack set the character of the Athletics in their first year when he talked Chick Fraser and Strawberry Bill Bernhard, a couple of established N.L. pitchers, into jumping to the American League. Neither pitched all that well and the A's finished fourth. Fraser nipped back to his old league the next year, and the Phillies got an injunction against Bernhard, forcing Connie to send him to Cleveland. They weren't missed. Mack won pennants in 1902 and 1905 on the arms of Eddie Plank, Rube Waddell, and Chief Bender. Other than his pitchers, Connie had lineups that included the likes of Socks Seybold, Lave Cross, Harry Davis, and Ossie Schreckengost—your basic journeymen. Only the pitchers were special.

Certainly Waddell was as special as they come—the ultimate left-headed left-hander. A genuine nut case who'd rather chase fire trucks than show up at the ballpark on time, Waddell missed games to watch parades, go fishing, wrestle alligators, tend bar, and, on at least one occasion, shoot marbles under the stands with the local kids. Of course, he was a child himself—from the neck up. Waddell's boozing, undependability, and generally weird behavior eventually drove all of his managers to throw up their hands and send him packing, but Mack put up with him longer than any other skipper—and got better results. Before Connie gave up on him, Rube gave the A's four 20-win seasons. He set a record that stood for sixty years with his 349 strikeouts in 1904.

Even after Waddell had agreed to join the A's in 1902, Mack had to send two Pinkertons to haul him in from Los Angeles. Connie tried all manner of devices to keep the Rube within bounds. He doled Waddell his pay in dribs and drabs. He set baby-sitters to keep an eye on him. When the Athletics fielded a pro football team in 1902, Connie signed Waddell as a player just to delay his off-season sprees. For publication, Rube was a substitute guard, but all he ever really did was lead cheers on the sideline.

When he was sober (and there), Waddell was one of baseball's most gifted pitchers. He had a crackling fastball, a deep biting curve, and superb control. In one game, he struck out sixteen batters. In another, he bested Cy Young 4–2 in 20 innings. In several exhibitions (though never in a regular-season game), he sat down his outfielders while he struck out the side. Still, many were the times Mack wondered if it was worth it. One night he caught Waddell sneaking into a hotel lobby after curfew. The Rube apologized abjectly and turned to go to his room. Just then a loaded pistol dropped from his pocket and went off. The bullet missed Connie by less than Rube's IQ.

In contrast to Waddell, Eddie Plank was a lefty with a white-bread head. Serious and sober, he was never a newsman's favorite because there wasn't much of a story there. He pitched, he won. No frills, no anecdotes.

Plank joined the A's in 1901, fresh from earning his degree at Gettysburg College. A college degree was pretty uncommon among players for that period, but Mack had great success with Plank, Chief Bender, Jack Coombs, and Eddie Collins.

Plank had fine control of his sidearm fastball and curve, and he used psychology on the mound. He'd fiddle and fuss while the batter waited. Fool with the resin bag. Tug his cap. Shake off a sign. Heist his socks. Mutter to himself. Adjust his belt. When he finally delivered, frustrated batters were ready to swing at anything still in the state of Pennsylvania.

Eddie didn't have much luck in the World Series—2–5, despite a 1.32 ERA. In four of his losses, the A's were shut out. Eddie knew all about shutouts—his 69 is the most in a career by a left-hander. Plank held the record for most lifetime wins by a lefty for ages and still holds the Athletics' top career mark for pitchers from either side of the mound, although he was probably not their greatest pitcher.

Mack's personal favorite was Bender, who arrived from Carlisle Indian School in 1903. He was called "Chief," as were all Indian ballplayers in those days, but Connie always referred to him as "Albert." Nevertheless, he was Mack's "chief" choice when a big game was on the line. Late in his long career, Connie still maintained he'd want Bender for an important game if he could have any of his former players in their prime.

Like Plank, Bender was dignified and reliable, but reporters liked him more than Eddie because they could always make up some Indian-related story to fill their columns. Bender's out pitch was a "talcum ball." That's right, he rubbed talcum powder on the ball so it would slip out of his hand without any rotation, like a knuckler. Technically, it was a sanitary spitball.

The A's near-dynasty in those early years lost pennants to Boston with Cy Young in '03 and '04 and to the epitome of a "pitcher's team," the 1906 Hitless Wonder White Sox. It's hard to believe Mack needed more pitching, but it took great pitching to beat him.

Dynasty I

By 1910, Mack had a good team to go with Plank and Bender. The A's became the first American League team to top 100 victories. The "$100,000 Infield" of Stuffy McInnis, Eddie Collins, Jack Barry, and Frank Baker would probably go for about $10 million plus incentives today. Regardless, pitching was still the backbone of the team.

Colby Jack Coombs was a great right-hander headed for the Hall of Fame until he was derailed by ill health. In 1910, he threw 13 shutouts on his way to winning 31 games, setting the A's record for season wins. Two more great seasons followed. Then, in the spring of 1913, he nearly died from typhoid. He never completely recovered the control or velocity that made him a winner. After he left the majors, Coombs became one of the country's most respected college baseball coaches at Princeton and Duke.

Perhaps it's only that Mack managed so many years, but he seemed to have cornered the market on terrific young pitchers whose careers were shortened by injuries and ill health. Besides Coombs, there were Andy Coakley, Rube Bressler, Cy Morgan, and Harry Krause in the early years, and Bill McCahan, Dick Fowler, and several others later.

The A's won in 1910 and '11. Mack always maintained the 1911 club was his best. It went 101–50, with Coombs winning 28, Plank 22, and Bender 17. Bender won two in the World Series victory over a solid New York Giants team.

What was essentially the same Athletics team took a year off to party and finish third in 1912, and then came back for pennants in 1913 and '14. Legend has it that Mack was so outraged by his four-straight loss to the Miracle Braves in the 1914 World Series that he broke up the team in spite. Actually, two wars were to blame: the baseball war with the Federal League that boosted salaries beyond what he was able—or at least willing—to pay, and the real war in Europe that made baseball's future uncertain. Losing Plank and Bender to the Feds wasn't tragic; both were near the end of the line. Worse was that he sold the A's future by retailing his young pitchers: Herb Pennock, Bob Shawkey, and Bullet Joe Bush.

The Athletics plummeted to last place and stayed there for seven years. They didn't recover for over a decade. Despite his team's bottom-dwelling there was never a question of firing Mack. He was universally respected as a strategist, judge of talent, and handler of men. He also owned the team.

Dynasty II

The key to the A's resurrection and eventually to their second dynasty was the $100,600 Mack paid for Lefty Grove in 1925. Lefty'd been ready for the majors for two or three years, but Jack Dunn, owner of Baltimore's International League champs, held on to his contract until he could get a then-fantastic price. Once he arrived, Grove established himself as the best left-hander of his time, some say ever. Mack called him "my best one" at times but sometimes rated Waddell ahead of him. Perhaps on those occasions Connie was grumbling about that hundred grand. Or maybe he actually preferred Rube's lunacy to Lefty's tantrums.

According to many people, Grove was a perfectly likable fellow away from a ballpark. A bit of a loner, perhaps, but all in all you wouldn't get upset if your daughter brought him to dinner. But put a baseball in his hand, and Lefty was mean as a snake with a belly rash. "Why, when he was just pitching batting practice," Doc Cramer said, "you hit one through the box and you'd go down on the next pitch. In *batting practice*." When he lost—which wasn't often—he'd go into the kind of rage they used to call "towering." Woe to the unwary glove, water bucket, bat, or *Homo sapiens* that crossed his path.

At 6' 3" with an intimidating scowl, Grove had the kind of fastball that made batters cringe and early in his career he was scary wild. After Mack sold him to the Red Sox in 1934, Lefty came down with a sore arm that turned him into a control-curver, but in his Athletics days he could, in Westbrook Pegler's words, "throw a lamb chop past a wolf."

Besides Grove, Mack had George Earnshaw and Rube Walberg on his 1929–31 dynasty. During the championship years, right-hander Earnshaw threw a fastball that was nearly the equal of Grove's. Walberg, an underrated lefty, was usually good for 15 to 18 wins a year.

Veterans like John Picus Quinn, Eddie Rommel, Roy Mahaffey, and Howard Ehmke rounded out baseball's best staff. Quinn won 247 games for various teams over twenty-three major league seasons. Rommel, who later became an outstanding umpire, had won 27 for Mack's seventh-place team in 1922 and was still effective as a knuckleballing reliever when the A's became champs. Mahaffey, a Phillies reject, won 15 for the A's in 1931. Ehmke was nearing the end of a fair career when Mack named him the surprise starter against the Cubs in the first game of the 1929 World Series. Connie knew Ehmke's sidearm delivery would be nearly unseeable coming out of a background of white shirts at Wrigley

Field. Sure enough, Ehmke gave up only one unearned run and fanned thirteen Cubs.

The 1929–31 A's weren't all pitching—they could have made it to the first division with Mickey Cochrane, Al Simmons, Jimmie Foxx, and a couple of other stalwarts—but their moundsmen put them over the top. Significantly, when Earnshaw and Walberg slipped a peg in 1932, Philadelphia finished second.

The Dark Ages

Another of those legends has Connie dismantling the team in a fit of pique over losing the '31 Series when the Cardinals' Pepper Martin stole everything but Mickey Cochrane's jock. This one gets less credence than the 1914 fantasy because most fans are familiar enough with the Depression to know why Mack *really* sold off his high-priced stars. The truth was Mack the Manager wanted to win; Mack the Owner wanted to avoid losing his stiff-collared shirt.

By 1936, the A's were back in the basement, where they stayed until after World War II. In the postwar era, a popular spring training picture was Connie Mack holding up a finger to indicate he was going for one more pennant, his tenth. But Lou Brissie, Joe Coleman, Phil Marchildon, Carl Scheib, and the rest were never quite in the Plank-Bender-Grove class. Alex Kellner was a 20-game winner in 1949, and little Bobby Shantz was a wonder in 1952, but neither could sustain that pace.

Mack finally gave up the managerial reins after the 1950 season. He died in 1956—two years after the *Philadelphia* Athletics.

After losing 103 games in 1954, the A's took flight west, leaving Philly to the Phillies. At first they tarried in Kansas City for a sad layover in which their practice of selling every promising player to the Yankees made them little more than a New York farm club. In 1968, they made the jump to Oakland, while K.C. gratefully waited for the Royals.

Dynasty III

A's owner Charley O. Finley got so much ragging in the press—most of it of the "Crazy Charley" variety—you'd think he was the reincarnation of Rube Waddell. Okay, he did keep a mascot mule named "Charley O." and he did advocate orange baseballs. Still, there were really no similarities.

Waddell was a nut. Finley was a shrewd promoter and businessman who had more ideas, good and bad, in a week than Rube had in his entire life.

One of Charley's better brainstorms was to hold on to his good players and watch them develop. Among the youngsters signed after Finley took over but before the team left Kansas City was a right-hander named Jim. Finley thought that too ordinary a monicker for a kid he expected to be extraordinary, so he christened him "Catfish."

He didn't need to spice up the name of his best lefty prospect; how many Vidas do you know? Nevertheless, one story has Finley offering Blue a bonus to change his name to "True."

In 1971, Jim and Vida won 45 games between them to lead the A's to the A.L.'s Western Division crown. Baltimore, however, had four 20-game winners in the East and only needed three of them to win the LCS.

After that, the A's were masters for three straight pennants and World Series triumphs. They weren't just successful, they were colorful in more ways than their green and gold uniforms. (And didn't Charley O. get laughed at when he first dressed them like that!) Finley's A's were an iconoclastic, mustachioed crew that squabbled in the clubhouse and then went out and beat the opposition to death. In addition to Catfish and Vida, the pitching staff boasted Ken Holtzman, Blue Moon Odom, and base-ball's best reliever, Rollie Fingers.

Oh, sure, Sal Bando, Bert Campaneris, Joe Rudi, and Reggie Jackson made major contributions and there were several other useful everyday players on that swashbuckling crew. But the swash that shined their buckle brightest was on the mound. In those three years, Hunter won 67 regular-season games, Holtzman 59, Blue 43, and Fingers saved 61. Hunter was 3–1 in three LCSs and Holtzman 2–0. Fingers saved a pair in each of three World Series, while Catfish went 4–0 and Holtzman 4–1.

In 1975, Charley O. made a serious error with Hunter's contract and Catfish became a free agent. When he signed with the Yankees for $3 million—a figure scarcely credible in those good olde days—it signaled the beginning of the end for Finley's A's. They lost the '75 LCS in three straight and after that Finley had to begin trading stars he couldn't afford to pay.

Dynasty IV

The Athletics were able to hold their team together long enough to win the required three pennants to qualify as a dynasty in 1988–90, although losing two out of three World Series tarnished things a bit. In this era of free agency, we may never see another dynasty anywhere.

These late A's looked modern as hell in their green and gold, but they won in the usual Athletics way. Oh, the Hendersons, Canseco, McGwire, and so forth helped, but the strength of the team was still its pitching. The big names were Dave Stewart, who was always ignored in the Cy Young voting, Bob Welch, and the Eck. But this team was loaded all the way down the staff: Mike Moore, Scott Sanderson, Storm Davis, Gene Nelson, Rick Honeycutt, and on and on. It seemed like every time you turned around, they had a good arm out there.

Old Connie would have been proud.

The Athletics slipped to the bottom of the standings in the last two years as Stewart, Welch, and other pitchers aged, were injured, or left through free agency. As the '93 season wound down, Todd Van Poppel and some other youngsters were just beginning to come on. Oakland has turned its future over to the next crop of arms. Who knows? They might be the best yet.

◯ 18 ◯

All-Star Yawn

The annual All-Star Game has become baseball's biggest bore. A civilized society would hand it a cup of hemlock and look the other way.

For three days every summer, the pennant races come to a screeching halt while a few baseball stars—inevitably the wrong ones—meet in a major league city for another pickup game. On Monday, all the media who could wrangle expenses out of assignment editors buzz around asking the same questions, and the players make appropriate noises about how they really want to win for "their" league, whichever league that happens to be this season. On Tuesday night, carefully timed so the one demographic group that might be interested in the outcome will have to be in bed by the fourth inning to be ready for school the next day, the game gets played. With luck, one side or the other will score a run—usually on a walk, sacrifice, error, and fielder's choice—before nine painful innings have elapsed. Most of the evening is spent with the greatest batsmen in the world doing Bob Buhl imitations. On Wednesday, nothing happens. Nothing. Except a lot of us suddenly realize we don't remember which league won the evening before. Then we thank God it's Thursday night and we can get back to playing real games.

It was NOT ever thus.

Once upon a time, the All-Star Game was a big deal that could really heat up your blood. It was a moment to be anticipated, savored, and remembered. What went wrong? Actually, a lot.

How It Got Broke

Remember 1957? That was the season that Cincinnati had a pretty good team—not a pennant-winner, but pretty good nonetheless. And it had been a long time coming. So, with a local radio station egging them on, Cincy fans proceeded to stuff the ballot box for their home team. They elected seven Reds to the National League's eight starting positions! Every slot except first base (where even rabid Reds fans couldn't bring themselves to vote against the Cardinals' Stan Musial) was filled by a Reds regular.

It wasn't that this showed the All-Star balloting to be nothing more than a popularity contest. Everybody already knew that. What hurt was that it proved that a few determined fans with pencils could manipulate the voting to elect anyone. Anyone!

Commissioner Ford Frick, as was his way, stepped in to make a bad situation disastrous. First, he arbitrarily removed Reds outfielders Gus Bell and Wally Post from the starting lineup to create an All-Star hybrid: half-Cincy, half-Frick. And then he took the voting away from the fans altogether and handed it to the managers and players, in effect removing the only good reason to hold an All-Star Game in the first place.

It wasn't until 1970 that Bowie Kuhn returned the vote to the fans. Supposedly there are safeguards to keep ballot-stuffing from happening again. But walk around your local ballpark a couple of weeks before the All-Star game. If you keep a sharp eye out, you just might come upon someone sitting there with a stack of ballots as high as an elephant's eye, busily filling them in with names of players on the home team. Apparently, several starting spots each year are dictated by a couple dozen busy ballot stuffers.

Of course, most of us don't really care that much whether the starting N.L. shortstop is Barry Larkin or Ozzie Smith. What we really could do without is all the bitching and moaning that goes on after the squads are named. Typically, it takes the form of some media guy complaining: "How can they leave Joe Dokes off the All-Star Team when he's hitting (fill in some appropriately high numbers)." If you didn't hear the same refrain every year, you might get the idea there's some sincerity involved, but odds are, he heard it somewhere else first. Like from Dokes. Dokes may have missed the cut because every team in his league must have at least one representative. Or it may be that in rounding out his squad the manager decided John Doe's glove would be more useful than Dokes' bat. Maybe Doe is better than Dokes. It doesn't matter.

Here are some guys who *really* had a right to complain when they were left off their league's All-Star squads: Hank Greenberg in 1935, Don Newcombe in 1956, Dave Parker in 1978, Keith Hernandez in 1979, Kirk Gibson in 1988, Robin Yount in 1989, and Terry Pendleton in 1991. Why should they feel particularly put-upon when they weren't put upon the squad in those years? Because at the end of each of those seasons they were named their league's Most Valuable Player! MVPs but not All-Stars!

The amount of greed involved in these things was made completely clear from 1960 to 1962 when they scheduled two games each summer. Two was exactly the wrong number because of the likelihood that the leagues would split (which happened in 1962). By making it blatant, the baseball establishment guaranteed that no one involved cared a fig if one league got the better of the other so long as more revenue flowed in.

That's why they play the thing at night, of course. Put it in prime time for a few more bucks. It doesn't matter that your wife hates you for making her miss "Roseanne," or that your kid calls you *Der Führer* when you send him to bed in the fourth inning, or that the next day you're so zonked out from staying up late you start snoring at your desk. None of that matters so long as baseball gets the most possible dollars.

Yet, even all that greed and trickery weren't enough to ruin the All-Star Game, so of late they've managed to make it one of the most boring games of the summer. A close, low-hit game during the season can be exciting because there's something at stake—even if it's only the pitchers' ERAs. Suspense builds. But, with the All-Star Game, there's no suspense because the outcome doesn't matter. All you can do is hope one of the endless parade of pitchers won't have it tonight so you can finally see some hitting! It doesn't matter which side. Anybody!

You put all this stuff together and there's no doubt you'll have a bad game. Even so, we might be able to get through it if it delivered real stars. Back when the whole mess started in 1933, players like Babe Ruth or Carl Hubbell were mythical figures glimpsed only from the distant bleachers or on the sports page. How one of these gods might do in competition with another seemed to have some importance.

Then television began taking us out to the ballgame weekly and we could watch Stan Musial adjust his jockstrap up close and personal. The close-up made Musial, Mays, and Mantle more human and less godlike.

When you could actually see a glistening bead of sweat roll off Hank Aaron's nose, you knew you were looking at someone in many ways like yourself.

Today, we see Bonds and Ripkin nightly in highlight tapes. And they're interviewed endlessly and often combatively. In the wake of Watergate, it seems like most reporters are determined to show us every wart. But the closer we get, the less in awe we are. There's hardly a player left that a baseball fan would pay to see. The so-called thrill of seeing most of the best players all together has become no more of a kick than paging through a fairly good baseball card collection.

In just over fifty years, the annual get-together has descended from an Olympian home run by Babe Ruth to an infield fly by who cares?

Memories Are Mis-Made of This

There's no doubt that back when it actually mattered, the All-Star Game provided some unique moments. In looking over the history of the game, I wasn't surprised that most of the events that have become legendary occurred before expansion. What came as something of a shock was that so often I mis-remembered the context and sometimes the events themselves.

For example, everyone remembers that Ruth hit a homer in the first All-Star game in 1933, but on more than one occasion I've read that Frankie Frisch hit the FIRST All-Star home run. Not so; the Babe drove one into the Comiskey Park right-field stands just inside the foul line in the third inning with Charley Gehringer on base to make the score 3–0. Three innings later, the National League scored its first run when Ruth misplayed Lon Warneke's looper into a triple. Warneke scored on Pepper Martin's ground out, and then Frisch hit the first *National League* homer to make it 3–2. The A.L. scored the final run of the game in the bottom of the sixth when Earl Averill's single drove in Joe Cronin.

A couple of good trivia questions came out of that first game. My favorite: who had the first All-Star RBI? Would you believe, with all those sluggers assembled, it was Lefty Gomez, a pitcher who hit like one? He singled Jimmy Dykes home in the second inning.

The American Leaguers wore their regular team uniforms (as is the practice to this day), but the National League had special unis with "NL" on the caps and "National League" across the chest. Connie Mack and John McGraw were the managers as much for sentiment as any other reason. McGraw had resigned as the Giants' skipper after thirty years the year before, so this was the last game he ever managed.

The original concept, as designed by Arch Ward of the *Chicago Tribune*, was for a one-time-only affair as part of Chicago's Century of Progress Exposition. The baseball establishment was generally against it, but Ward got Commissioner Kenesaw Landis' approval by directing the proceeds to the Players' Pension Fund to help desititute former players. Landis ran baseball as democratically as Ivan the Terrible ran Russia, so that made it a done deal. The public took to it right away, and even before the first ball was thrown out, everyone knew there was going to be another game the next year.

Carl and Ted

It was a good thing they played a game in 1934, because it was graced by the most famous incident in All-Star history: Carl Hubbell's strikeout streak. What is seldom remembered is that King Carl began the game less than royally. Since it was held at the Polo Grounds, he was the obvious choice to start for the National League, but he got into immediate do-do by giving Gehringer a single and walking Heinie Manush. Up came Babe Ruth. Hubbell went to his screwball, which was a pitch, if not unknown, at least seldom seen in the American League. Ruth went down on a called third strike. Lou Gehrig was retired swinging. And Jimmie Foxx was also dispatched on strikes. Frankie Frisch led off the bottom of the first inning with a home run, to give Hubbell a lead. In the second inning, Hubbell struck out Al Simmons and Joe Cronin before Bill Dickey nicked him for a single. Then he got his sixth strikeout by fanning (another trivia stumper?) Lefty Gomez. Hubbell put down the A.L. with only one walk and no strikeouts in the third inning. He then left the game to a great cheer as he exited through the outfield into the clubhouse in center field.

It was a spectacular performance, and there are only two other things to add.

First, Hubbell's National League team did not win the game. The A.L. jumped all over King Carl's successors to score nine runs to seven for the Nationals.

Second, Hubbell did not do the game's best pitching. The most spectacular, yes; the best, no. In the fifth inning, the N.L. had closed the score to 8–7 by wreaking havoc on Gomez and Red Ruffing. In came Mel Harder for the A.L. with no outs and a man aboard. The Cleveland curveballer went on to throw five shutout innings, allowing only one hit and one walk. Deservedly, he received credit for the win, but somehow the memory of his superior work got lost in memories of Hubbell's strikeouts.

A somewhat similar situation occurred in 1941 when Ted Williams blasted a grand slam in the bottom of the ninth at Detroit to win the affair 7–5. Williams, who also doubled in four trips, certainly came through in the clutch and deserved all the praise he got. But often forgotten is National Leaguer Arky Vaughan, who had four RBI on *two* homers and a single. Newspapers all over the country had already set Arky's name in headlines when Williams changed the story.

Another Williams home run was the big story in the 1946 All-Star Game when he connected with Rip Sewell's famous blooper. Sometimes called the "eephus," Sewell's pitch was really a sky-high lob that he was often successful in getting over the plate. Although the ball came in like a dead fish, it was on such an extreme downward trajectory that it was hard to hit square. Moreover, the batter had to supply all the power so that it was generally agreed that a home run was impossible. But in the bottom of the eighth inning, Williams changed that perception. He fouled off the first blooper, let one go for a ball, and then took a strike on a fastball. Sewell nodded: here it comes again. The blooper arched high. Ted took a step or two forward and uncoiled. Bam! into the right-field stands! Williams laughed all the way around the bases, and the fans loved it.

Good thing, too. Up to that point, the game was a real drag. The American League won 12–0.

Hurts

Williams was also the key player in one of those All-Star Game injuries that make people ask if the show is worth the risk. In the first inning of the 1950 game, played at Comiskey Park, he made a nice catch of Ralph Kiner's drive and then ran into the left-field wall with his left elbow. Despite the pain, he stayed in the game and even singled once in four at bats. An examination after the game revealed a fracture. Ted, who'd been on his way to a typically great season, was out until mid-September. His Red Sox finished a scant four games behind the Yankees that year, leaving Red Sox fans convinced that they'd lost the pennant at the All-Star Game.

Cleveland fans can't delude themselves that the All-Star Game cost them a pennant, but many of them are certain that the game cost them a catcher in 1970. That was the year, with the game tied 4–4 in the twelfth inning, Pete Rose steamrollered American League catcher Ray Fosse at home plate, separating backstop from ball and scoring the winning run. Up until that time, Fosse had been one of the few bright spots in Cleveland's annual humiliation. A young, bright receiver in his first year as a regular, Fosse had his batting average comfortably above .300 at the midsummer break.

Then Rose, playing before a home crowd at Cincinnati, ran through him and left him dazed in the dust. From that point on, according to Clevelanders, Fosse ceased being an All-Star and fell pell-mell toward journeyman. However, many make the counterargument that his early promise was just another case of Cleveland's flash-in-the-pannism.

Had Rose's crash occurred in the heat of a pennant race, it would have been universally praised as a gritty play. But many question the appropriateness of such a high injury-risk collision in what is essentially an exhibition game.

The most famous All-Star injury happened in 1937 at Washington when Cleveland's Earl Averill lined a shot off Dizzy Dean's right foot. A toe was broken, and when Dean returned to the mound less than two weeks later (with the St. Louis Cardinals' blessing), he altered his motion to favor the toe. And THAT led to a sore arm and a premature end to Dean's career.

A couple of things usually forgotten: Diz didn't pitch all that well even before he got his toe stubbed; he gave up two runs on four hits and a walk to take the loss for the N.L. But Averill's smash was turned into the final out of the third inning when Billy Herman picked up the ricochet and threw to first.

Windy

The All-Star Game usually brings out the worst in headline writers. Maybe they think of it as a challenge. More likely, they figure their sins will be forgiven by baseball fans because the game is meaningless. When the National League won the rain-shortened 1952 game on Hank Sauer's home run, there was a rush to work "Swingin' in the Rain" into the headline.

The 1967 game went fifteen long, mostly dull innings before the National League put an end to the misery, 2–1, on Tony Perez's home run. Inevitably, a few newspapers attempted to look literate by headlining

"Long Day's Journey into Night." That was terribly unfair to Eugene O'Neill, as any one of his plays has more action than your average All-Star Game. If a literary reference is absolutely necessary, try Shakespeare's *Much Ado About Nothing*.

As final proof that the outcome of the game matters little, if at all, take the first of the two games played in 1961. By the top of the ninth at Candlestick Park, the National League led 3–1, but the A.L. tied the score with a pair of runs. The N.L. couldn't score in the bottom of the ninth, sending the game into extra innings. The American League forged ahead with a run in the top of the tenth, but the National League came back to score twice in the bottom of the frame to win. Exhibition or not, any game with a pair of last-ditch rallies—one by either side—is worth remembering, right?

Wrong. Today, it could take you a week to find a fan who remembers even one of the rallies, yet this is one of the most famous All-Star Games of all. Why? Because little Stu Miller relieved for the National League in the top of the ninth. And when the irresistible force of the Candlestick wind hit Miller flush, he was literally blown off the mound for a balk to set up the tying run.

Like most All-Star Games, even this one turned out to be more wind than substance.

⚾ 19 ⚾

To Hell with Babe Ruth

They say that during World War II, U.S. Marines crouching at night in shallow foxholes on South Pacific islands would sometimes hear Japanese soldiers call out what they thought was the ultimate insult to Americans: "To hell with Babe Ruth!" I guess the idea was that any Marine hearing such blasphemy was supposed to lose his head completely and go charging blindly into the jungle, spraying lead. As far as I can ascertain, the Marines kept their cool. Maybe the Japanese should have tried, "To hell with Budweiser!"

Anyway, of late there have been several books published and even a couple of movies made that show the Babe as less than admirable in many ways. It's generally agreed he drank, smoked, cursed, and womanized to gargantuan degrees. He was not nearly so lovable to those who knew him well as he appeared at a distance to the general public.

But before we say a collective "to hell with Babe Ruth," let's admit one thing: put a bat in his hands and he was the best.

Baseball statisticians are always coming up with new ways to rate ballplayers. The test of validity is whether Ruth finishes on top or not. If he doesn't, take the system back to the drawing board. Years and years ago, baseball statisticians looked at batting averages, but Ruth as much as anyone made them go beyond that because, while they were sure he did the most damage with his bat, his BA wasn't at the top. Actually, it was near there; he ranks ninth lifetime. But that merely proved some tinkering with the system was needed. Most of the new-type rating stats take into consideration both how often a batter made hits and how far he hits them.

The Sultan of New Stats

Here's a quick survey of some of the newer stats and how Ruth rates:

PRODUCTION: One of the simplest and most accurate new stats, this combines a batter's On Base Percentage with his Slugging Average. In short, OBP says how often; SLG says how far.

For players with careers of over ten years, Ted Williams has the top On Base Percentage (.483), with Ruth right behind (.474). Ruth's lifetime Slugging Average (.690) leads everyone, with Williams second (.634). Taking the two stats together as Production, Ruth's 1.163 is the all-time best, followed by Williams and Lou Gehrig.

The Babe also had the three highest single-season totals in 1920, 1921, and 1923. Williams' 1941 season ranks fourth, and then Ruth has three of the next four highest-ranked individual seasons: 1927, 1926, and 1924.

BATTING RUNS: One of statistician Pete Palmer's inventions, this measures how many runs a batter would deliver beyond or below what a league-average batter would produce in a season or a career. The runs are derived from the kinds of hits, etc., not from runs scored and RBI. In other words, how many more runs would Ruthian hitting cause than would absolute "C" hitting?

Ruth brought about 1,322 more runs over his career than would have an average Joe Blow. Williams (1,166) and Ty Cobb (1,032) are the only others to get above 1,000 lifetime.

As far as individual seasons go, Ruth again owns the top three spots (the order is 1921, 1923, and 1920 this time) and six of the best eight seasons ever.

RUNS CREATED: Writer Bill James came up with this measurement of run contribution produced by a batter's batting and baserunning. Unlike Batting Runs, which measures distance away from the norm, this produces a total. In its simplest form, it's Hits plus Walks times Total Bases divided by At Bats plus Walks, but other stats like stolen bases and caught stealing can be added in to increase accuracy.

Longevity is a factor here. Ty Cobb, who played 532 more games than Ruth, came very near to creating as many runs, with 2,803 to the Babe's 2,838. Other high totals belong to Stan Musial (2,625), Hank Aaron (2,550), and Williams (2,538).

Ruth's 1921 and 1923 stats rank at the top in individual seasons under the James formula, with his 1920 season fourth. Surprisingly, Hugh Duffy wins third place with his all-time-high batting average season of 1894.

TOTAL AVERAGE: Writer Tom Boswell's contribution to the world of baseball stats essentially measures the bases gained against the bases lost. Add total bases, steals, walks, and hit by pitch, then divide the total by the number of at bats (minus hits), caught stealings, and grounded into double plays.

There are 21 careers that averaged at least 1.000, with the old Yankee Charley Keller twenty-first. Ruth, who once again leads all, is at 1.399, well ahead of Williams at 1.320.

In individual seasons, Ruth takes first and second (1920 and 1921), Williams is third (1941), and the Babe chimes in fourth with 1923.

Whew! No matter how he's measured, Ruth always stands tall.

The Greatest—Relatively

It's easy to see why those movies took swats at Ruth's character. If they wanted to introduce any conflict into the plot—instead of producing an hour-and-a-half-long highlight film—they needed to give the Babe some demons. There wasn't any way they could denigrate his hitting.

Well, I'm not going to try to do anything those smart Hollywood people couldn't do. I'm convinced that Babe Ruth was the greatest hitter of all time.

Relatively.

Ah, "relatively" is such a nasty little word! When applied to baseball statistics, it usually means something like comparing Bill Terry's .401 batting average in 1930 to Carl Yastrzemski's .301 in 1968. Then you show that Yaz outhit his league by 71 points and Memphis Bill outhit his by 98. And THAT shows Yaz would have hit .374 in 1930 and Terry .328 in 1968. In other words, had they both played under the same conditions, they would have been a lot closer in batting average.

Those things are fun to brood about, but that's not quite the "relatively" I'm thinking of here. My "relatively" is how a few circumstances combined to allow the Babe to compile those three great seasons (1920, 1921, and 1923) that are the real cornerstone of his career record and which keep him ahead of all others in the various ways of measuring lifetime marks. Take away those three seasons and Ruth would still rank high, but Williams, Cobb, Musial, and a few others would edge past him in career achievement as measured by our new and improved stats.

Right off you're going to say I can't "take away" a season or three like they never happened. Well, bless your soul, we do it all the time in a way.

For certain seasons, when the times were out of joint, we always soft-pedal what the real numbers tell us in favor of what we think the situation permitted. Roger Maris will never get full value for his 61 homers because he did it in an expansion year. Hal Newhouser's 29 wins in 1944 are yawned at because they came during a war. Even old Hugh Duffy's unmatched batting average of 1894 fades because it came right after they moved the pitchers back fifteen feet. And Bill Terry's .401? Well, EVERY-BODY hit that year!

So what I'm saying is that circumstances combined to give Babe Ruth a batting edge in the early '20s. Because of that edge, we are permitted to mentally take a little off the top of his stats for those years. And in doing so we bring his career record back to earth. Once that's done, it's possible—quite possible—that someone like Williams, who didn't have the same advantages Ruth did, will look like a better hitter on an absolute, pure-hitting scale.

To put it another way, in taking those early 1920s years at face value, there's no question that Ruth did the most hitting. But he may not have really been the most hitter.

Okay, what were these circumstances that helped the Babe? First, he came to the majors as a pitcher. Second, somebody assassinated the Archduke Ferdinand. Third, Harry Frazee had a couple of bad years on Broadway. And fourth, baseball owners wanted to increase their profits. Let's examine these circumstances in detail.

Only as a Pitcher

As a hitter, what advantage did the Babe derive in coming to the majors as a pitcher? Simply this: had he not been a pitcher, he might never have gone to the majors at all. And, if he had gotten there, he would have been a very different kind of hitter.

We've all seen film of Babe Ruth's swing. He lifted his right foot and then stepped toward the pitcher with a long stride, putting every ounce into it—and he had a lot of ounces. At the same time his hands come down and back in a sort of hitch that allowed him to bring the bat around like a buggy whip. Even today, that swing looks more powerful than the flailings of any modern-day slugger. It's an "all out" swing, aiming for the seats. And when he missed, which was often, he practically screwed himself into the ground.

When Ruth arrived in the majors, no one else batted that way. And for a very good reason. It didn't work. Remember, the ball was as dead as Custer's army. Even swinging as hard as Ruth did—and connecting—produced only long fly outs for most batters. The proper way to hit against the dead ball was to use a compact, controlled, level swing and either bounce the ball between the infielders or line-drive it just over their heads. This would be what we call a "contact hitter."

Ruth was stronger than the average bear, and occasionally—very occasionally—he could hit one into the seats swinging from the heels like he did. His manager no doubt found it useful to have a hitter he could put up in a do-or-die situation when only a home run could stave off defeat. Ruth could be the pinch hitter of last resort. That was okay. Because he was a pitcher, Babe didn't take up an extra spot on the roster. But, had he been an outfielder, his rare home runs couldn't have justified his being on the team.

Babe's batting averages as a major league pitcher weren't all that bad. In his first three full seasons at Boston, he topped .300 twice. But, long before he could have reached the majors as an outfielder, some smart baseball manager would have thought, "This kid could hit .350 if he only knew how to bat." And the Babe would have been taught to cut down his swing. He was kind of muleheaded. Maybe he would have refused to alter his style. Maybe he would have sat on the bench.

It didn't happen that way, of course, because Babe was a pitcher. And since pitchers weren't expected to hit well, they could bat any way they pleased. And that is exactly what Ruth continued to do.

The Archduke

While Ruth was starting out as a Boston pitcher, the Archduke was starting World War I by getting himself killed. By 1918, the U.S. was involved. The baseball season was shortened because all the men were supposed to "work or fight" by Labor Day, and a lot of players either joined the service or went into defense work early. Boston found itself short an outfielder or two. Ruth was pressed into service as an outfielder–first baseman in 75 games (he also pitched 20) and came through with a .300 batting average and eleven home runs—enough to lead the league.

It's safe to say that Ruth would never have been put into the lineup if Boston had possessed its full contingent of players. Ed Barrow, who is always tagged as a genius for sending Ruth into the outfield, didn't want to do it. Finally, Harry Hooper convinced Ed that SOMEBODY had to go out there and it might as well be the kid with the big swing.

When 1919 rolled around, Babe was a full-time outfielder. He became front-page news when his home run total began to threaten all existing records. The big one, it was decided, had been set by Ned Williamson back in 1884 when he hit 27 dingers. That was a remarkable total, although few people in 1919 remembered it had been done in a bandbox stadium with 180-foot foul lines. When the Babe hit 29—and in a real ballpark—folks were aghast.

No one was going to tinker with his swing at that point. Or send him back to pitching either. He had become baseball's biggest draw. Which brings us to Harry Frazee.

The Yankees' Angel

Harry owned the Red Sox, but his passion was backing Broadway shows. Unfortunately, his shows backed him—into a corner. Just as Babe Ruth was making baseball's biggest hits, Harry was financing Broadway's biggest flops. And, the next thing he knew, Harry needed money— desperately.

As luck would have it, just down from Harry Frazee's Broadway office was the office of Colonel Jacob Ruppert, who also owned a ball club, the New York Yankees. It wasn't a very good ball club, not nearly as good as Harry's if you looked at the players under contract. But the Colonel DID have lots of that thing that Harry needed—cash. An exchange was arranged. Ruppert got Ruth. Harry got $125,000 plus a $350,000 loan. Red Sox fans were no doubt thrilled that the money allowed Harry to continue paving Broadway with greenbacks. Certainly Harry was pleased. For the next couple of years he kept dealing good players to New York for good cash from Ruppert. Soon, the Yankees began winning pennants and Harry had a smash hit in "No, No, Nanette!" And the Sox fell into last place for a decade.

Back to Ruth. The deal put him in a new home park—the Polo Grounds. For those of you too young to remember, the Polo Grounds were oddly shaped. Playing there was like being inside a huge Spam can. The center-field fence was something like seven miles away from home plate and the power alleys were equally deep. But if you could pull the ball down the foul line, you had a home-run shot of about 280 feet in left and 256 in right. In a league filled with contact hitters, those near and dear foul lines produced only occasional Chinese homers, but in 1920, George Herman Ruth, who pulled everything he could lay a bat on, was given a target only 256 feet away. I've read that very few of his homers were actually cheap shots down the line, but that misses the point. With the wall that close, he was justified in going for it every time.

Long Ball Equals Long Green

As if that inviting target wasn't enough, baseball's owners gave Ruth another advantage in 1920. They livened up the baseball. Having seen fans flock out to watch the Babe hit homers in 1919, they ordered up more of the same—much more—by injecting a massive dose of rabbit into the ball. Of course, everybody hit the same baseball, but Ruth was the one man in the game whose batting style allowed him to take full advantage. Batting averages went up for contact hitters because the ball whizzed through the infield faster, but for Ruth, it was up, up, and away.

Not content with invigorating the ball, the owners also passed rules limiting what pitchers could throw. Spitballs were outlawed except for a handful of hurlers who made their livings off that pitch. Gone completely were shine balls, emery balls, talcum balls, and various other trick deliveries. A few pitchers saw their careers go in the dumper because they lost their number-one pitch. For most, however, the loss was of their second or third pitch. Great! At that moment in history, half the pitchers in the league were reduced to throwing Ruth a fastball, a fastball, or a fastball!

A quick footnote: legend has it that the various trick deliveries were outlawed as a reaction to the fatal beaning of Cleveland shortstop Ray Chapman in August of 1920. In point of fact, the pitches were banned before that season began.

There may have been no "good" way to pitch to Ruth. Lefty Hub Pruett had success feeding him screwballs, but he didn't face the Babe that often. And, at any rate, almost no one else in the American League threw a screwball at that time. We might guess from watching films of his batting that the best thing to do with Ruth would be serve him plenty of change-ups. However, few pitchers of the period had a change-up in their reper-toire, and if they did, it was usually a talcum ball or one of the other banned deliveries.

Sincere Flattery

Again, all the other batters in the majors had the same advantage that Ruth did of batting against a limited diet of fastballs and occasional curves. We might then expect that they would have been popping homers right and left.

Not so.

Ruth smashed 54 homers in 1920; George Sisler was second with a mere 19. In 1921, the Babe upped his record to 59; Ken Williams and Ruth's teammate Bob Meusel tied for second at 24. In 1923, Williams cracked 29 homers, but Ruth was still way ahead with 41.

On first glance, you'd say that Ruth was simply that much more powerful than anyone else, but I think it goes deeper than that. Every other hitter in the league had been trained as a contact hitter. Only Ruth (because he came up as a pitcher, remember) always swung from his heels. Batters like Ken Williams might swing pretty hard sometimes, but they weren't going to completely revamp their hitting style at that late date.

So, for a period of five or six years—until the next generation of sluggers could come up through the minors with Ruth as a model—the Babe was in a class by himself. By 1930, Ruth could still lead the American League in homers with 49, but Hack Wilson had 56 in the National League and eight other batters blasted at least 30.

In summary, then, a number of factors combined with the Babe's natural abilities to push his batting stats out of sight during the early 1920s. And, because his records for 1920–21 and 1923 were so far beyond anything that had gone before or has occurred since, he ranks at the very top in any statistical measurement of hitting. And what were those factors? First, an unusual batting style (that he was only able to bring to the majors because he was a pitcher). Second, his move to the outfield (which only happened because World War I brought about a shortage of ballplayers). Third, his sale to the Yankees (to save Harry Frazee's bacon), which put him into the "friendly" Polo Grounds. Fourth, the introduction of a livelier baseball in 1920 (because owners saw profit in more home runs). And fifth, the banning of various trick pitches (also to increase hitting and, naturally, receipts).

So, "relatively," Ruth will probably always rank number one. But if we soft-pedal those "special" early 1920s seasons—well, who knows?

⚾ 20 ⚾

The Little Things That Mean a Lot

He sidles toward you: eyes narrowed, spurs clinking, gun hand hovering near the baseball encyclopedia stuck in his belt. You know how it goes. You write a couple of books about the game and the next thing, they're calling you "Expert"—and looking to knock you off.

So you think you know all about baseball, eh, Chubby?

No, not really. I—

Okay, let's see just how "expert" you are.

I don't—

What was Joe Cascarella's earned run average in 1938?

Who?

Joe Cascarella! Joe Cascarella! 4.57!

That's very interesting, but—

Awright, how many doubles did Oscar Melillo hit in 1927?

Probably—uh—

Eighteen! Say, what kind of tinhorn expert are you, anyhow?

Well, definitely not THAT kind. There are people who memorize the record book and can quote page after page easier than I can recite my zip code. To me, that's like committing the telephone book to memory—the odds are awfully long against your ever wanting to call most of those numbers. Who needs it? I can pick up a book. I can turn pages. I know the alphabet. I don't HAVE to spend hours memorizing what I can look up in a minute.

Nevertheless, some people are going to judge any so-called "expert" by memorized numbers and otherwise useless minutia. I've done radio shows where the host, thinking he'll make me look good, fired one minutia question after another and expected me to regurgitate stats, scores, and years like some Pavlovian parrot. I'm sure the audience was less than dazzled by the number of times I promised to "check on that one after the show."

People who can spout Donie Bush's 1920 slugging average from memory usually say they are dealing in trivia. I beg to differ. That's not trivia—it's micro-minutia. Flatulent factoids. Dead data. Trivia—real trivia—is engaging, elating, and brings a smile to the lips, a thump to the heart, and a pleasant tightening to the pit of the stomach. Knowing the answers doesn't prove you know baseball. Only that you love baseball. You love it so much that during your lifetime of watching, listening, and reading you've inadvertently learned all this useless *stuff* without even trying.

Rule number one: Don't study. Anyone who sets out purposely to learn nine million niggling little facts isn't playing the game fair and will make for a REALLY boring dinner companion. A knowledge of baseball trivia is something that's arrived at naturally—a by-product of your love affair with the game, like an inability to read the word "niggling" without thinking "knuckleball."

In the movie *City Slickers*, a woman says she likes baseball but can never understand why men get excited about trivial information like—and it's obvious she's pulling an example out of the air—like who played third base for the 1960 Pirates? On screen, Billy Crystal and his three friends yell out: "Don Hoak!" I've heard that in any theater audience, at least half the men over forty chime in and a lot of those left snap their fingers and grimace as they try to peel Hoak off the tips of their tongues.

The third-base-for-the-Pirates question is close to the perfect baseball trivia question. It's much better in fact than the most famous question of all: who played third base in the Tinker, Evers, Chance infield? Admittedly, everyone knows the answer to that one by now, but even before Harry Steinfeldt became a trivia staple, his question wasn't quite the ideal that every Trivialist looks for.

The trouble with Harry is that he's just a little too—well—trivial! Aside from the fact that he played in that famed infield, is there any other reason to remember him? Not really. He was a solid ballplayer—like a thousand others.

Rule number two: An outstanding trivia question should have an answer your opponent, the answerer, knew at one time but has since forgotten. Therefore, most of the really good ones involve a player or event that took place during the time your opponent was a baseball fan. Think about what it is you want to accomplish with the question. You want your opponent to kick himself for having forgotten a piece of his own life. If you ask him something he couldn't possibly know anyway, he won't be frustrated; he'll just shrug it off. You might as well ask him about a stone lying on the dark side of the moon. He never knew the answer, never wanted to know the answer, and doesn't care if anybody else knows the answer. Harry Steinfeldt is on the dark side of the moon. Or at least very close to it. If your opponent hasn't made a study of the 1906 Cubs, he very well may have never heard of Harry. So, when you reveal the BIG ANSWER, you may get only apathy.

On the other hand, if your opponent is in his forties and has followed baseball since he was a kid, no doubt at one time he did know the whole starting lineup for the 1960 Pirate champions. He probably hasn't thought about them in years, but he used to know all their names. More important, he *knows* that he *used to know* them. This will drive him up the wall. He's ripe! Don't ask him who played shortstop—he might remember Dick Groat was MVP that year. Forget second base—Mazeroski hit the home run to win the Series. And outfielders can be confusing as to which one is left field, right field, or center. But third base for Pittsburgh in 1960 is perfect. The guy was good, but not great. There's no one defining play in his career, yet his name will be easily recognized. Your opponent once knew that name like the back of his hand. It's still rattling around somewhere in his head. He can almost picture the third baseman in his mind! Blond. Terrific competitor. Who was that guy? His name began with an "H"! HEINIE GROH! No. Wait, give me a second—

You can get hours of pleasure watching someone drive himself crazy because he is certain the correct answer is hiding somewhere just behind his sinuses. He'll keep squirming so long as he's sure he can come up with it. But ask him a question about the distant past—Harry Steinfeldt, for example—and he knows he never knew THAT! At which point, he gives up, ruining your fun.

Here's an example: "What was the first name of the guy who married my aunt Lillian?" Give up? Of course you do. His name was "Clarence!" Do you believe me? Maybe. Do you care? Not a whit!

And why should you? You never met my aunt Lillian OR my uncle Clarence. You didn't forget—the answer is one you never knew or cared to know. Here's an equally pointless baseball question: "Who played third base for the 1923 Phillies?" Unless you're a native Philadelphian of eighty or more years, there's no reason why the name Russ Wrightstone should leap to your lips.

Ah, but ask him the "Whiz Kids" third baseman!

Rule number three: Trivia questions should ask for names, not numbers. I won't say it's impossible, but I don't remember ever hearing a really good question that had a number for an answer. Baseball is filled with numbers, but only a few have any emotional significance. 60. .406. 31. 755. $7.2 million. Most other numbers lack humanity.

Playing baseball trivia is a kind of one-upmanship. It doesn't prove that you are smarter. Or even that you know more about baseball. As I said before, all it proves is love. You love baseball more than your opponent and prove it by the readiness with which you can babble out baseball names. Every time you bubble up a new old name, a whole avalanche of memories and associations come with it. Bill Serena! Wilbur Wood! Max Alvis! Numbers, on the other hand, are specific and lack any accompanying memories.

Which is the better question:

"How many games did Juan Marichal win in 1968?"

"When Bob Gibson won the Cy Young in '68, what N.L. pitcher won the most games?"

Obviously the second one. The first is answered with a flat 26. BORING! The second opens up all sorts of additional areas of speculation, like why DIDN'T Marichal ever win a Cy Young? Or is a great Earned Run Average more important than a great won-lost record?

Rule number four: The answer to a trivia question should be unique, surprising, or amusing. This is a judgment call. Sometimes, as with Don Hoak, the player's fame is sufficient to carry the day. Sometimes, a little more is needed. Compare the following:

"What Red Sox hitter led the A.L. in RBI in 1967?"

"What Red Sox hitter led the A.L. in RBI in 1968?"

No, they do not have the same answer.

Consider the first question. It might get by because it's not usually asked this way. More common would be "What Red Sox hitter won the Triple Crown in 1967?" Oh, of COURSE! Yaz! If you could sneak it past your opponent in this form, it would be the trivia equivalent of striking him out with an eephus pitch in the last of the ninth. But realistically, your chances are slim. Your opponent will probably mentally run through the BoSox lineup, and when he gets to Yastrzemski, he'll pull the trigger.

The second question is much better. Here, he mentally ticks off the lineup, screams Yaz, and you get to bellow: "No! It's Hawk Harrelson!" You got him because he THOUGHT you were asking the '67 question.

I'm sure you remember Russ Wrightstone, the Phillies' third sacker in 1923. Russ may have been a terrific guy, but as a major league infielder he was neither unique, surprising, nor anything else. To demonstrate the difference, suppose we asked, "What Phillies second baseman hit .218 in 1959, the only year he played in the majors?" After considering Mike Goliat, Chico Fernandez, and Putsy Cabellero, you settle on Sparky Anderson. Ol' Sparky may not have done much as a second baseman, but he went on to a great managing career. So "Sparky Anderson" is an answer with significance even though his .218 year made barely a ripple.

Which reminds me, name the only Reds outfielder to homer in the 1940 World Series.

I must confess a liking for questions that sound easy but are actually hard and for questions that sound hard but are actually very easy. Three of my favorites:

"In 1935, Wally Berger of the Braves led the National League with 34 home runs; who finished second on the club?"

"When Ernie Shore pitched his perfect game, who started on the mound for the Red Sox?"

"When Babe Ruth hit his 60th home run in 1927, whose home run record did he break?"

I'm sure you knew the answer to each of these questions was Babe Ruth. In baseball trivia, nothing has more significance than Babe Ruth.

A trivia question I enjoyed was "Can you name three Hall of Famers who homered in their first major league at bat?" Just about everybody I asked knew Hoyt Wilhelm and Earl Averill right off. And then they fumed and fussed looking for that third name. You could practically see them running the whole Baseball Hall of Fame roster through their minds. When at last they surrendered and I murmured "Ace Parker, who's in the *Pro Football* Hall of Fame," they wanted to kill. Great fun. A variation on the same idea is, "What Hall of Famer led the Reds in batting during the 1919 World Series?" If they don't stop to think about it, they'll say Edd Roush and you can hit them with Greasy Neale, the Reds outfielder who entered the football hall as a coach.

You have to be careful though. Sometimes a question sounds good, but the answer is a letdown. I once had a question I was very proud of: "How many touchdowns did Christy Mathewson score in 1902?" At the asking, people looked startled. Was there a mistake? Did I mean home runs? I would then explain that Mathewson played some football games for the professional Pittsburgh Stars in 1902. So far, so good. But of course no one had the answer and so they gave up quickly, leaving me with nothing to do but reveal the not-very-interesting fact that Christy scored two touchdowns. Oh.

Some trivia rules are really a matter of courtesy. We call them "unwritten." I forget what we call what I'm doing to them right now.

Any question containing the name Owen Wilson must be about three-base hits.

A question asking anyone to name all the teams Dick Littlefield pitched for must be allowed extra time.

Who, what, and where questions are almost always better than when, why, or how questions.

For trivia purposes, Hoss Radbourn won 60 games in 1884 regardless of what the record books end up saying.

Any question combining Thurman Munson, Ken Hubbs, and Tommy Gastall will put a damper on the evening.

Questions that require a demonstration of a pitcher's windup are not permitted indoors. Or near any glass.

If YOU don't know the answer, don't ask the question.

At some point in the evening, Fleetwood Walker must be mentioned.

Top-shelf trivia must have fermented for at least five years. (Mickey Morandini becomes eligible in 1997.)

End-of-season batting averages only; none of this "What was Stan Musial hitting on the morning of August 16, 1953?" The only exception is Ted Williams' BA on the morning of the final day of the 1941 season.

Any trivia question directed at the author of this book must be submitted in writing three weeks in advance.

⚾ 21 ⚾

The Hall of Fame's Ten Biggest Mistakes

When you murmur "Hall of Fame" in a baseball fan's ear, he immediately thinks of the Hall of Enshrinees with all those plaques on the wall. That's what gets Cooperstown nationwide publicity each year. If you've ever been there, you know that the Hall of Enshrinees (or whatever they call it) is a lot less interesting than the rest of the museum or, for that matter, than the library. Or some of the shops that sell trinkets on the main street. Or the gorgeous upstate New York scenery.

The plaque-place is just rows and rows of little greenish tablets with not-very-convincing likenesses of the 213 players, managers, umpires, and executives who've been enshrined. Most likely there aren't many fans who've heard of them all.

But even though most fans don't know every one of the enshrinees, every fan worth his salt is an absolute expert on someone who's NOT IN but SHOULD BE. Give any fan a chance and he'll twist your ear telling you about some favorite player whose unenshrinement is a dirty rotten crime. Anyone from Roger Maris to Bobo Holliman.

However, I'd rather talk about who is IN who should be OUT. None of that griping about who got bypassed for me! No soapbox. I'll stick with the slipups who slipped in.

Sure as it don't rain in Indianapolis in the summertime, there are some people with plaques on the Hall wall who really belong in a lesser shrine,

153

say the "Hall of Very Good." And—alas!—there are a couple of enshrinees who couldn't even make it there.

Sometimes I worry about the Hall of Fame. If they have 213 enshrinees
after operating for fewer than sixty years, where are they going to put all
the plaques they'll have accumulated two hundred years from now? Will
they start adding additions onto the building till it stretches all the way to
Utica? Or will they make the plaques smaller? Micro-dots maybe, and
you rent a microscope at the door.

Of course, if some purist sportswriters have their way, the Hall won't
have any crowding problem. They'd like to make enshrinement much
more exclusive. A Super Hall. To qualify for election, according to the
purists, a player needs to be a Babe Ruth clone with a touch of Mother
Teresa. The merely great need not apply.

The fact that this would make for many years in which no one got
elected bothers the purists not at all. One columnist I read even insisted
he'd be perfectly happy to travel to Cooperstown on a designated date
during non-enshrinement years just to pay homage to those already in and
to watch a summer exhibition game. Say, between Cleveland and Montreal. *Sure* he would!

Some would suggest occasional recall elections of the enshrinees to
weed out the undeserving. If 60 percent of the voters had forgotten the
guy, out he'd come. They could melt down his plaque and cast a new one
for the latest choice. Then they could rename the place "The Hall of
Fleeting Fame."

But to get serious about this, it's important that the Hall hold an election
every year and enshrine somebody just to remind us that it's there. If
enshrinements came along only every five years, nearly all of us would
spend four years not thinking about the Hall at all. Attendance at the
museum would drop off. Funds would get tight. The library would stop
buying books. Those main street shops would close. Greyhound would
take Cooperstown off its schedule. Pretty soon you'd see guys dressed in
oldtyme baseball uniforms standing on street corners ringing bells: "Help
save the Hall of Fame, mister? Put a penny in the pot."

I never quite understood the purists anyway. What do they hope to gain
by limiting the Hall to twenty or thirty big names? Such a Super Hall
would be boring to the point of fatality. Worse, somebody would come
along and want to limit *that* to Babe Ruth. As it stands, there are maybe
twenty thousand folks who *might* have been elected to the Hall (counting
players, managers, umpires, and executives), but only about one percent
have been enshrined. That's exclusive enough for me.

Besides, it's the borderline Famers who make the Hall interesting. Wouldn't you rather hear about Chick Hafey or Addie Joss, guys you can't quote chapter and verse on, than get another dose of Ty (yawn) Cobb?

When you come right down to it, the Super Names don't NEED enshrinement. They're already famed enough. If for some reason Joe DiMaggio had never been elected to the Hall (perhaps an obscure bylaw barring native San Franciscans) would we stop toasting his career in word and song? Of course not. Everyone knows DiMag was one of the best. Putting his plaque in Cooperstown was simply a necessary bit of business. If it weren't there, the Hall would look silly.

It's the borderline guys who benefit from being named. Enshrinement is how we tell Harry Hooper from Duffy Lewis, Catfish Hunter from Vida Blue, and Travis Jackson from Dick Bartell. Enshrinement lifts the borderline guys out of the top five percent where they languish nearly forgotten and into the top one percent where their plaque ensures they will be remembered. At least a little.

Actually, the BEST place for a borderliner to get publicity is to be ALMOST-BUT-NOT-QUITE elected. How many times each year do you see Nellie Fox's name? And out of those, how many times is it in connection with his not yet being in the Hall of Fame? I'll bet at least three out of every four mentionings. You can say the same thing about Phil Rizzuto and Bill Mazeroski. NOT getting elected keeps their names cropping up.

I remember some years ago there was a big push to have Chuck Klein elected. He got a lot of ink right up until he received the necessary votes, but I don't think I've seen his name in a newspaper a dozen times since. Enshrinement for some is a lot like entombment.

When sportswriters start bitching about the Hall's lack of exclusivity, they always point out some of the "mistakes" elected—nearly all by the Veterans Committee. Actually, about two-thirds of the enshrinees were put there by the Veterans or some other committee. The Baseball Writers have been pretty exclusive all along.

At the risk of being a minority of one, I enjoy seeing those mistakes enshrined. They humanize the Hall. I'd be the last to suggest drumming them out. Not because I think they really belong in the top one percent, of course. It's more that they represent all the borderliners who will forever fall on the wrong side of the border. If Wes Ferrell never goes in, at least we have Rick.

Everybody seems to have his list of Hall of Famers who shouldn't be there. Here's mine, in descending order.

The Mistakes

10. HEINIE MANUSH—This outfielder compiled a .330 BA over 17 seasons. He hit .378 in 1926 to lead the American League and two years later hit another .378 to not lead.

That's the trouble. Heinie played at a time when just about any good hitter—especially an outfielder—hit at least .350. He had very ordinary power and was no great shakes with a glove. The tip-off is that he spent almost his whole career being traded around among second-division teams. He was available. If he was truly a better-than-middling player, wouldn't the Yankees have dealt for him?

9. RAY SCHALK—As a defensive catcher, Ray was quite good. But defense has gotten almost no one else into the Hall of Fame, so we have to look elsewhere for a reason to enshrine Ray. Well, he was honest. He was one of the unstained on the Black Sox team. And he stuck around for 18 seasons.

On the other hand, he was a really rotten hitter—.253 lifetime even though he played through the hit-happy 1920s. Frankly, I think he got into the Hall by being confused with Wally Schang, a catcher who caught as well, hit much better, and played on a whole raft of championship teams. And, apparently, Schang didn't get in 'cause some voters thought he was Schalk.

8. LLOYD WANER—When he was elected, they said he got in on Paul's statistics. It was probably more a case of fame outreaching fact. Everybody's heard of the "Big Poison–Little Poison" combo, so they must have been great, right?

Paul was. Lloyd wasn't. Lloyd had no power and never walked, making him a soft .316 lifetime hitter in an age of .350 sluggers. He WAS a first-rate flychaser and had 678 hits in his first three seasons, but after a 1930 injury, he was just ordinary. Still, by putting him in, they don't have to keep answering the same question over and over: "If Paul was 'Big Poison,' who was . . ."

7. GEORGE KELLY—"Highpockets" had a great arm, but on a first baseman, so what? He had some power and drove in over 100 runs five times just like lots of guys. He DID have his best years in seasons when the Giants won four pennants, and that was something.

Still, all things considered, most of us would rather have Boog Powell, Frank Howard, or Norm Cash playing first for us. He was still alive in 1973 when he was named to the Hall, and I have to think some of the people who voted for him thought, "Wouldn't this be a nice treat for good ol' George?"

6. FORD FRICK, ET AL.—Frick is just one of several executives who did their job for a long time and then got elected to the Hall for no better reason than that they didn't screw up too badly. Will Harridge and Warren Giles are two more. As long as competent bureaucrats get enshrined, the exclusion of people like Gil Hodges is kind of sinful.

5. FRED LINDSTROM—Like Kelly, Lindstrom was still alive when he was elected by the Veterans Committee in 1976. That and the fact that he hit .379 one year got him a plaque. Still, he was a regular only eight seasons, batted in fewer than 800 runs, and had a lower batting average than Lloyd Waner with only a little more power.

At age eighteen, he was the goat of the 1924 World Series when a couple of grounders hit pebbles and bounced over his head to let Washington beat the Giants. If you figure the pebbles weren't really his fault (though why he didn't clean his space we'll never know), you may think it was nice to see an old man receive an honor toward the end of his life after such a bad start.

Better they should have enshrined the pebbles.

4. JESSE HAINES—Need we say it? Another case of a good ol' boy who was still around to be patted on the back when he was elected by the Vets in 1970. Well, he did win over 200 games, but so have ninety others. He had three 20-win seasons, but there must be two hundred who've done that. In other words, he was a good pitcher but no Hal Newhouser.

In case you didn't know it, Jesse's real claim to fame is that he developed a blister on his finger. It got him relieved with the bases full in the 1926 World Series so Pete Alexander could come in and strike out Tony Lazzeri.

3. TOMMY McCARTHY—A lot of players from the last century get a "who's he?" from modern fans, but Tommy deserves it. He was a good right fielder who supposedly had a knack for trapping the ball and throwing the runner out at second. And the records say he was fast.

But come on! A .292 career hitter when Ed Delahanty, Dan Brouthers, and dozens of others called .350 a "slump"? I've heard that he was the boyhood hero of someone on the committee that elected him in 1946. And I've heard that everybody thought he was some *other* Tommy McCarthy. All I know is when I see his name in the Hall of Fame, I figure there's hope for Jim Busby.

2. CANDY CUMMINGS—I dealt with Cummings and his curveball claim earlier. Candy went in because the electors believed that he really

invented the curveball. But so what? Why should that get the guy into the Hall of Fame? Should we enshrine the inventors of the knuckleball, the slider, the split-finger fastball? The resin bag? Whose idea was this anyway?

1. MORGAN G. BULKELEY—You can put up some kind of defense for all the other Hall of Fame mistakes—even McCarthy and Cummings. But not for Bulkeley. There's simply no excuse.

Apparently back in 1937, they wanted to honor the game's founders. They had Ban Johnson as the first American League president, so they thought they'd even things out by electing the first National League president too. That was Bulkeley.

In truth, however, ol' Morg was a figurehead president and barely that. When Chicago's Bill Hulbert talked seven other team owners into starting the National League in 1876, he wanted a president from an eastern club because that's where the money was. Some say they drew straws and Bulkeley of Hartford got the short one. As president, he held no meetings, issued no directives, enforced no rules, created no precedents, and when the time for the next league meeting rolled around the next year, he didn't even attend!

If you want to find someone actually connected with baseball who had LESS influence on the way it turned out than Morg did, you might consider batboys (but only those for visiting teams).

There is an upside, of course. Every time we see Bulkeley's bulky name listed among the Hall of Fame enshrinees, we're reminded that Bill Hulbert was actually the National League's creator and *second* president. And, if we get enough reminders, maybe someone will wake up and put him in the Hall.

⚾ 22 ⚾

The Hall of Fame Is Shafting My Youth

Okay, maybe that title's a little strong. It's not like Cooperstown deliberately set out to get me. Nevertheless, the Hall is doing irredeemable harm to my self-esteem and I may sue.

As you well know, it's during those wonderful-awful growing-up years that our psyches are formed. If you're a baseball fan, you take on certain opinions, beliefs, hunches, and so forth that stay with you all your days. One is that the players you rooted for when you were still a couple of years away from shaving were the greatest of all time. It's not something you prove with slide rules or coefficients or any other kind of stats; you just KNOW IT. You may see many wonderful players during the rest of your life, but they never quite measure up to the ones you grew up with.

My personal wonderful-awful years were the 1940s and 1950s: an era that I revere. A number of critics, including a few who grew up later, have suggested that baseball was at its absolute peak in those very years I remember so well. They argue that black players were at last entering the majors and expansion had not yet watered down the talent level.

And yet the Hall of Fame indicates the greatest period for baseball was between World War I and World War II. Can you understand what that sort of thing does to my preconceived prejudices?

I touched on the Hall of Fame previously when I pointed out some of the mistakes they've made. In thinking it over, though, I may have given the wrong impression. You might get the idea that I'm one of those super-purists who want to restrict the Hall to a couple of superstars like Ruth and Cobb and then keep everybody else out. I know I didn't SAY that, but maybe you missed what I DID say.

As a matter of fact, I'm a whole lot more concerned that some curious twists in the voting procedures seem to work against the players I idolized when I was a kid. Frankly, I'd rather see two "iffy" choices go into the Hall than to leave out one really deserving candidate. Especially if I cheered for him when I was twelve.

To get this straight, I'm going to put up a chart. (Well, it worked for Ross Perot, didn't it?) My chart, on the next page, shows in which historic baseball period the various enshrinees in the Hall of Fame played.

Okay, the first column shows the periods. The nineteenth century is lumped together as 1871–1900; then the twentieth century is divided into twenty-year periods up to 1980. The second column shows the total number of players who played in each period. When players' careers were split between two periods, they were assigned to the period in which they played the most games. Only players are counted here; managers, executives, umpires, and Negro Leaguers are not included. Columns three and four show how many players had careers of fewer than ten years and how many had careers of more than ten years. The final three columns show the number of Hall of Fame players from each period, the percentage of all the players from the period in the hall, and the percentage of ten-year players in.

A Period for Pitchers

As you can see, the period between World War I and World War II has contributed more players to the Hall than any other period. Nearly one out of every five players during that period who lasted for ten years is a Hall of Famer. Does that seem a bit much to you? The reason for so many of those guys going in is sometimes said to be the unusually high batting averages of the period. But what is really surprising is that fourteen pitchers from the period have been enshrined. That's two more than from the dead ball days of 1901–20 and two more than the 1961–80 period, two eras when the pitcher was king. In alphabetical order the 1921–40 pitchers in the Hall are Stan Coveleski, Dizzy Dean, Red Faber, Lefty Gomez, Burleigh Grimes, Lefty Grove, Jesse Haines, Waite Hoyt, Carl Hubbell, Ted Lyons, Herb Pennock, Eppa Rixey, Red Ruffing, and Dazzy Vance.

Not surprisingly, the Earned Run Averages for the Hall of Fame

Period	Total Players in Period*	Period's Players w/<10-yr. Careers	Period's Players w/>10-yr. Careers	HOF Memb	HOF% Tot	HOF% +10
1871–1900	2,041	1,879	162	28	1.4	17.3
1901–1920	2,648	2,434	214	31	1.2	14.5
1921–1940	2,174	1,876	298	57	2.6	19.1
1941–1960	2,227	1,939	288	27	1.2	9.4
1961–1980	2,532	1,984	548	27	1.1	4.9
1981–1990*	1,868	1,675	193	0	0.0	0.0
Totals	13,490	11,787	1,703	170	1.3	10.0
Totals without 1981–90	11,622	10,112	1,510	170	1.5	11.3

* By the ends of their careers, many players listed in the 1981–1990 totals will belong in the 1991–2000 period; many others will have played ten years, with the majority of seasons in the 1981–1990 period.

pitchers from this hot hitting period are generally higher than those of pitchers from other periods. However, what must give one pause is that even when their ERAs are adjusted to other periods and compared with all the pitchers in history, six of them do not make the top 100 ERAs all-time—Grimes, Haines, Hoyt, Pennock, Rixey, and Ruffing.

There WERE some pitchers from the period between the wars who are not in the Hall of Fame but whose ERAs make the adjusted top 100 list—Tommy Bridges, Wes Ferrell, Dolf Luque, Eddie Rommel, Urb Shocker, and Lon Warneke. The difference seems to be that their career victory totals are lower than most of those enshrined.

Catching Up

The period from 1960 to 1980 is lower in enshrinees than the others, but that's to be expected. This is the period the Baseball Writers are concentrating on now. In recent years Tom Seaver, Rollie Fingers, Ferguson Jenkins, Reggie Jackson, Rod Carew, and Gaylord Perry have been elected. We can assume that the majority of enshrinees for the next few years will be from this period. So let's not worry about them.

The period that gets less than its due is the 1941–60 era. My era! Less than half as many players from what many consider the "Golden Age" of baseball have been named to the Hall than have been taken in from the twenty years immediately preceding. How is this possible?

Lord knows what goes through the minds of the electors, but we'll hazard a couple of guesses. First off, the Veterans Committee was for years controlled by people, including former players, who were rooted in the 1920s and '30s.

Thirty of the fifty-seven players from the 1921–40 period got their tickets to the Hall from the Veterans Committee: Earl Averill, Dave Bancroft, Jim Bottomley, Max Carey, Earle Combs, Stan Coveleski, Kiki Cuyler, Red Faber, Rick Ferrell, Lefty Gomez, Goose Goslin, Burleigh Grimes, Chick Hafey, Jesse Haines, Billy Herman, Waite Hoyt, Travis Jackson, George Kelly, Chuck Klein, Tony Lazzeri, Fred Lindstrom, Ernie Lombardi, Heinie Manush, Sam Rice, Eppa Rixey, Edd Roush, Red Ruffing, Arky Vaughan, Lloyd Waner, and Hack Wilson. Without being critical of any individual selection, we still have to note that the majority of players with marginal Hall of Fame credentials are on this list.

The Vets Committee has not been nearly so generous with players from the 1941–60 period, although they did tag Bobby Doerr, George Kell,

Johnny Mize, Hal Newhouser, Pee Wee Reese, Red Schoendienst, and Enos Slaughter. You'd think perhaps that this would all even out in the long run—that the Veterans Committee would eventually be made up of selectors rooted in the 1940s and '50s, and that then they would elect scads of their old friends just like earlier committees. But for the last couple of years, the Vets Committee has been hamstrung by new rules that allow it to elect only two new enshrinees each year, only one of whom can be named as a former player.

Furthermore, the Committee is being pressured to name more former Negro League players to the Hall. Anyone who doesn't watch baseball with a sheet over his head knows that there are many more deserving Negro Leaguers than the mere eleven so far enshrined. But by putting that burden on the already restricted Veterans Committee (instead of on a special committee where it belongs), we are practically assured that numerous deserving players from the 1941–60 group will never make it to Cooperstown.

Another strike against players from that period is that the 1942 through 1945 seasons were war years. Voters seem to like to ignore those seasons, arguing that the overall quality of baseball was lower during that time. While that's probably true, it wasn't as bad as all that, and it can also be argued that there were other periods when the quality dipped. Regardless, why should a player be punished if the other players in the league didn't play up to his level? Or even worse, because his career was shortened because he served in his country's military?

Three and Four Stars

The fact is that there are two classes of Hall of Famers: the four-star players whose credentials are so overpowering that they must be enshrined and the three-star players who are just a step below. Their enshrinement has often depended on a push from an old friend or a small circle of admirers. That's all right. The players who slipped through are still good players. The Hall of Fame needn't blush while nailing up their plaques.

But now, with so many three-star players from the period between the wars already in the Hall, the same standards are not being used to judge the players of the 1941–60 period. The result is a skewing of history that makes it appear as though baseball's greatest age came twenty years earlier than it really did.

In addition to the Veterans Committee choices, here are the 1941–60 players in the Hall of Fame: catchers, Yogi Berra and Roy Campanella; pitchers, Bob Feller, Bob Lemon, Robin Roberts, Warren Spahn, and Early Wynn; second base, Jackie Robinson; shortstops, Ernie Banks and Lou Boudreau; third base, Eddie Mathews; outfielders, Joe DiMaggio, Ralph Kiner, Mickey Mantle, Stan Musial, Duke Snider, and Ted Williams. Pound for pound, that's a heckuva crew. Add in the Vets choices (Newhouser, Mize, Doerr, Schoendienst, Reese, Kell, and Slaughter) and you could probably win any all-time all-star league pennant.

But what of the others? We'll call them three-star players for the sake of simplicity, but some of them were surely better than that. And, if the 1941–60 period was indeed the period when baseball was at its best, as so many insist, doesn't it then follow that the Golden Age's three-stars would have been four-stars (or at least 3.5) in another era?

I submit Walker Cooper, Sherm Lollar, Birdie Tebbetts, Del Crandall, Curt Simmons, Allie Reynolds, Billy Pierce, Lew Burdette, Virgil Trucks, Don Newcombe, Sal Maglie, Roy Face, Gil Hodges, Phil Cavarretta, Mickey Vernon, Ted Kluszewski, Joe Gordon, Nellie Fox, Junior Gilliam, Phil Rizzuto, Alvin Dark, Marty Marion, Al Rosen, Bob Elliott, Ken Boyer, Richie Ashburn, Dixie Walker, Minnie Minoso, Carl Furillo, Larry Doby, Dom DiMaggio, Jackie Jensen.

◉ 23 ◉

Do Catchers Make the Best Managers?

One day I woke up to discover that more current major league managers are ex-catchers than any other position.

Ex-catchers have ALWAYS been in the majority among managers. I didn't "discover" it; I already knew it. As long as I can remember, former catchers have made up the bulk of the Manager Pool. I don't think it's a baseball rule (like the infield-fly) but it might be a rule of baseball (like the guy who just made a great catch always leads off the next inning).

Anyway, as I say, the revelation that a carload of ex-catchers are still gainfully employed was about as surprising as ketchup in a slasher movie. But getting reminded got me to thinking. Just why, I asked myself, do all those erstwhile backstops get hired in the first place even if they never get their teams there? First place, that is.

The answer that came immediately to mind was that catchers make the best managers.

Well, maybe. But managers are supposed to be smart. If not smarter than other baseball players, at least smarter than baseball bats. But, catchers spend their careers letting hefty young men throw hard objects at them. At speeds up to 90 m.p.h.! And catchers don't dodge around while this is happening; they just SQUAT there! How smart can these guys be?

The fella who coined the phrase "Tools of Ignorance" for catching equipment had a point.

Why Hire a Catcher?

So I worked out a Letterman List of reasons why team owners hire ex-catchers to manage:

10. Catchers have to get along with all kinds of cranky people: pitchers, managers, umpires. Owners figure they won't make a fuss when they're fired.

9. When not in a game, a catcher is likely to be out in the bullpen where he can't get blamed for anything.

8. After years of catching, their fingers are so gnarled and crooked they can't hold a job in the typing pool (except for bosses who like letters starting "Dgar Siy").

7. Most catchers are weak hitters, and any position player who stays in the majors while batting .218 is automatically considered "a smart player," thus making him a "smart manager."

6. Catchers are always slow runners, so owners get a better look at them when they pass by. After a while they assume they know them better than any of the other players on the team.

5. A manager's biggest decisions are about pitchers. Pitchers themselves are too egocentric to manage, but catchers work with pitchers and already know the route to the mound.

4. Because they have to gather up all that equipment after a game, catchers leave the field last. This gives them a reputation of being "really into the game."

3. Catchers spend a lot of time looking at the dugout for signs; the owners' box is usually behind the dugout; owners misconstrue the catchers' stares and think a relationship exists between them.

2. After a game, most catchers are too tired to be clever or controversial and so writers avoid them. Since they're seldom quoted, catchers acquire a reputation for sagacity. (For some reason, this seems to be particularly true in New York, where the less you say, the wiser you are. There are exceptions, of course. Yogi Berra was a New York catcher who was widely quoted whether he said anything or not.)

1. Because catchers spend half the game giving signs with their fingers, owners figure closed-caption fans will like them and hire a catcher-manager as a sop to the handicapped.

Why Become a Manager?

Okay, that's taken care of. There are plenty of great reasons for hiring ex-catchers to be managers. Next, why do they take the job? Oh, sure, it's fun to order everybody around. ("Take two and hit to right, Lefty!") Especially when almost all of them make more money than you. ("Next time, hit it with your wallet, Lefty.") And, after years of being ignored, those post-game interviews managers give to the press must be a thrill. ("Lefty puts his pants on one leg at a time and that's how we play the season, one game at a time. And how I talk. One word at a time.")

But, on the other hand, at least one out of every three games you're going to be everybody's whipping boy. ("I let Lefty bat against Glavine 'cause I figured he was due. Yes, triple plays are rare.") Players win games; managers lose them. Ask anybody. ("Sure, putting on a double steal when we're down by six is unusual, but I wanted to jump-start our offense. Yes, triple plays are rare.") And no matter what you do with pitchers, you'll be criticized. ("I had Lefty pitch to McGwire because he's handled him so well before. No, the longest grand slam I ever saw was . . .")

What kind of a job is it when a good day is one where you don't get booed? By your own family?

And, sooner or later, you're gonna get fired. Usually, sooner. ("Our manager has just received an absolute, ironclad vote of confidence from our team owner, who, by the way, is calling a press conference for tomorrow morning at ten.")

So why agree to this misery? Does a cat volunteer to be kicked?

As best I can see, it's simply that ex-catchers really aren't prepared to do much else. Let's face it, holding your hand in front of a speeding missile isn't job training for anything else except a career as a Ping-Pong paddle. So, after twenty-five years of catching, a guy finds himself fat and mid-fortyish, with hands like two bowls of walnuts and knees that sound like a Chinese New Year when he crosses a room. All his old teammates are going on TV as analysts and saying clever things like, "Yes, Fred, the Sox may hit-and-run here although there's a good chance they won't." Unfortunately, few ex-catchers are designed for television. Generally, the only athletes who are less photogenic chase wooden rabbits around tracks.

So when an ex-catcher is offered a job as a manager, he grits his teeth and bends over.

But Do Catchers Make the Best Managers?

Of course, what I've been doing with all this inquiring into motives is just putting off the tough question. You can tap-dance forever about WHY people do things. When push comes to shove is when you try to evaluate not why but HOW WELL. Sure, there are numerous ex-catchers chewing sunflower seeds in major league dugouts, but are they any good at managing? More important, are they significantly better (or worse) than ex-shortstops or ex-outfielders? Because, if they aren't, there's no baseball-justification for hiring ex-catchers so often.

The first thing I thought of was taking all the managers ever and adding up their records. But, after I mulled that over, I decided that there were too many variables. How many owners have hired incompetents? Certainly enough to skew the data. At least four owners I can think of— Chris Von der Ahe, Charley Ebbets, Judge Fuchs, and Ted Turner— hired themselves. Well, actually, so did Connie Mack, but that doesn't count.

Another variable is the good manager who gets hired by a bad team, fired the next year, and never gets another chance. This also has happened hundreds of times.

Besides, adding up ALL the managers and ALL their records sounded like an awful lot of work. So it wasn't too hard to convince myself that the best route was to look at the records of guys who managed at least 1,500 games. That would get rid of the doofuses. Anybody who managed for nearly ten years (or longer) must have been considered COMPETENT. Maybe even good.

Okay, so here are the records of all those managers with at least 1,500 games under their belts through 1992.

DO CATCHERS MAKE THE BEST MANAGERS?

	Years	No	W–L	Pct	Pen
Walter Alston	1954– 76	23	2040–1613	.558	7
Sparky Anderson	1970– 92	23	1996–1611	.553	6
Cap Anson	1875– 98	21	1296– 947	.578	5
Lou Boudreau	1942– 60	16	1162–1224	.487	1
Frank Chance	1905– 23	11	946– 648	.593	4
Fred Clarke	1897–1915	19	1602–1181	.576	4
Joe Cronin	1933– 47	15	1236–1055	.540	2
Alvin Dark	1961– 77	13	994– 954	.510	2

Patsy Donovan	1897–1911	11	684– 879	.438	0
Chuck Dressen	1934– 66	16	1008– 973	.509	2
Leo Durocher	1939– 73	24	2008–1709	.540	3
Jimmy Dykes	1934– 61	21	1406–1541	.477	0
Lee Fohl	1915– 26	11	713– 792	.474	0
Frankie Frisch	1933– 51	16	1138–1078	.514	1
Clark Griffith	1901– 20	20	1491–1367	.522	1
Charlie Grimm	1932– 60	19	1287–1067	.547	3
Ned Hanlon	1889–1907	19	1313–1164	.530	5
Bucky Harris	1924– 56	29	2157–2218	.493	3
Whitey Herzog	1973– 90	18	1281–1125	.532	3
Rogers Hornsby	1925– 53	14	701– 812	.463	1
Ralph Houk	1961– 84	20	1619–1531	.514	3
Miller Huggins	1913– 29	17	1413–1134	.555	6
Fred Hutchinson	1952– 64	12	830– 827	.501	1
Hugh Jennings	1907– 24	15	1163– 984	.542	3
Tony LaRussa	1979– 92	14	1134– 949	.544	3
Tommy Lasorda	1976– 92	17	1341–1201	.528	4
Al Lopez	1951– 69	17	1410–1004	.584	2
Connie Mack	1894–1950	53	3731–3948	.486	9
Billy Martin	1969– 88	16	1253–1013	.553	2
Gene Mauch	1960– 87	26	1902–2037	.483	0
Jimmy McAleer	1901– 11	11	736– 889	.453	0
Joe McCarthy	1926– 50	24	2125–1333	.615	9
John McGraw	1899–1932	33	2784–1959	.587	10
Bill McKechnie	1915– 46	25	1896–1723	.524	4
John McNamara	1969– 91	18	1150–1215	.486	1
Danny Murtaugh	1957– 76	15	1115– 950	.540	2
Steve O'Neill	1935– 54	14	1040– 821	.559	1
Paul Richards	1951– 76	12	923– 901	.506	0
Bill Rigney	1956– 76	18	1239–1321	.484	0
Wilbert Robinson	1902– 31	19	1399–1398	.500	2
Red Schoendienst	1965– 90	14	1041– 955	.522	2
Frank Selee	1890–1905	16	1284– 862	.598	5
Billy Southworth	1929– 51	13	1044– 704	.597	4
George Stallings	1897–1920	13	879– 898	.495	1
Casey Stengel	1934– 65	25	1905–1842	.508	10
Chuck Tanner	1970– 88	19	1352–1381	.495	1
Bill Virdon	1972– 84	13	995– 921	.519	0
Earl Weaver	1968– 86	17	1480–1060	.583	4
Dick Williams	1967– 88	21	1571–1451	.520	4
Harry Wright	1871– 93	23	1225– 885	.581	6
Don Zimmer	1972– 91	13	885– 858	.508	0

Now, let's look at them by position.

FORMER PITCHERS IN ORDER OF WINNING PERCENTAGE

	Years	No	W–L	Pct	Pen
Tommy Lasorda	1976–92	17	1341–1201	.528	4
Clark Griffith	1901–20	20	1491–1367	.522	1
Fred Hutchinson	1952–64	12	830– 827	.501	1

Didn't I tell you that ex-pitchers are too egocentric to make good managers? Or they're thought to be. Roger Craig is a good one who hasn't managed enough games to make our list. Hutch might have been the best, although Lasorda is hell in a tight race.

Here's a real oddity. The pennant-winning managers in both the National League's and the American League's first seasons were both 20-game-winning pitchers that year for Chicago teams—both then known as the "White Stockings." Al Spalding and Clark Griffith. Actually, Spalding was 47–13, which makes him a 20-game winner × 2.

FORMER FIRST BASEMEN IN ORDER OF WINNING PERCENTAGE

	Years	No	W–L	Pct	Pen
Frank Chance	1905–23	11	946– 648	.593	4
Cap Anson	1875–98	21	1296– 947	.578	5
Walter Alston	1954–76	23	2040–1613	.558	7
Charlie Grimm	1932–60	19	1287–1067	.547	3

It's sort of surprising that there are only four men on this list in that three of them are in the Hall of Fame. Maybe four should be. Chance and Anson were great in their day, but baseball has changed so much that you'd have to go with Alston as the best under today's conditions. Had Gil Hodges not died prematurely, he'd surely be on the list. Perhaps at the top.

FORMER THIRD BASEMEN IN ORDER OF WINNING PERCENTAGE

	Years	No	W–L	Pct	Pen
John McGraw	1899–1932	33	2784–1959	.587	10
Chuck Dressen	1934– 66	16	1008– 973	.509	2
Don Zimmer	1972– 91	13	885– 858	.508	0
Jimmy Dykes	1934– 61	21	1406–1541	.477	0

McGraw was probably the greatest for his time, but can you imagine him managing a team today? ("What do you mean you're filing a grievance with the players' union? Just because I called you a *&%$@*!") And, with today's contracts, let's see if Mac could make those cute August trades he was so good at.

Dykes was as good a manager as never won a pennant. Zim, I always thought, was underrated. But then, he looks like an ex-catcher. Dressen brought in Branca to pitch to Thomson in '51, but he won the next two years. Of course, with those Dodgers, J. Fred Muggs might have won.

FORMER OUTFIELDERS IN ORDER OF WINNING PERCENTAGE

	Years	No	W–L	Pct	Pen
Frank Selee	1890–1905	16	1284– 862	.598	5
Billy Southworth	1929– 51	13	1044– 704	.597	4
Harry Wright	1871– 93	23	1225– 885	.581	6
Fred Clarke	1897–1915	19	1602–1181	.576	4
Whitey Herzog	1973– 90	18	1281–1125	.532	3
Ned Hanlon	1889–1907	19	1313–1164	.530	5
Dick Williams	1967– 88	21	1571–1451	.520	4
Bill Virdon	1972– 84	13	995– 921	.519	0
Casey Stengel	1934– 65	25	1905–1842	.508	10
Chuck Tanner	1970– 88	19	1352–1381	.495	1
Jimmy McAleer	1901– 11	11	736– 889	.453	0
Patsy Donovan	1897–1911	11	684– 879	.438	0

Yes, there are twelve outfielders listed, but there are three times as many outfielders in a game as any other position, so it breaks down to four per field. Interesting that there are only three Hall of Famers on the list. Moreover, Clarke made the Hall as much as a player, and Harry Wright was successful mostly in the old National Association. That leaves Stengel, who probably had as much impact on how the game is played as any manager since McGraw. (And as much impact on the English language as any baseballer since Dizzy Dean.)

Selee, who won five times in Boston in the 1890s and then built the Cubs team that Chance took the bows for, really deserves more recognition. Williams won pennants with three different teams. That ought to be worth something. Herzog was another good one, regarded as the best around until he pulled the plug. Still, I'm betting that if anyone else on this list gets to the HOF, it'll be Hanlon, who won the pennants Selee didn't.

FORMER SHORTSTOPS IN ORDER OF WINNING PERCENTAGE

	Years	No	W–L	Pct	Pen
Hugh Jennings	1907–24	15	1163– 984	.542	3
Leo Durocher	1939–73	24	2008–1709	.540	3
Joe Cronin	1933–47	15	1236–1055	.540	2
Alvin Dark	1961–77	13	994– 954	.510	2
Lou Boudreau	1942–60	16	1162–1224	.487	1

There are people who want to make Leo the best ever, but I think they are mainly macho types who judge a manager by how much dirt he can kick on an umpire's shoes. Frankly, I can't see it. He lost in '42 and '46 when he should have won, and we all remember the '69 Cubs. He WAS terrific in '51 if you don't notice he let himself get so far behind to start with. I'll give him this: the man really knew how to ride a hot streak.

Cronin won a pair of pennants but chewed up his pitching staff too much. Boudreau played too many hunches and didn't have enough Beardens. Jennings let Cobb push him around.

FORMER CATCHERS IN ORDER OF WINNING PERCENTAGE

	Years	No	W–L	Pct	Pen
Al Lopez	1951– 69	17	1410–1004	.584	2
Steve O'Neill	1935– 54	14	1040– 821	.559	1
Ralph Houk	1961– 84	20	1619–1531	.514	3
Paul Richards	1951– 76	12	923– 901	.506	0
Wilbert Robinson	1902– 31	19	1399–1398	.500	2
George Stallings	1897–1920	13	879– 898	.495	1
Connie Mack	1894–1950	53	3731–3948	.486	9
John McNamara	1969– 91	18	1150–1215	.486	1
Lee Fohl	1915– 26	11	713– 792	.474	0

Okay, here's the moment you've been waiting for and it's kind of anticlimactic, right?

Sure, there's Connie Mack. He managed forever because he wouldn't fire himself. He finished last more times than all the horses I ever bet on put together. But he did win nine pennants, and he DID know how to handle men. He's one of the few old-timers who could manage successfully today. I just wish he'd retired to the front office after 1931. THEN he'd have a heckuva record!

Of the others, Houk was good, though he couldn't win after the Yankees went downhill, and Richards was smart as a whip but always seemed to be looking to do something else. Uncle Robby has become a legendary caricature because of the "Daffiness Boys" of the late '20s, but he won in 1916 and 1920 when he shouldn't have. Stallings had that one great, "miracle" year. And everybody forgets O'Neill, who had a very good record.

For my money, I'll take Lopez as the best of the ex-catcher managers. Sure, he only won two pennants and no World Series, but how many times did he finish second with the third- or fourth-best team? All you can really ask of a manager is that he get the most possible out of a team. The Señor always did that and sometimes more!

Anyway, with ten ex-catchers among the "top" managers (at least in longevity), it might seem to you that backstops are best. However, look at the last chart.

FORMER SECOND BASEMEN IN ORDER OF WINNING PERCENTAGE

	Years	No	W–L	Pct	Pen
Joe McCarthy	1926–50	24	2125–1333	.615	9
Earl Weaver	1968–86	17	1480–1060	.583	4
Miller Huggins	1913–29	17	1413–1134	.555	6
Sparky Anderson	1970–92	23	1996–1611	.553	6
Billy Martin	1969–88	16	1253–1013	.553	2
Tony LaRussa	1979–92	14	1134– 949	.544	3
Danny Murtaugh	1957–76	15	1115– 950	.540	2
Bill McKechnie	1915–46	25	1896–1723	.524	4
Red Schoendienst	1965–90	14	1041– 955	.522	2
Frankie Frisch	1933–51	16	1138–1078	.514	1
Bucky Harris	1924–56	29	2157–2218	.493	3
Bill Rigney	1956–76	18	1239–1321	.484	0
Gene Mauch	1960–87	26	1902–2037	.483	0
Rogers Hornsby	1925–53	14	701– 812	.463	1

How's that for a crew! Fourteen managers and at least thirteen of them are Grade A! (Hornsby made McGraw look like a "player's" manager.) Oh, the others, the Grade A guys, had their idiosyncrasies. Mauch and Rigney never won pennants, but they were widely and deservedly respected. Frisch is a little iffy, but he deserves points for surviving the

Gashouse Gang. And though Billy-Ball wasn't always worth the side-show, he still gets all but the marshmallow vote.

McCarthy's record is so good that he surmounts the "push-button" label and even the '48 Red Sox. Huggins couldn't tame Babe Ruth, but some seasons he had him housebroken. Weaver will make the HOF someday, and Sparky and LaRussa are likely to get there too.

Harris, and to only a slightly lesser extent Murtaugh and Schoendienst, are "managers for all seasons"—solid baseball people who knew how to treat their men so that the effort was always there. McKechnie, my personal favorite, was like that too. He did the same thing as Dick Williams—won pennants with three different teams.

What about Playing Managers?

I know some of you are chafing at the bit to remind me that a lot of these ex-whatevers weren't ex when they did their best managing. In baseball's first fifty league years, most managers were players. As late as the 1930s, the player-manager was still common, with Charlie Grimm, Joe Cronin, Mickey Cochrane, Frankie Frisch, Gabby Hartnett, and Bill Terry winning pennants.

The last P-M to win a pennant was Boudreau in 1948. There hasn't been what you'd call a successful player-manager since. But who can say why? Is it because the job has gotten so complicated that a normal human can't play well and manage well at the same time? Or is it because player-managers are almost as rare as left-handed shortstops over the last fifty years? One thing for sure, if there aren't any player-managers in the league, the odds are against a P-M winning the pennant.

Admittedly, a lot of the men on our lists above were ONLY successful at managing during the time they played, but that seems to cut across all the positions. The only catcher on our list who did much managing while still active was Connie Mack, but Mickey Cochrane and Rough Carrigan were very successful as player-managers and unsuccessful after they stopped playing.

I think player-managing is a side issue that has no real bearing on the question here. Why'd you bring it up? The real question is what position best prepares a man to manage a major league team.

Now if we add all the charts up and make a Master Chart, here's what we see:

Pos.	No	Yrs	W–L	Pct	Pen	PPY
First Basemen	4	74	5569– 4275	.566	19	3.895
Third Basemen	4	83	6083– 5331	.533	12	6.917
Second Basemen	14	268	20590–18194	.531	43	6.231
Outfielders	12	208	14992–13284	.530	42	4.952
Shortstops	5	83	6563– 5926	.526	11	7.545
Pitchers	3	49	3662– 3395	.519	6	8.167
Catchers	9	177	12864–12508	.507	19	9.315

("PPY" is "pennant frequency," or number of seasons managed divided by number of pennants won.)

Outfielders are good at bringing in pennants and first and third basemen (in limited numbers) have the edge in winning percentage. But overall, second basemen win the brass ring. (Where does that expression come from? Who wants a BRASS ring?)

So catchers—although some have been terrific—don't make the best managers, according to the numbers. And, as SABR-metricians keep telling us, numbers are all that matter. (If SABR-metricians judged Miss America, you could forget the talent competition, and Miss Congeniality would be the one with square roots instead of dark roots.)

Anyway, in summary, Mr. Clubowner, if you're looking for a manager and don't want to take the trouble to look at a candidate's individual strengths and weaknesses, hire an ex–second baseman. The odds of getting a good one are pretty high.

⚾ 24 ⚾

Oops! It's OPS!

All right, I admit it. I'm as bad as everyone else. When they print those little stat boxes of league leaders in my morning newspaper, the first thing I squint at is the batting averages. I couldn't be more ashamed if I was hooked on a kids' cereal.

Yes, I know, as you know—as EVERYBODY knows—that a player's batting average is his least important stat next to his shoe size. I'm not stat illiterate! I just need to be reminded sometimes. Bear with me while I repeat the catechism:

A batting average shows only how often hits are made—not how often a player reaches base—and it doesn't differentiate among the hits. A single is worth just as much as a home run in a batting average. If you just look at the batting average, Lloyd Waner (.316) was a better hitter than Hank Aaron (.305).

Better rating systems are On Base Percentage (OBP) and Slugging Average (SLG), both of which are added on at the end of those little newspaper stat boxes and with only the top three or four players listed.

	OBP	SLG
Hank Aaron	.377	.555
Lloyd Waner	.353	.393

Isn't that more like it?

OBP = One Better Procedure

The OBP is far better than batting average in determining a player's ability to reach first base because it includes his walks. How many times has someone said, "A walk's as good as a hit"? Well, in the OBP, it really is. To get an OBP, you add up a player's hits, *walks*, and *hit by pitches* and divide that by his at bats, walks, and hit by pitches. Or, as Miss Ziegler used to tell us:

$$\frac{H + BB + HBP}{AB + BB + HBP} = OBP$$

For your information, the highest OBP ever was .551 by Ted Williams in 1941 when his batting average was a paltry .406. Think of it this way: every twenty times Ted strode to the plate that year he made six hits and five walks. Only nine men have ever reached .500 OBP over a whole season. Williams did it three times and Babe Ruth five, but Ted also had two .499 seasons. You'd never in a million years guess the only other player to top .500 in OBP more than once.

Although it's a better measure than a batting average, nobody ever said the OBP was perfect and sure enough it has four faults. First, the number of times a player walks is not always listed in your run-of-the-mill statistic charts and the number of times hit by pitches is very rarely included. Of course, except for Don Baylor or Ron Hunt, the occasional HBPs won't make a whole lot of difference. But if you really want to be accurate, you have to do some digging to get all the numbers.

Second, when they made OBP an official stat, they decided to count sacrifice flies as at bats. They're not counted in figuring batting averages. Some of those weigh-a-ton stat books like *Total Baseball* ignore sacrifice flies altogether. That certainly gets my vote; I'm always in favor of a stat that can be safely ignored.

The third problem with OBP is that I habitually write it as OPB and sometimes even OTB. Actually, I guess that's *my* problem.

Fault number four, as you've been screaming all along, is that it doesn't say *how far* a batter gets on base. It shows us *quantity* but not *quality*, just like a batting average. In OBP, a triple or a walk are all the same—one time on base.

SLG = Still Looking for the Greatest

Okay, that's where a Slugging Average comes in. In SLG, you add up the total bases on all the player's hits and divide by his at bats. Or:

$$\frac{1 \times S + 2 \times D + 3 \times T + 4 \times HR}{AB} = SLG$$

There are two big criticisms of SLG. The first is that because it's not as well known as the batting average, a lot of people are in the dark as to what it means. Like, is .401 any good?

As a rule of thumb, an SLG that's twice as high as a batting average means a darned good year. Barry Bonds topped the majors last year with .624. The only hitter ever to top .800 was Babe Ruth, who did it twice with .847 in 1920 and .846 in 1921. In 1927, the year he hit 60 homers, his SLG was .772, which happens to rank third all-time. And in the fourth all-time spot is teammate Lou Gehrig's .765, also in 1927. Ruth actually has seven of the eleven top SLGs ever recorded.

A better criticism of the SLG is that it makes no provision for walks (or being hit by pitches). So we're back to one of the big drawbacks of batting average. Of course, you could do SLGs with BBs and HBPs added into the Numerators and Denominators. But adding BBs to an SLG screws it all up royally. Remember, we're talking about *quality* here. It turns out a walk is *not* as good as a hit. Statisticians explain that a team benefits a smidgeon more from its singles than it does from its walks. I don't really understand all the math involved, but I think it comes down to three walks only load the bases but three singles usually produce a run.

OPS = One Possible Solution

Pete Palmer, Bill James, and several others who would have had front seats in Miss Ziegler's class have invented marvelously intricate formulae to rate hitters. These take into account hits, walks, total bases, steals, sacrifices, ballpark factors, wind resistance, temperature, pitchers' SAT scores, the rainfall on Venus, and I don't know what all else. For all I know, Miss Ziegler had some spectacular way of analyzing hitters' stats that works better than the Rosetta Stone.

I'm not about to disagree with all the math majors. I have more than enough trouble balancing my checkbook (but I'm getting better; as of the beginning of this month my balance was either 63 cents or $630,000—or somewhere in between). If these statisticians say their ratings are more accurate than any of the traditional statistical measures, I have to believe them. The only trouble is that their wonderful formulae won't do me a whole lot of good any time I'm in a situation where I have to do the figuring myself—like this year's stats or, for that matter, last year's, if I don't have the books with me. Try carrying *Total Baseball* in your hip pocket when you go to the grocery and you'll end up mooning the checkout lady.

Fortunately, there's a simpler way, one that even I can work out with a hand calculator in a few minutes (or a pencil and paper in a fortnight). It may not be quite as accurate as Linear Weights, Runs Created, or the other super-math formulae, but it's head and shoulders above batting average, on base percentage, and slugging average as a tool for assessing a hitter's performance. All you do is add the player's OBP and SLG together.

And?

And nothing. That's it. The total of OBP and SLG, sometimes called OPS and sometimes called Production, gives you the best of both. The OBP tells you about quantity and the SLG about quality. Even most of the experts admit that it's the most accurate of the simple (i.e., user-friendly) hitter rating tools.

The top eight all-time OPS seasons belong to Ruth and Williams, with the Babe getting six of them. Not surprisingly, they lead all in career OPS. The top ten in lifetime OPS:

1.	Babe Ruth	1.163
2.	Ted Williams	1.116
3.	Lou Gehrig	1.080
4.	Jimmie Foxx	1.038
5.	Hank Greenberg	1.017
6.	Rogers Hornsby	1.010
7.	Mickey Mantle	.979
8.	Joe DiMaggio	.977
	Stan Musial	.977
10.	Johnny Mize	.959

ADJ = Ad-Damned-Justment

Naturally, that's not good enough for the statisticians. They prefer an *adjusted* OPS. By that they mean you figure in things like the time and place for each individual and adjust his numbers accordingly. You know, like a power hitter will hit better in Wrigley Field than in Shea Stadium. (Well, actually anybody will hit better in Wrigley than in Shea, especially lately.) Or there are certain times in history when the pitchers had it all over the hitters and other times when the hitters were on top. So they *adjust* the OPS to allow for those things.

When I first heard of adjusting numbers, I thought "Uh-oh! They must be changing doubles and triples to home runs." Happily, that's not how it's done, they tell me. Instead, they just rate a player's OBP and SLG against the league average to see how much better or worse he did. Then they allow some for different ballparks and that's it.

I'm of two minds on adjusting an OPS. From one side, I'm against it. And not just because I wouldn't have the faintest idea where to start if I had to do the adjusting myself. (What IS the "ballpark factor" for Candlestick? Does it change between day and night games?) I think what bugs me most is that here they have a nice simple little stat that any seventh-grader can understand and they have to go and encode it in their mathematical gobbledegook.

But from the other side, I do see some advantages in adjusting. I did a quick survey of some years in baseball history to see how the differences stacked up in batting average, OBP, SLG, OPS, and in Runs Per Game.

	BA	OBP	SLG	OPS	RPG
1894 NL	.309	.373	.435	.808	14.73
1906 AL	.249	.302	.318	.620	7.33
1920 AL	.284	.347	.387	.734	9.51
1930 NL	.303	.360	.448	.808	11.37
1941 AL	.266	.341	.389	.730	9.49
1961 AL	.256	.331	.395	.726	9.05
1968 AL	.230	.299	.339	.639	6.81
1992 NL	.252	.318	.368	.686	7.76
1992 AL	.259	.331	.385	.716	8.64

I figured 1894 was a good year to look at because that's when the full effect of moving the pitchers back was felt; 1906 was the year of the "Hitless Wonders" White Sox; 1920 saw the advent of the lively ball; in 1930 the baseball used by the National League was so souped up it could have won at Indy; 1941 was when Williams was our last .400 hitter; 1961 was THE expansion year; and 1968 was "The Year of the Pitcher" when hitters had a summer's siesta. Naturally, I checked out 1992 as the most recent season for which I had numbers.

I wasn't surprised that 1906 and 1968 came out looking so similar, but 1894 really surprised me with an OPS as high as the N.L. in 1930. Homers weren't as common in the 1890s, but they made up for it in doubles and triples so that the 1894 SLG matches that of 1930. My guess is that the Runs Per Game was three more in 1894 largely because of fielding, what with poor infields and terrible gloves. The league *earned run* averages are much closer—5.32 in 1894 to 4.97 in 1930.

Anyway, the differences in various years were so great that I was pretty much convinced that adjusting the career OPS was a good idea. So I turned to see what the statisticians came up with. I was expecting to see some new top ten names, like George Brett, Hank Aaron, or maybe Rafael Belliard.

Instead . . .

1. Babe Ruth   209
2. Ted Williams   186
3. Lou Gehrig   182
4. Rogers Hornsby   176
5. Mickey Mantle   173
6. Dan Brouthers   171
7. Joe Jackson   169
8. Ty Cobb   167
9. Pete Browning   166
10. Jimmie Foxx   161

(The numbers show how much more than an "average" hitter these people hit over their careers.)

Okay, I can accept Dan Brouthers. And Jackson and Cobb could certainly hit despite their other weaknesses. But Pete Browning?

A Few Words about Pete

If that name doesn't ring a bell, here's a quick synopsis: Louis Rogers "Pete" Browning played from 1882 through 1894, mostly in the old major league American Association, which he led in batting a couple of times, but he also spent time in the Players League and the National League. He ended up with a terrific career batting average of .341. On the other hand, he only played 1,183 games in thirteen seasons. Admittedly schedules were shorter in those days, but his managers also kept him out of the lineup a lot because he was a horrible fielder—so bad, in fact, that no one has ever seriously suggested him for the Hall of Fame despite his gaudy batting average.

Pete was very persnickety about his batting and wanted his bats just so. One day in the 1880s when he was playing for Louisville, he met a feller who offered to turn out a bat on his lathe that would be the candy. When he got it, Pete loved the bat so much he ordered more and told his friends. And that's how the famous bat-making company Hillerich and Bradsby got started. Ol' Pete was the original Louisville Slugger.

You'd think it would be poetic justice that the first Louisville Slugger have his Slugging Average adjusted to lift his OPS and put him into the company of all those later sluggers, but I'm not so sure. The American Association, where Pete spent the majority of his career, was replete with lousy hitters. From 1882 through 1886 the league Slugging Average never once got as high as the American League's SLG in 1968, the Year of the Pitcher. So, if you plop somebody like Browning who *could* hit in with all those A.A. batters who couldn't, he's going to make a heckuva splash. And then, a hundred years later, when you start this adjusting stuff, wouldn't he jump to the fore just because his league-mates couldn't hit a lick?

Let's Think about This

See, the problem with adjusting batting averages, OBPs, SLGs, or OPSes is that every season and league becomes the same. If the league batting average is .230 and Joe Blow hits .300, he's 70 points above the norm; if the league average is .300 and John Doe hits .370, he's 70 points above the norm. They both have the same adjusted batting average. That might make sense if we knew for sure that there weren't a lot of better hitters around during Doe's time (pulling up that league average) than there were during Blow's time. Some would argue that today's sluggers with their batting gloves and batting coaches are better schooled, are bigger and stronger, and have better reflexes than in the old days.

But you can't prove that with the numbers.

Anyway, as I said, I'm of two minds about adjusting an OPS. Fortunately, we don't have to always concern ourselves with who was the greatest going back to the days of Chester A. Arthur. Most of us are more vitally interested in knowing who is the best around right now. That's simple. To paraphrase Casey Stengel, "You could look it OPS."

No, Casey never even once finished a season with an OBP over .500. The only one to do it twice besides Ruth and Williams was—believe it or not—John J. McGraw, who also happens to be one of two men to manage ten pennant winners.

Now, who was the only other manager to do that?

⚾ 25 ⚾

Why Cy's Arm Stayed Young

Don't bet on Greg Maddux to win the National League's Cy Young Award this year. No one has done it back to back in twenty-seven seasons. Sandy Koufax actually strung three in a row from 1963 through '65, and they would have held an investigation if he'd done it again.

No matter what pitcher gets the award this season, you can be sure he'll know more about pitching than he will about Cy Young. Ask a major league pitcher to identify Cy Young and he might guess Marcus Welby's brother. A few may remember that Cy won "oh, a lot of games back in—gee, I think Lincoln was President, yuh know?"

He won 511, to be exact. If the Cy Young Award was for lifetime achievement, the first winner would be Cy Young.

That figure is so absurd that it's unreal. Five hundred and eleven games? Sure, and my golf score is in the low 70s. Five hundred and eleven? Right, and I get forty-five miles to a gallon in the city. Honest. Five hundred and eleven. No wonder they named the award after him. They should have named a state after him.

So how did he win more games than most guys pitch? Well, there is a trick to it. Ol' Cy pitched from 1890 to 1911, in baseball's equivalent of the Dark Ages—the Dead Ball Era. That's "dead" as in "not lively." The baseball they used then had about as much rabbit as burger-stand rarebit. You had to hit it twice and kick it once to get it into the outfield. Home runs were as common as Iranian Peace Prizes.

Delivered from the imminent likelihood of throwing a gopher ball, pitchers in those days could coast along, really raring back and cutting loose only about a dozen times a game. That wasn't too hard on anybody's arm. Tuesday's pitcher was ready to go again by Thursday. Guys pitched 400 innings a season and figured they should moonlight a night job.

Ol' Cy was good. But he was also available for a long time. While he was winning a ton, he also lost 313. And pitched 7,356 innings.

By way of comparison, fireballer Nolan Ryan, who began pitching about the time Prohibition went out, has thrown 5,319 innings going into 1993 and will catch Ol' Cy in August, 1998, if he reconsiders his retirement. Nobody pitches 400 innings anymore. Or even 300 for that matter.

It's not that they don't make arms like they used to. They just don't make baseballs like they used to.

Today's baseball has more bounce than a check at a crap game. With a good wind, you can bunt it into the second row of the bleachers. And, since anytime he lets go of anything but the resin bag a pitcher is liable to be watching his outfielder's back, he has to bear down on every pitch. The strain of pitching that way would wear out Atlas.

If any pitcher tried to throw a Cy Young 400 innings now, they'd have to reattach his arm with bailing wire by July 4. About 250 innings is today's upper limit. Anything more than that and a pitcher has to start asking his friends to comb his hair for him.

And that would be true for Ol' Cy if he were around today. At 250 innings a season, Young wouldn't have come close to 511 wins.

What would a typical Cy Young year look like? Divide 250 into those 7,356 innings and you get 29.424. Divide THAT into his career wins and losses and you'll have his average record: a rounded-off 17–11. Not bad, but put him in the 1992 National League and Greg Maddux still gets the Cy Young Award. Maddux was 20–11.

⚾ 26 ⚾

Fie on the Cy Jinx!

Bob Welch and Doug Drabek, two pretty fair country pitchers, waddled out of the starting blocks in 1991. At mid-year, both were still far off the pace they set in 1990 when each won his league's Big Pitcher McGoo. Aha! quoth the Raven, the Cy Young Jinx strikes again!

Quoth me: Nevermore!

Baseball has its share of legitimate jinxes. Like it's ill-fated to pitch in Wrigley Field when the wind's blowing out. It's ill-advised to bat against Clemens unless the umpire's name is Cooney. It's hapless to try sneaking a nothin' fastball past Cecil on a 3–0 count and hopeless to bounce a grounder at Ozzie with a man on first. It's unlucky to be traded to Cleveland. Appear on *SI*'s cover at your peril.

With so many real jinxes—some of them career-threatening—ballplayers need a spurious, *manufactured* jinx as much as they need an umbrella in the Astrodome. Yet, nearly every season, you'll hear earnest, grown-up men (in long pants and everything) talk seriously about the Cy Young Award Jinx as though it's a real and true monster to be feared like those things that hide under my bed when I turn out the lights. Enough! Enough of this blather!

There is no Cy Young Award Jinx.

There never was!

How We Got the Cy Young

To start at the beginning, there once was no Cy Young Award. (Ergo, no jinx.) Come the end of each season in the Good Ol' Days, they handed out Most Valuable Player trophies and called it quits until the next spring. But some people weren't satisfied. Sometimes a pitcher would get named MVP and all the position players would gripe and grumble about calling someone Most Valuable who only played every four or five days. And the pitchers were equally PO'd because one of them won the MVP only once in a blue moon and they KNEW the guy on the mound was ALWAYS the most important player in the park.

Finally in 1956, after enough back-and-forth pitching bitching, Commissioner Ford Frick came out in favor of a special award for pitchers, and the Baseball Writers Association of America voted that henceforth and forsooth they'd vote for one.

Naturally they needed a name for the new honor. They couldn't just call it "Good Pitchin' Trophy." Somebody suggested "The Ford Frick Trophy" and when the laughter died down they decided to name it after a dead pitcher. Cy Young, having cleverly timed his dying to the previous November, came immediately to mind.

It's worth noting that had old Cy succumbed twenty or thirty years earlier, the writers might have named the award after Christy Mathewson or Walter Johnson, who were even better pitchers. Then it could be referred to familiarly as a "Christy" or a "Wally," both of which have a nice show-biz ring. You can't say a pitcher won a "Cy" and expect to be taken seriously.

The funniest part of the whole thing was that Don Newcombe, who took the first Cy Young in 1956, also won the MVP for the National League that year. You should have heard the position players on that one! Marine drill sergeants blushed.

For reasons best known to himself, Frick favored a single pitchers' award to cover both leagues instead of one for each. Maybe he figured they'd save on the engraving. The writers humored him until he retired in 1965 and then, after a decent interval, started in 1967 to vote an award for each league like they'd always wanted to. They had the approval of William Eckert in this. (Note: diligent research has failed to reveal anything more about this fellow Eckert. Apparently he had some obscure connection with baseball during the 1960s, but I've been unable to find anyone who can further identify him. If you can help, dial 555-ECK-WHOM.)

Troubles in Cy-Land

Aside from the fact that the Cy Young winner could still be named MVP, some other bugs showed up in the system. Like the way they voted.

During the period when there was only one award covering both leagues, one writer from each team in both leagues voted for one pitcher only. Sometimes, you had American League writers voting for National League pitchers on the basis of what some of their fellow voters had written. And vice versa. Over a stretch of five years (1962–66) every Cy Young went to a Los Angeles pitcher, which speaks well for West Coast pitching or West Coast writing. Or both.

When they went to an award for each league, they widened the voting to two writers from each city (voting only for a single pitcher in his league) because two heads are better than one unless you're a coin. Well, you could see it coming. A limited number of votes—sooner or later there was going to be a tie.

In 1969 they got it. Ten A.L. writers voted for Mike Cuellar, ten voted for Denny McLain, and four writers must've watched some other pennant race. So, after the barn was stolen, the B.W.A.A. locked up the horse by having their guys vote their first, second, and third choices, marked five points, three points, and one point. A unanimous first choice in the American League can get 140 points, in the National League 120, until 1993 when expansion added 20 more points.

The biggest complaint nowadays is that nearly every year they vote the awards to the wrong pitchers. At least that's what you read in the newspapers. Of course, those end-of-season columns about how the newest Cy Young choice was a mistake are mostly written by the guys who voted for the wrong horse and are determined to prove they were really smarter than anybody else.

That stuff gets stale and has nothing to do with the Cy Young Award Jinx.

Which doesn't exist.

What Is the Jinx and Who Gets Bit?

When the previous year's Cy Young Award winner staggers off to a rocky start, as often happens, some Chicken Little is sure to shout "Jinx!" The idea is that winning that award somehow makes a star thrower turn into a bum. Presumably, if no one had recognized his terrificness, he would have gone on being terrific. Which is a thought worthy of Yogi Berra!

Even though the thesis lacks logic the way the Tigers lack pitching, the jinx-shouters will tell you a Cy is cause for sighing. Today an award, tomorrow an ash heap. Better a black cat should walk under your ladder!

As proof that the Jinx exists, the shouters will dredge up the examples of Steve Stone, Jim Lonborg, Pete Vuckovich, John Denny, Mark Davis, LaMarr Hoyt, Randy Jones, and several other flingers who won a Cy Young one year and crapped out the next. Even some pitchers who later returned to greatness slumped the year after they won a Cy: Steve Carlton, Bret Saberhagen, Frank Viola, Ron Guidry, Jim Palmer, and Tom Seaver, to name an impressive few. So this year, both of last year's winners were candidates for the Jinx as soon as they started thanking the little people.

If there is a Jinx.

Which there isn't.

How to Get There from Here

Before explaining why there isn't a Jinx, we should spend a moment considering what it takes if you decide you want to go out and win a Cy Young. Allowing for the dictum that there's an exception to every rule, here are the rules:

1. You should be a starter. Although eight relievers have won Cy Youngs, the other fifty-six trophies have gone to starters. Middle relievers can forget it altogether. The next one to get a vote will be the first.

2. You should pitch for a pennant-winner or near-winner. Oh, sure, Carlton won with the last-place Phillies in 1972, but those kind of seasons come along once every twenty years. Ask Murry Dickson. If your team wins a pennant, the writers can blame it on you when they hand you the Cy dingus.

3. Your team should score a ton. No matter how well you pitch, you'll need to be bailed out a couple of times after you give up four or five runs.

4. Your team should have a good closer. Otherwise you'll get a lot of no-decisions after leaving with a 2–1 lead through seven.

5. You must stay healthy. You can't pile up the wins sitting on the DL. And total wins are the most important stat. Forty-four of the fifty-six starters who've won the award led their league in victories.

6. You should have been around long enough so that the writers know

you can pitch. Nobody believed David Cone's 20–3 in 1988 or Orel Hershiser's 19–3 in 1985, because they seemed to come from nowhere.

7. You need a reasonably low ERA, but you don't have to lead the league. Just stay under 3.00. Let the crown go to some guy who pitches 164 innings.

8. Toss a lotta shutouts. No-hitters don't seem to mean much, but a few whitewashings—especially in a row—impress.

9. Hope no other pitcher in your league has a "career-type year." Otherwise you'll only win the Dave Stewart Award.

10. You have to be lucky. Not only because of all the above but also so that your team gets five runs when you give up four, four when you give up three, three when . . . etc.

Why There's No Jinx

What are the odds of a pitcher—any pitcher—hitting all ten of those rules two years in a row? About the same as Jose Oquendo winning a home run contest. I mean it's POSSIBLE but . . .

Let's take the case of Joe Hypothetical, the 19XX winner. He made 35 starts—8 so great he couldn't lose (though he didn't get a decision in one), 8 very good, 7 average, 6 just below average, and 6 where he got his clock cleaned. Because his team scored a ton of runs and had a good closer AND because he was lucky, his record came out like this:

	Starts	*Win–Loss*
Great	8	7–0
Very Good	8	6–1
Average	7	5–1
Sub-par	6	3–2
Poor	6	0–3

No one else in the league won 20 games, and Joe's 20–7 was good enough to get the award. He spent the winter on the banquet circuit taking bows and tellin' 'em how he was just happy to contribute. His agent spent the winter getting Joe's contract renegotiated.

So the next year, the team's slugger jumped to the Yankees as a free agent, the closer came up with a sore arm, and Joe's luck evened out. He pitched almost as well, but . . .

	Starts	Win–Loss
Great	7	5–0
Very Good	9	4–3
Average	6	2–3
Sub-par	7	1–5
Poor	6	0–6

. . . his 12–17 got him listed as a victim of the Jinx.

So, if only because the Luck Factor gravitates toward the middle, it's practically built in that a Cy Young winner will slump the year after. As a matter of fact, only three of the fifty-six starters who've won Cy Gizmos ever improved their win-loss records the next year. To demonstrate that there's no Jinx, we first have to distinguish between normal tailing-off and *Götterdämmerung*. Then we have to take the really awful follow-up seasons and see if they are out of proportion to what could normally be expected in this best of all possible worlds.

In the accompanying chart, you'll find the top three vote-getters in each year's Cy Young voting (sometimes fewer than three if only one or two pitchers received votes and sometimes four when there was a tie for third). The votes are listed. Then the pitcher's win-loss record in his Cy Young year, followed by his record the next year, and finally the difference, subtracting points for fewer wins and more losses and adding points for more wins and fewer losses. Win-loss records aren't the only criteria for Cy Young voting, but they are the most important.

Two notes:

First, relievers' records in wins and saves are given in the chart, but those guys really don't belong in the study and will be ignored. Relievers are notorious for roller-coaster career swings. How many times was Hoyt Wilhelm given up for dead? They may be subject to their own special jinx, but it has nothing to do with Cy Young.

Second, the 1981 records given here are derived by multiplying the real records by a third to make up for the strike.

Now, your job, should you decide to accept it, Mr. Phelps, is to identify the real, unexpected tailspins. That's not as easy as you might think. Don Drysdale went from 25–9 in 1962 to 19–17 in '63, a *minus* 14 difference. Yet he was still a very good pitcher. On the other hand, Vernon Law's sore arm dropped him from 20–9 in 1960 to 3–4 the next year. That's only a difference of 12, but it put Pittsburgh out of the pennant race.

Injuries ruined the "next" season for Law in 1961, Koufax in 1967,

Lonborg in 1968, Blue in 1972, Palmer in 1973, Jones in 1977, Stone in 1981, Vuckovich in 1983, Denny in 1984, Sutcliffe in 1985, and Saberhagen in 1990. That's eleven out of fifty-three, or over 20 percent. But, if that seems like a lot, consider how often any team can get its five regular starters through a whole season without at least one of them putting in serious time on the DL. If the proportion of injuries is not a jinx.

Perhaps it's even fated. The career of the Phils' Danny Lynne Jackson has been shaped by his initials.

Speaking of what's to be expected, Early Wynn took his Cy Young at age thirty-nine and Gaylord Perry was thirty-nine when he won his second. Who was surprised when they slumped at age forty? Only Nolan Ryan. Several pitchers like Gibson and Palmer won Cy Youngs in their mid-thirties and didn't repeat. That's not a jinx; that's Nature.

A few Cy Youngers won when they suddenly had seasons all out of relation to anything they'd ever done before. Vuckovich, Denny, and Stone again, both 1990 winners, Mike McCormick, and even Bob Turley fit into that mold. They had "career years." They weren't jinxed the next year; they just stopped overachieving.

Then there were a couple of winners who jinxed themselves. Newcombe with alcohol, Hoyt with drugs, and McLain with gambling.

The point here is that the examples of the Cy Young Jinx turn out to be explainable as either a normal tailing-off or caused by "natural" things like injuries, age, lack of greatness, or self-destruction. When something is "natural" or "explainable" it qualifies as a jinx the way Gregg Jefferies qualifies for a Gold Glove. You can get rich betting against a Cy Young winner or ANY OTHER BIG WINNER duplicating his record the next year.

And the proof is that the same sort of "jinx" things happened with just about the same regularity to the pitchers who finished second and third in the Cy Young voting. Some of the also-rans' tailspins were far more inexplicable. What happened to Bob Friend in 1959? Or Larry Jackson in 1965? Or Ernie Broglio?

Where did Joel Horlen go wrong?

Steve Blass ranks with Amelia Earhart as a mystery.

Somebody could write a best-seller called *When Bad Things Happen to Nice Pitchers*. But it'd be longer than the biography of Warren Peace. Look at the chart!

Year/Pitcher/Team	Votes	Year	Nxt/Yr	Diff
1956				
Don Newcombe, Bkn (N)	10	*27– 7	11–12	−21
Sal Maglie, Bkn (N)	4	13– 5	6– 6	−8
Warren Spahn, Mil (N)	1	20–11	*21–11	+1
Whitey Ford, NY (A)	1	19– 6	11– 5	−7
1957				
Warren Spahn, Mil (N)	15	*21–11	*22–11	+1
Dick Donovan, Chi (A)	1	16– 6	15–14	−9
1958				
Bob Turley, NY (A)	5	*21– 7	8–11	−17
Warren Spahn, Mil (N)	4	*22–11	*21–15	−5
Bob Friend, Pit (N)	3	*22–14	8–19	−19
Lew Burdette, Mil (N)	3	20–10	21–15	−4
1959				
Early Wynn, Chi (A)	13	*22–10	13–12	−11
Sam Jones, SF (N)	2	*21–15	18–14	−2
Bob Shaw, Chi (A)	1	18– 6	13–13	−12
1960				
Vernon Law, Pit (N)	8	20– 9	3– 4	−12
Warren Spahn, Mil (N)	4	*21–10	*21–13	−2
Ernie Broglio, StL (N)	1	*21– 9	9–12	−15
Lindy McDaniel, StL (N)	1	12w*26s	10w9s	−19
1961				
Whitey Ford, NY (A)	9	*25– 4	17– 8	−12
Warren Spahn, Mil (N)	4	*21–13	18–14	−4
Frank Lary, Det (A)	2	23– 9	2– 6	−18
1962				
Don Drysdale, LA (N)	14	*25– 9	19–17	−14
Jack Sanford, SF (N)	4	24– 7	16–13	−14
Bob Purkey, Cin (N)	1	23– 5	6–10	−22
Billy Pierce, SF (N)	1	16– 6	3–11	−18
1963				
Sandy Koufax, LA (N)	20	*25– 5	19– 5	−6

Year/Pitcher/Team	Votes	Year	Nxt/Yr	Diff
1964				
Dean Chance, LA (A)	17	*20– 9	15–10	−6
Larry Jackson, Chi (N)	2	*24–11	14–21	−20
Sandy Koufax, LA (N)	1	19– 5	*26– 8	+4
1965				
Sandy Koufax, LA (N)	20	*26– 8	*27– 9	0
1966				
Sandy Koufax, LA (N)	20	*27– 9	Ret.	−18
1967—NL				
Mike McCormick, SF	18	*22–10	12–14	−14
Ferguson Jenkins, Chi	1	20–13	20–15	−2
Jim Bunning, Phi	1	17–15	4–14	−12
1967—AL				
Jim Lonborg, Bos	18	*22– 9	6–10	−17
Joel Horlen, Chi	2	19– 7	12–14	−14
1968—NL				
Bob Gibson, StL	20	22– 9	20–13	−6
1968—AL				
Denny McLain, Det	20	*31– 6	*24– 9	−10
1969—NL				
Tom Seaver, NY	23	*25– 7	18–12	−12
Phil Niekro, Atl	1	23–13	12–18	−16
1969—AL				
Mike Cuellar, Bal	10	23–11	*24– 8	+4
Denny McLain, Det	10	*24– 9	3– 5	−15
Jim Perry, Min	3	20– 6	*24–12	−2
1970—NL				
Bob Gibson, StL	118	*23– 7	16–13	−13
Gaylord Perry, SF	51	*23–13	16–12	−6
Ferguson Jenkins, Chi	16	22–16	*24–13	+5

1970—AL

Jim Perry, Min	55	*24–12	17–17	−12
Dave McNally, Bal	47	*24– 9	21– 5	+1
Sam McDowell, Cle	45	20–12	13–17	−12

1971—NL

Ferguson Jenkins, Chi	97	*24–13	20–12	−3
Tom Seaver, NY	61	−10	21–12	−1
Al Downing, LA	40	20– 9	9– 9	−11

1971—AL

Vida Blue, Oak	98	24– 8	6–10	−20
Mickey Lolich, Det	85	*25–14	22–14	−3
Wilbur Wood, Chi	23	22–13	*24–17	−2

1972—NL

Steve Carlton, Phi	120	27–10	13–20	−24
Steve Blass, Pit	35	19– 8	3– 9	−17
Ferguson Jenkins, Chi	23	20–12	14–16	−10

1972—AL

Gaylord Perry, Cle	64	*24–16	19–19	−8
Wilbur Wood, Chi	58	*24–17	*24–20	−3
Mickey Lolich, Det	27	22–14	16–15	−7

1973—NL

Tom Seaver, NY	71	19–10	11–11	−9
Mike Marshall, Mon	54	14w*31s	15w*21s	−9
Ron Bryant, SF	50	*24–12	3–15	−24

1973—AL

Jim Palmer, Bal	88	22– 9	7–12	−18
Nolan Ryan, Cal	62	21–16	22–16	+1
Jim Hunter, Oak	52	21– 5	*25–12	−3

1974—NL

Mike Marshall, LA	96	15w*21s	9w13s	−14
Andy Messersmith, LA	66	*20– 6	19–14	−9
Phil Niekro, Atl	15	*20–13	15–15	−7

Year/Pitcher/Team	Votes	Year	Nxt/Yr	Diff
1974—AL				
Jim Hunter, Oak	90	*25–12	*23–14	−4
Ferguson Jenkins, Tex	75	*25–12	17–18	−14
Nolan Ryan, Cal	28	22–16	14–12	−4
1975—NL				
Tom Seaver, NY	98	*22– 9	14–11	−10
Randy Jones, SD	80	20–12	*22–14	0
Al Hrabosky, StL	33	13w*22s	8w13s	−14
1975—AL				
Jim Palmer, Bal	98	*23–11	*22–13	−3
Jim Hunter, NY	74	*23–14	17–15	−7
Rollie Fingers, Oak	25	10w24s	13w20s	−1
1976—NL				
Randy Jones, SD	96	*22–14	6–12	−14
Jerry Koosman, NY	69.5	21–10	8–20	−23
Don Sutton, LA	25.5	21–10	14– 8	−5
1976—AL				
Jim Palmer, Bal	108	*22–13	*20–11	0
Mark Fidrych, Det	51	19– 9	6– 4	−8
Frank Tanana, Cal	18	19–10	15– 9	−3
1977—NL				
Steve Carlton, Phi	104	*23–10	16–13	−10
Tommy John, LA	54	20– 7	17–10	−6
Tom Seaver, NY-Cin	18	21– 6	16–14	−13
1977—AL				
Sparky Lyle, NY	56.5	13w26s	9w9s	−21
Jim Palmer, Bal	48	*20–11	21–12	0
Nolan Ryan, Cal	46	19–16	10–13	−6
1978—NL				
Gaylord Perry, SD	116	*21– 6	12–11	−14
Burt Hooten, LA	38	19–10	11–10	−8
Vida Blue, SF	17	18–10	14–14	−8

1978—AL
Ron Guidry, NY	140	*25– 3	18– 8	–12
Mike Caldwell, Mil	76	22– 9	16– 6	–3
Jim Palmer, Bal	14	21–12	10– 6	–5

1979—NL
Bruce Sutter, Chi	72	6w*37s	5w*28s	–12
Joe Niekro, Hou	66	*21–11	20–12	–2
J.R. Richard, Hou	41	18–13	10– 4	+1

1979—AL
Mike Flanagan, Bal	136	*23– 9	16–13	–11
Tommy John, NY	51	21– 9	22– 9	+1
Ron Guidry, NY	26	18– 8	17–10	–3

1980—NL
Steve Carlton, Phi	118	*24– 9	#19– 6	–2
Jerry Reuss, LA	55	18– 6	#15– 6	–3
Jim Bibby, Pit	28	19– 6	#9– 4	–8

1980—AL
Steve Stone, Bal	100	*25– 7	#6–10	–22
Mike Norris, Oak	91	22– 9	#18–13	–8
Rich Gossage, NY	37.5	6w*33s	#4s30s	–5

1981—NL
Fernando Valenzuela, LA	70	#19–10	19–13	–3
Tom Seaver, Cin	67	#*21– 3	5–13	–26
Steve Carlton, Phi	50	#19– 6	*23–11	–1

1981—AL
Rollie Fingers, Mil	126	#9w*42s	5w29s	–17
Steve McCatty, Oak	84.5	#*21–10	6– 3	–8
Jack Morris, Det	21	#*21–10	17–16	–10

1982—NL
Steve Carlton, Phi	112	*23–11	15–16	–13
Steve Rogers, Mon	29	19– 8	17–12	–6
Fern. Valenzuela, LA	25.5	19–13	15–10	–1

1982—AL
Pete Vuckovich, Mil	87	18– 6	0– 2	–14

Year/Pitcher/Team	Votes	Year	Nxt/Yr	Diff
Jim Palmer, Bal	59	15– 5	5– 4	−9
Dan Quisenberry, KC	40	9w*35s	5w*45s	+6
1983—NL				
John Denny, Phi	103	*19– 6	7– 7	−13
Mario Soto, Cin	61	17–13	18– 7	+7
Jesse Orosco, NY	19	13w17s	10w31s	+11
1983—AL				
LaMarr Hoyt, Chi	116	*24–10	13–18	−19
Dan Quisenberry, KC	81	5w*45s	6w*44s	0
Jack Morris, Det	38	20–13	19–11	+1
1984—NL				
Rich Sutcliffe, Chi	120	16– 1	8– 8	−15
Doc Gooden, NY	45	17– 9	*24– 4	−11
Bruce Sutter, StL	33.5	5w*45s	7w23s	−20
1984—AL				
Willie Hernandez, Det	88	9w32s	8w31s	−2
Dan Quisenberry, KC	71	6w*44s	8w*37s	−5
Bert Blyleven, Cle	45	19– 7	9–11	−14
1985—NL				
Doc Gooden, NY	120	*24– 4	17– 6	−9
John Tudor, StL	65	21– 8	13– 7	−7
Orel Hershiser, LA	17	19– 3	14–14	−16
1985—AL				
Bret Saberhagen, KC	127	20– 6	7–12	−19
Ron Guidry, NY	88	*22– 6	9–12	−19
Bert Blyleven, Min	9	17–16	17–14	+2
Dan Quisenberry, KC	9	8w*37s	3w12s	−30
1986—NL				
Mike Scott, Hou	98	18–10	16–13	−5
Fern. Valenzuela, LA	88	*21–11	14–14	−10
Mike Krukow, SF	15	20– 9	5– 6	−12

1986—AL

Roger Clemens, Bos	140	*24– 4	*20– 9	−9
Teddy Higuera, Mil	42	20–11	18–10	−11
Mike Witt, Cal	35	18–10	16–14	−6

1987—NL

Steve Bedrosian, Phi	57	5w*40s	6w28s	−11
Rick Sutcliffe, Chi	55	*18–10	13–14	−9
Rick Reuschel, SF	54	13– 9	19–11	+4

1987—AL

Roger Clemens, Bos	124	*20– 9	18–12	−5
Jimmy Key, Tor	64	17– 8	12– 5	−2
Dave Stewart, Oak	32	*20–13	21–12	+2

1988—NL

Orel Hershiser, LA	120	*23– 8	15–15	−15
Danny Jackson, Cin	54	*23– 8	6–11	−20
David Cone, NY	42	20– 3	14– 8	−11

1988—AL

Frank Viola, Min	138	*24– 7	13–17	−21
Dennis Eckersley, Oak	52	4w*45s	4w33s	−12
Mark Gubicza, KC	26	20– 8	15–11	−8

1989—NL

Mark Davis, SD	107	4w*44s	2w6s	−40
Mike Scott, Hou	65	*20–10	9–13	−14
Greg Maddux, Chi	17	19–12	15–15	−7

1989—AL

Bret Saberhagen, KC	138	*23– 6	5– 9	−21
Dave Stewart, Oak	80	21– 9	22–11	−1
Mike Moore, Oak	10	19–11	13–15	−10

1990—NL

Doug Drabek, Pit	118	*22– 6	15–14	−15
Ramon Martinez, LA	70	20– 6	17–13	−10
Frank Viola, NY	19	20–12	13–15	−10

Year/Pitcher/Team	Votes	Year	Nxt/Yr	Diff
1990—AL				
Bob Welch, Oak	107	*27– 6	12–13	−22
Roger Clemens, Bos	77	21– 6	18–10	−7
Dave Stewart, Oak	43	22–11	11–11	−11
1991—NL				
Tom Glavine, Atl	110	*20–11	*20– 8	+3
Lee Smith, StL	60	6w*47s	4w*43s	−7
John Smiley, Pit	26	*20– 8	16– 9	−5
1991—AL				
Roger Clemens, Bos	119	18–10	18–11	−1
Scott Erickson, Min	56	*20– 8	13–12	−11
Jim Abbott, Cal	26	18–11	7–15	−15
1992—NL				
Greg Maddux, Chi	112	*20–11	?	?
Tom Glavine, Atl	78	*20– 8	?	?
Bob Tewksbury, StL	22	16– 5	?	?
1992—AL				
Dennis Eckersley, Oak	107	7w*51s	?	?
Jack McDowell, Chi	51	20–10	?	?
Roger Clemens, Bos	48	18–11	?	?

#—All 1981 records raised by ⅓
* Led league

⚾ 27 ⚾

Legitimizing the Fireman

It took a long time—about eighty years—but the poor pitiful relief pitcher finally gets his due these days. Firemen finally became legitimate in 1960. Now, they're indispensable.

A manager with a bad bullpen in June begins planning where he'll go fishing in August. By the dog days some other schnook will be trying to make chicken salad out of his chicken-feathered firemen. It's as simple as E-R-A. Winning begins with the last man on the mound. Any modern manager who can't find a solid closer will soon find *himself* no longer gainfully employed.

Search your memory. You can count the pennant winners with less-than-reliable relievers on the fingers of your Johnny Bench Junior Model X-15.

Oh, sure, if you go back far enough . . .

"Smile When You Call Me That, Pardner"

Once upon a time, back when men were men and baseballs had the bounce of feldspar, getting relieved in the late innings damaged a pitcher's reputation more than being caught in a hotel room with a ballet instructor. A pitcher who couldn't go nine innings might as well have worn a tutu to the mound. Sissy!

Shucks, Iron Man McGinnity used to pitch doubleheaders just to get warmed up. Jack Taylor went from 1901 to 1906 without letting any reliever set a toeplate on HIS mound. Cy Young threw 749 complete games.

Of course, ol' Iron Man threw a baseball that was dead as a Civil War soldier. And Jack stuck around long enough some days to lose games 9–8. And Cy started his career when the pitcher only had to throw 50 feet, for gosh sakes! Let's not go overboard with this stuff.

In 1904, nine out of ten games were finished by the pitcher who started. And, of the ten percent that saw a reliever, only about every tenth game saw a reliever pick up what we'd call a "save" today—which means the game was usually out of control before a manager went to his bullpen.

What a Good Little Starter Did on His Day Off

Up until about 1920, a team could do okay with a reliable rotation of starters. When things went absolutely kaflooey and a reliever absolutely HAD to be brought in to get the damned game over with, there was always some creaky veteran on his last legs or a fuzzy-cheeked kid just up from the Three-I League. But, if the issue was still in doubt, any peerless leader would call in one of his starters. Three Finger Brown, the Cubs' great of the Tinker-to-Evers-to-Etcetera era, was the N.L. save leader from 1908 to 1911 and never missed a start. Of course, Tri-Digit didn't KNOW he was the save leader and neither did anybody else, because that particular stat hadn't been thought up yet. But we'll get to that in a minute.

The most famous relief job of the pre-1920 years was that 1917 day in Boston when a hotheaded lefty starter walked the first batter and then berated the umpire so loudly and profanely that the man in blue booted him from the premises. Right-hander Ernie Shore, another regular starter, hustled in. The runner on first was cut down trying to steal second and Shore got the next twenty-six batters on his own. He's credited with a perfect game, but when you hear about it today, it's mostly in an anecdote about the lefty—fellow named Ruth—who soon gave up pitching for other pursuits.

"Hey! Who Changed the Ground Rules?"

Within a couple of years, young Ruth was hitting the ball to the nether regions and fans were pouring into the ballparks in record puddles to watch him. Since getting good people to pay good money at the box office is the ultimate aim of Organized Baseball, the Powers-That-Were reasoned more Ruths would equal more tickets sold. But, cloning being what it was back then, more Ruths just weren't available. So they did the next best thing. They injected the baseball with a healthy dose of rabbit serum, enabling lesser mortals to produce hits that were Ruthian.

And right then and there, the whole art of pitching changed. For whereas before a hurler could sling along nice and easy, only working up a sweat when a runner or two made threatening movements toward home plate, now any lackluster lob was liable to be larruped to Louisiana. And not only did every pitch have to be the real thing, but there were no more "down-the-middle" pitches. Pitchers began living on the edge—of the plate. And that meant many more throws per inning. A lot more! Scientists can work out the $E = mc^2$ of it, but the upshot was that a guy burned up more energy in six innings than he used to in nine innings and a night on the town.

The Senator from Texas

Pitchers and managers were slow to catch on to the new way of things. The first manager to tumble to the revolution was Bucky Harris. The Washington "Boy Manager's" starting staff featured thirty-six-year-old Walter Johnson and thirty-five-year-old George Mogridge. Like most middle-aged men, these two tended to commence puffing after a good workout—say, about the seventh inning. That was a problem, but also on Bucky's club was a well-built young Texan, Fred Marberry, who threw a fastball that was nigh unto unhittable for about three innings.

Eureka! said Bucky.

Under Harris, Fred Marberry became baseball's first great relief specialist. In 1924 and '25, he rode to the rescue 90 times and won 14. More important, he saved 30 games, which was considerably more than the margins by which the Senators eked out two straight pennants. In 1926, he was even better, though the rest of the Senators weren't. Fred won nine in relief and saved 22. His 31 relief points (wins plus saves) wouldn't be matched for twenty-one years.

Of course, when we say "save," we're talking about a stat that no one ever heard of in 1926. All they could say for certain back then was that the game got close, Marberry came in, and the Senators usually won. Rather imprecise. Like measuring the base paths by paces. It would take forty-three years before *saves* became official, but modern stat freaks have gone back and examined the records so that WE know things like Marberry saved 101 games over 14 seasons. Not bad, considering they made him a starter later on.

If You Liked the Movie, You'll Love the Game

But to get back to 1926, that's when the single most famous save took place. The Cardinals were nursing a 3–2 lead in the seventh inning of the seventh game of the World Series, when the Yankees loaded the bases on Redbird starter Pop Haines. In trooped ancient Grover Alexander, reportedly somewhat loaded himself, to strike out Tony Lazzeri and then nail down the Series with two more shutout innings.

Admittedly, nobody ever thought of Alexander as a relief pitcher in the career sense. He'd already started and won two games in that Series. So his save did nothing to advance the cause of bullpenners in general. *Regular* relievers still got the kind of respect that would make Rodney Dangerfield cringe. Nevertheless, Alexander's effort WAS famous. Eventually, they even built a movie around it, an honor more often accorded war heroics and guys who carry tablets down from mountains.

One year later the Yankees had a wonder in sinker-baller Wilcy Moore, a thirty-year-old rookie. Moore got 13 of his 19 wins in relief and saved 13 others. Sure, he was helped by pitching for the '27 Yankees, which wasn't your average baseball team. That crew was kind of an Inevitability for its pitchers. Hold a game close long enough and Gehrig, Ruth, Meusel, Lazzeri, or one of the other guys would poke one into the stands to win it. Still, the only important roster change from the '26 Yankees—the ones that couldn't get it done against the Cardinals—was Wilcy Moore.

Despite his fine season, Moore wasn't a headliner with the Bombers— the plaudits went to the hitters—and the next year he was regularly bombed by other American League teams.

Murphy's Law

The 1930s saw some good relief work, but the lot of the fireman was still to be regarded as a second-class citizen. The best-known incident involving a reliever was a loss—Mace Brown's 1938 gopher ball to Gabby Hartnett in the gloaming at Wrigley. Brown was a pretty fair fireman, but he never lived down "the pitch that cost the Pirates the pennant." Like he did it all himself!

The best reliever of the period was the Yankees' Johnny Murphy, whose curveball served him consistently on seven pennant winners between 1936 and 1943. Murphy was smarter than your average bear-down guy, and when manager Joe McCarthy told him to forget about starting and take up permanent residence in the bullpen, Johnny got it down in black and white that he'd be paid as though he were a starter. He was probably the only reliever before World War II to make any money doing it. His 107 saves say he deserved every cent.

Most relievers during the seasons between the wars were underpaid, but at least they worked fairly regularly. About half the games played saw relievers.

Mighty Casey Struck (Him) Out

Brooklyn's Hugh Casey also threw a curveball—though many said it was so wet it sloshed. He emerged as the Dodgers' stopper in 1941 against the Yankees, just in time to splash a third strike past Tommy Henrich in the World Series. Catcher Mickey Owen developed sudden hydrophobia and avoided the pitch. "Old Reliable" Henrich scampered reliably to first and the Yankees went on to score four runs and for all practical purposes wrap up the Series.

Casey came back after the war to do some good relief work for the Bums, and that made him mini-famous. In those days, you'll recall, Brooklyn was "America's Team," a love affair they broke off when they became "Los Angeles's Team"—as though money could buy happiness! Lots of money. Anyway, Casey won two and saved one in the '47 World Series, but it didn't get him bupkis 'cause in the same Series the Yankees had the first Superstar Fireman.

Paging Mr. Page

They called Joe Page "The Gay Reliever," but that didn't mean he minced in from the bullpen; it referred to his love of the Good Life. Fireman Joe left legends in New York high life that Mickey, Billy, and Whitey could only dream of later. His fastball made managers salivate but his fast lane made them growl. Bucky Harris (remember him?) became the Yankee skipper in 1947 and discovered Page marinating in the doghouse, still under the mistaken impression he was a starter. Bucky, sensing the ghost of Fred Marberry, re-apprised Joe of his destiny and set him to relieving. The Yanks rode Page's lefty fastball to a surprise pennant, while Fireman Joe tied Marberry's 31-relief-point record with 14 wins and 17 saves. In the World Series, Casey probably pitched a *poco* better than Page, but everybody remembered that Fireman Joe won Game Seven by stopping the Dodgers on one hit over the last five innings.

When Page was only so-so in '48, Harris was fired and the Yankees brought in an old-timer named Stengel, who the smart money said was only there for a year of comic relief. Instead, all the relief came from Page—back to being the blazing Fireman Joe. With 13 wins and 27 saves, he became the first man to register 40 relief points. And for the first time in the world's long history, folks began using "genius" and "Stengel" in the same sentence.

For an encore, Page saved the finale of the '49 Series, but it was his last hurrah. The next October, Casey didn't even call him in for a bow in the Yanks' four-game sweep of the Phillies' Whiz Kids.

Prove It!

By mid-century it was obvious to just about anybody who could tell a baseball from a bass fiddle that relief pitchers were pretty important to winning pennants. Just how important was hard to measure, though. You couldn't get too excited by a low ERA—the important runs he gave up were usually charged to the guy he relieved. Wins were an unreliable yardstick because firemen were used in different ways.

F'rincetance, what exactly did a high number of relief wins mean? Did the guy give up a few late runs and then vulture a win when his team rallied? That's true today, but back then, a top reliever might be called in as early as the fifth or sixth inning with his team trailing. Okay, but he also might be needed to get the last out in the ninth with his team one run up. Wasn't that worth something? Slowly, a few figure filberts were feeling their way toward identifying *saves*.

The Old Whiz

In 1950, the reliever of the year was Jim Konstanty of those Phillies. Anything but a "Whiz Kid" himself, he was a ripe thirty-three and had been pretty much a career minor leaguer until he added a palmball and slider to his very forgettable fast one. Everybody knew Jim was the biggest reason the formerly Phutile Phillies got to the World Series. The baseball writers were so sure of it they did something they've only done once since—named a reliever the league's Most Valuable Player. But when it came to justifying their choice for posterity, they had to say things like he had the league's second-best ERA, had relieved in nearly half the Phillies' games, and had 16 wins to show for it. Living in a more enlightened age, *we* can add the biggie—Jim saved 22 games. Now if you remember, Philadelphia won that pennant on the last day of the season, so had it not been for Konstanty Brooklyn would have had yet another chance to lose to the Yanks.

Konstanty stuck around for years, but he never hit those heights again.

All of which brings up a complaint you used to hear a lot in the 1950s. By then, relievers were getting good press, but, often as not, last year's stopper was this year's bust. Very few were the firemen who could string several good seasons together.

One theory held that many relievers relied on a trick pitch like a knuckler, palmball, forkball, or whatever and the batters simply caught on to its vagaries. That may have been true in a couple of cases, but it couldn't explain why some of the one-trick tossers would come back a year or so later and win again.

"Their arms just plumb wore out" didn't really address the problem. How come a fireman could quash blazes right through a World Series and then, after a winter of rest, be unable to get anybody out?

A theory that makes sense is that a reliever's arm builds up lesions during a long summer of rescue work. They heal over the winter, but the next spring, he has to get enough work to break them loose. Meanwhile, it takes him longer than the other pitchers to get up to speed and so he's knocked around during the exhibition season. Pretty soon his manager loses confidence in him and starts calling on others in the clinches. This further impedes headway on the old soupbone, to say nothing about what it does to the fireman's head.

One-year Wonders aren't as common as they used to be in the bullpen. Partly that's because of advances in kinesiatrics, and also smart managers have learned to be patient until their relief ace rounds into form.

Career Move

The 1950s saw the floodgates—well, anyhow, the bullpen gates—open. Firemen won no more MVPs in the period, but fans stopped spitting after they said "bullpen." No wonder! Starters finished their games only about a third of the time.

Some of the relief stars were short-term comets, like Brooklyn's Joe Black and the Yankees' Ryne Duren, the guy with pop-bottle glasses who terrified batters with his potentially lethal combination of poor sight and wildness. Pretty soon, all the hitters *knew* Ryne's shtick of throwing a warm-up fastball against the backstop was pure hokum, but they were never certain enough to dig in.

Some relievers, like Lindy McDaniel, Clem Labine, Turk Farrell, and Roy Face, were men for all seasons. Hoyt Wilhelm, the master of the knuckleball, came up in 1952 and stayed for twenty-one years, 123 relief wins, and 227 saves. Wilhelm and Rollie Fingers are the only relievers in the Hall of Fame so far, but what can you expect from the folks who gave us Morgan Bulkeley?

Speaking of obscure people, Larry Sherry of the Los Angeles Dodgers (and didn't that sound strange back then?) went almost unnoticed through the 1959 season—5–2 as a starter, two relief wins, and a mere three saves. Oh, he earned his keep, but nobody was building a shrine to his baseball card. Then, in the World Series, he came on like Godzilla—relieving four times and getting two wins and two saves. As everybody knows, two and two equals world championship.

In one way, the most spectacular year ever by a reliever was the one Roy Face faced in '59. Roy was a small man with unusually long fingers, allowing him to throw a wicked forkball, or, as everybody says today, "split-fingered fastball." His 18–1 in 1959, all in relief, gave him a percentage that would look okay in a fielding column. But it wasn't Roy's best season. He vultched a lot of those wins off Vernon Law, who might have won 20 if Roy had been a little sharper. In '60, Face saved 24, the Pirates won the pennant, and Law got the Cy Young.

By the end of the '50s—with firemen answering the bell in three out of every four games—the stigma of being a "career reliever" was almost gone. More and more, the boss of the bullpen wasn't a failed starter or a kid waiting for his first start. Instead, he was someone physically and psychologically capable of doing the job—and proud of it!

Legitimacy!

The most important news for relievers in 1960 was that, largely through the lobbying of Chicago writer Jerome Holtzman, *The Sporting News* began recording and publishing saves. Finally, for the first time since Cal McVey used to give Al Spalding an inning off, relief pitching was recognized by the baseball establishment as legitimate. *TSN* was the bible of baseball, and league statisticians got the Word slowly. Saves were made an official stat in 1969. Might as well, by then everybody who was anybody talked about saves as though they were real anyway. When we look for that moment in time when relief pitching stepped full grown out of the shadows into the glaring light of legitimacy, we should focus on 1960. The bible said so.

The save wasn't perfect—in fact, for a while they tinkered with it to make it easier or harder for a fireman to get one. In its present incarnation, a save is earned by a pitcher who finishes a win but isn't the winner himself if he (a) protects a lead of three runs or less for one inning or more, or (b) faces the potential tying run on base, at bat, or on deck, or (c) pitches effectively for three innings regardless of the team's lead.

Sometimes it gets a little silly. In a 1993 game, Rob Dibble came in for the Reds in the ninth inning with a three-run lead. He got a couple of outs but also loaded the bases on walks. Then he gave up a hit. Two runs scored. Dibble cut off the throw from the outfield and then threw wildly to third, allowing the runner to get up and race home. Suddenly the Reds left-fielder came out of nowhere, grabbed the ball, and fired it home for the final out. Dibble, who had not pitched well and had fielded worse, was credited with a save. So, it's probably only a matter of time before the "blown save" becomes official too.

Unofficial but widely used is the "Rolaids Formula," which credits a pitcher with two points for each win or save and deducts one for each loss. Corporate sponsorship makes relievers practically as legitimate as bowl games and golfers.

Today's bullpen ace probably never heard of Joe Page or Roy Face and he'd think Marberry was something that grows along country fences. He's too busy to worry about origins. After all, he directly affects the outcome of more than 40 games a year—more than any MVP hitters. The premier fireman is a high-wire walker who plays only the center ring. He's paid nearly as well as ex-Presidents who visit Japan for pitching only ninth innings, and then only when there's a "save opportunity." It's probably in his contract that way.

Call it progress.

⚾ 28 ⚾

Butterfingers!

Unless you happen to be a Dodgers fan, the Dodgers were a lot of fun to watch in 1992. Not at bat, of course—they scored less often than anyone else in the game. No, the Dodgers weren't offensive on the offensive, just dull. But when they went to the field, they made a barrel of monkeys look like a wake. Those guys could muff, drop, boot, dribble, throw away, and just plain mess up with a Picasso's creativity. Balls batted in their direction were treated as strange gods to be worshiped from afar, occasionally patted, but almost never completely embraced. Somehow, the '92 Dodgers made the '92 Phillies look like Ozzie Smiths and Brooks Robinsons. Watching Los Angeles in the field was like watching the last twenty minutes of a *Die Hard* movie. Great fun!

Along about the end of August I said to myself, "Self, this has GOT to be the worst-fielding team that has ever mishandled a routine grounder." So I looked up the all-time major league record just to see when the Dodgers would fumble past it. Yoicks! They weren't even close.

In fact, the '92 Dodgers couldn't even approach their CLUB record in faulty fielding. Back in 1905, the Dodgers team that used to be the only one in franchise history to finish last flubbed an astounding 408 times (in only 155 games). That's about as bad as it gets in this century. The 1901 Tigers had 410 miscues, but the American League was major in name only that year. The 1900 Giants erred 439 times, but many people don't count it a new century until '01.

211

The Bad Ol' Days

I knew going in that I couldn't depend on the 1800s. The nineteenth century was chock full of staggering feats of ineptitude, but it doesn't really count. Most of the players played without gloves, infields were as smooth as a back road in Georgia, and by the third inning the ball (which was kept in play through fire, flood, or locust attack) usually looked like it came out of Love Canal. Even good teams made over four hundred errors a season; five hundred wasn't uncommon. Our great-grandfathers weren't unusually sloppy; they just had too many strikes against them (to use a baseball metaphor).

Well, SOME of those olde teams deserved coal in their stockings. The 1890 Pittsburgh Gosh-Awfuls (I forget their real nickname, but they were possibly the worst team ever to play in a major league) made 607 errors. Even the Pitiful Pittsburghs had steadier hands than the 1883 Phillies, who somehow committed 639 errors in only 99 games! The Mount Holyoke School for the Blind had a better fielding average!

But once you get into the 1900s, you start paying attention to records.

Actually, last year's Dodgers (who eventually made 174 errors) would have been wonders in the first decade of this century. Remember Tinker, Evers, and Chance—so wondrous afield they were always bursting the Giants' gonfalon bubble? Well, in their prime—1906–1910—the T. E. and C. Cubs made 194, 211, 205, 244, and 230 errors. The kicker is that every one of those figures except the next-to-last was the league LOW for the season.

In the next decade, the Philadelphia Athletics had four men so remarkable they were called the "$100,000 Infield." (Ah, the good old days when six figures meant serious money!) You might think they were overpriced if I told you the A's of 1910–1914 errored 230, 225, 263, 212, and 213 times, but, again, those were league-leading marks. (Okay, can you name the four members of that infield? If you said Stuffy McInnis, Eddie Collins, Jack Barry, and Home Run Baker, you win an Old Rubering—or maybe a Rube Oldring. Now, for a tough question: what the heck's a "gonfalon"?)

By the 1920s, even bad teams were erroring under 300. The 1921 Red Sox led the A.L. in fewest goofs with 157, with everybody else above 200. In 1925, the Cubs led with 198, New York had 199, and the rest of the N.L. was in the two hundreds. The '27 Yankees made 195 errors—21 more than the '92 Dodgers.

Since World War II, two hundred errors in a season is rare. The last team to do it was the 1963 Mets with 210. You might be interested in knowing that this is exactly the same number of errors the fabled 1962 Mets made, but in '63 they played one more game, so there WAS some improvement.

Bigger, Faster . . . But Better?

As you can see by looking up the records (which I just did, thank you), there are lots fewer errors today than once upon a time. If things continue at their present pace, a team will go through the whole 2046 season without a miscue. If you're twelve years old, you probably assume that the fielders are much better now than they were when I was twelve years old.

Well, you're wrong.

Modernists never get tired of prating that players are bigger and faster now than ever before, but bigness is no advantage at all in fielding and speed can't replace getting a good jump on the ball. There are great fielders today, good ones, average ones, and poor ones. I doubt if the ratio of good to bad has changed, but the situation has changed a lot.

Some of the reasons we've already mentioned.

Like gloves. Look at the pictures of those early-century gloves and you'd think players had some dread dermatological disease afflicting their non-throwing hands. Catch a ball with one of those things? I wouldn't even slide into one!

But gloves got a lot more glove-like. Eventually Bill Doak came up with that thingamabob between the thumb and index finger. Pre-formed pockets appeared. Today, there's no problem in getting the ball to stick in a modern glove—real flies escape flypaper more easily. Catching a base-ball has become as iffy as fishing with hand grenades, but it DOES seem like at least once a game a fielder can't get the ball OUT of his glove.

Another improvement is the playing field. The artificial surfaces are like playing on a pool table and the un-artificial surfaces are almost as good. I'll grant you groundskeepers are better than ever.

Maybe my memory's faulty, but I seem to remember that every September there used to be lots of games played on grass fields the day after they'd been subjected to football games—in spikes!

A related ballpark factor is that there are fewer parks with unique nooks and crannies. The more stadiums are designed with a cookie cutter, the less an outfielder needs to know.

Since 1920, the baseballs get changed more often than a newborn. And various illegal pitches have been outlawed since 1920 (which hasn't gotten rid of them but has made them less common). In the early days, the balls used to come at fielders covered with powder, mud, spit, and who knows what. Now, you could eat off them. Most scientific studies agree that it's easier to catch a ball you can see and easier to throw one that doesn't come wrapped in stuff Macbeth's witches tossed in the pot.

One reason for fewer errors you don't hear much about is that there are fewer balls to field during a game. No kidding! Look at the chart on the next page. Column one (OUT/G) is the number of outs recorded by both teams in an average game; it's been basically the same throughout the century. Column two (H/G), the hits-per-game, hasn't changed much since the start of the century, but the one hit you can't make an error on, the home run (see column four—HR/G), has to be subtracted, and it's gone up. Likewise the strikeouts-per-game (SO/G), and very few errors are made on whiffs. The stolen bases-per-game (SB/G)—and a lot of errors happen on stolen base attempts—hasn't got back up to what it was in the first two decades. If you add all the error-possible situations and subtract the error-impossible situations, you find that today's average game has about seven fewer circumstances in which an error might happen than the average game eighty or ninety years ago.

Finally—and this is just an opinion—I think a basketful of today's hits would have been called errors when I was a kid. As I recall, "too hot to handle" once meant that an infielder was left lying dazed with his socks around his ankles. Now, it seems that a mishandled ball is assumed to have been "too hot" BECAUSE it wasn't handled.

I don't know exactly why scorekeepers have got so compassionate. It's one of those enduring mysteries like the Meaning of Life or the whereabouts of Jimmy Hoffa. My guess is that we pay more attention to streaks today and scorekeepers are a little faint of heart where a possible record is at stake. Or maybe it's just easier to pick on the pitcher by charging him with an earned run. He'll probably be gone by the next inning anyway.

Summing Up

Even if you don't buy the last argument, gloves, parks, rules, and style of play have all combined to reduce errors. It's even possible for a real curmudgeon to argue that while fielding averages have gone up, absolute skill has gone down.

	Out/G	H/G	SB/G	HR/G	SO/G	TOT	E/G
1902 NL	53.17	17.56	2.42	−0.17	−6.93	66.05	4.24
1912 NL	53.57	18.29	2.57	−0.47	−7.55	66.41	3.27
1922 NL	53.40	20.29	1.22	−0.85	−5.45	68.61	2.70
1932 NL	53.99	19.56	0.72	−1.05	−6.24	66.98	2.32
1942 NL	53.92	16.95	0.68	−0.87	−6.83	63.85	2.14
1952 NL	53.53	17.12	0.64	−1.47	−8.48	61.34	1.85
1962 NL	53.53	17.80	0.97	−1.78	−11.12	59.40	1.92
1972 NL	54.18	16.86	1.03	−1.46	−11.34	59.27	1.74
1982 NL	54.15	17.58	1.83	−1.34	−10.60	61.62	1.73
1992 NL	54.01	17.01	1.60	−1.30	−11.67	59.65	1.44

	Out/G	H/G	SB/G	HR/G	SO/G	TOT	E/G
1902 AL	52.80	18.90	2.38	−0.47	−4.96	68.65	4.26
1912 AL	52.98	17.49	2.92	−0.25	−8.32	64.82	3.98
1922 AL	53.70	19.48	1.10	−0.85	−5.77	67.66	2.49
1932 AL	53.68	19.54	0.88	−1.15	−6.55	66.40	2.44
1942 AL	53.69	17.65	0.88	−0.87	−6.78	64.57	2.30
1952 AL	54.00	17.21	0.60	−1.28	−8.30	62.23	1.82
1962 AL	53.83	17.39	0.69	−1.92	−10.55	59.44	1.69
1972 AL	53.78	15.88	0.92	−1.26	−10.95	58.37	1.65
1982 AL	53.75	18.12	1.23	−1.83	−9.62	61.65	1.56
1992 AL	53.78	17.64	1.50	−1.57	−10.75	60.60	1.46

Being of a nonconfrontational nature, I'm more inclined to take the middle ground—good fielders have abounded in all places and ages. Everywhere but in Los Angeles in 1992.

The All-Time Bad-Fielding Team (since 1901)

First Base: Jerry Freeman, Washington 1908 (154 games, 41 errors, .975 fielding average), is a strong candidate, but, in point of fact, there have been lots of worse fielders on first than butterfingered Jerry—big, hulking guys who had adequate hands but the range of a sequoia. Zeke Bonura led the league three times in fielding average because he was master of the "ole" wave. The real all-timer here has got to be Dr. Strangeglove, Dick Stuart, who led his league in errors at first base seven straight years and played on the same dime all seven. The two most legendary fielders in baseball history were both Pirates—Honus Wagner and Dick Stuart. Talk about Yin and Yang!

Second Base: Kid Gleason, Detroit 1901 (135 games, 64 errors, .925 fielding average). Poor Kid. First his arm goes bad and he has to switch from pitching. Later, he managed the Black Sox. And in between, THIS! The thing is, almost no one gets put at second base unless he has pretty good hands, so there aren't a lot of real butchers here. The real test isn't how they mess up grounders; it's how they make the DP pivot. Bobby Avila was one of my favorite players, but even I didn't think he was any more than middling in the midfield. And Rod Carew eventually got shifted to first base even though he wasn't a power hitter. That ought to tell us something. Nevertheless, we'll stick with the Kid strictly on his '01 errors. Incidentally, he got his total down to 42 the next year but then ballooned to 52 and 46 in '04 and '05.

Shortstop: Johnny Gochnaur, Cleveland 1903 (134 games, 98 errors, .869 fielding average—but he batted a robust .185). If there was a Bad Ballplayer Hall of Fame, Johnny G. would be a charter enshrinee. It wasn't enough that he was terrible at bat and worse in the field, the poor guy played next to Nap Lajoie so fans could make easy comparisons. This almost looks like some kind of publicity stunt. Speaking of tough times in Cleveland, remember Ray Boone, an ex-catcher, being put on the spot as the successor to Lou Boudreau? He made 33 errors in 1951 and it seemed (to at least one heartbroken young fan) like every one of them cost a ballgame. Two years later, he was at Detroit playing third base and he turned out to be pretty good at it.

Third Base: Butch Hobson, Boston Red Sox 1978 (133 games, 43 errors, .899 fielding average). As the last major leaguer to field under .900 in over 100 games, the present Red Sox skipper is an automatic. Personally, though, I have a soft spot for Bob Dillinger, the old St. Louis Brown. I only saw him play once, but the memory lingers. There used to be a tendency to bring a heavy-hitting outfielder in and stick him on third to keep his bat in the lineup. Bob Elliott, Bobby Thomson, and Sid Gordon come to mind. Frank Thomas was less successful at it. Bobby Bonilla tried it for a couple of years recently, but you don't see it all that often anymore. Probably the insurance people stopped covering the seats behind first base.

Outfield: Guy Zinn, New York Yankees 1912 (106 games, 20 errors, .899 fielding average). Another automatic on FA alone.

Outfield: Roy Johnson, Detroit 1929 (146 games, 31 errors, .928 fielding average). Actually, Johnson may have not been a true liability. He had a league-leading 25 assists the same year and matched that in 1931. On the other hand, he made 46 errors in 1932–33.

Outfield: Cy Seymour, Cincinnati 1903 (135 games, 36 errors, .902 fielding average). Seymour had the perfectly good excuse that he'd been a pitcher up until a couple of years earlier. Then they turned around and stuck him in center, the field where he'd get the most business. It wasn't really his fault. Still, messing up one out of every ten plays won't win any prizes.

Of course, it's only fair to point out that, like first basemen, some of the immovable objects who have stood guard in major league outfields have hurt their teams far more than these error-prone three. On the other hand, sometimes it seems like any big guy who can hit is automatically labeled "no field." When I was growing up, Pirate fans groused about Ralph Kiner's outfielding. He was slow, but I never saw him make a bad play. On reputation, Smead Jolley was something special, and Babe Herman is in all the anecdote books. They were both born before their time. They'd be All-Stars in today's American League.

My personal favorite outfielder was Kent Tekulve. One day, Pirate manager Chuck Tanner made one of those clever switches where he sent his ace fireman (Tekulve) to left field while he brought in another reliever to pitch to one batter. Sure enough, the batter lifted a high can of corn to left field and every Pirate heart stopped while Tekulve circled under it like a guy trying to calibrate the trajectory of pigeon droppings. If you could freeze that moment of fear and anticipation, Kent would be a cinch for this team. But then he had to go and ruin everything by catching the ball.

Catcher: Oscar Stanage, Detroit 1911 (141 games, 41 errors, .952 fielding average). This isn't as bad as it looks. Oscar also led the A.L. in putouts and assists that year. Red Dooin of the Phillies made 40 errors only two years earlier and he was considered a standout fielder. Judging a catcher's real defensive ability has very little to do with errors. Yankee fans said Yogi Berra was the worst catcher who ever came down the pike in 1947. Big deal! He made eight errors. Then, after a lot of hard work, he became the best in the business and still led the league in errors three times.

The Answer

You probably thought I was going to leave you hanging about that "gonfalon" thing. So what'd you guess it was? An Italian rowboat? A Danish cheese? A bowdlerized oath? A dead falon?

Wrong, wrong, wrong! A gonfalon, friends, is a banderole. Now, don't you feel much better?

⚾ 29 ⚾

A Song for May, 1993

All right, class. On the downbeat:

> *'Twas that dirty little coward*
> *Who shot Mr. Howard*
> *That's laid Jesse James in his grave.*

Very nicely done, class. Now let me explain why we're singing today.

I can't say whether Tony Perez is (or could have become) a top major league manager. My heart says a decent, intelligent man who'd paid his dues as a player and coach and who had the respect of his players could probably do the job, but you never know. Maybe Tony had some fatal flaw that would have prevented him from getting the most out of his team—like maybe he was too decent or too intelligent. Maybe by the end of the 1993 season, we'd have all decided that Tony didn't have the necessaries to match up against Leyland, Lasorda, Cox, Torre, Baker, and the other skippers in the National League. Maybe.

But I wish we'd had a chance to find out.

Instead, Cincinnati General Manager Jim Bowden pulled the plug on Perez two days ago, after only about a quarter of the season had passed. You can get a longer tryout on a toaster! Bowden was quick to shoulder the blame—the blame for hiring Tony in the first place. Presumably the contrite G.M. didn't feel this was a mistake that should in any way endanger HIS job. At any rate, he didn't offer to resign, throw himself on a burning pyre, leap into the nearest volcano, or any of the other penances suggested by irate Reds fans.

Tony Perez was a Reds hero when Bowden was still learning to fit his Lincoln Logs together and hide his G.I. Joe behind them. I'll bet that doll was better hidden than the cynicism lurking behind Bowden's mask when he announced the firing. Despite Jimbo's crocodile tears, it's plain as the hurt on Tony's face that the thirty-two-year-old G.M. did just what he'd planned to do all along at the earliest possible convenience. Of course, he needed a pretext; who remembers how the Nazis said Poland invaded *them*? When the Reds lost six of seven, Bowden moved quick as a jackal; Cincy might not have another decent bad stretch to give him an excuse. If you think it was just a coincidence that little Jimmy had managerial usetabes-and-wannabes Davey Johnson, Jack McKeon, and Bobby Valentine stashed on his staff, you probably don't see any connection between sunrise and the rooster crowing either.

When Bowden named Perez manager in the winter of '92, he genuflected all over himself about how Tony had "swept us off our feet" with "his analysis of the club, his philosophy on how to run the game, his thoughts on discipline." Bowden was so overwhelmed he gave Perez a one-year contract and even let him name one of his own coaches. Gee! A whole year! On paper. Tony might have interviewed like the second coming of Casey Stengel, but Bowden's bull about his brilliance was strictly for Bowden's benefit—to make it look like the decision to hire Tony was all his idea—when everyone who can tell a baseball from a bass fiddle knew he was under pressure to make a PR move after Marge Schott's attack of foot-in-mouth disease.

So, no sooner had Bowden hired a manager he didn't really want than he went out and got Johnson, McKeon, and Valentine, and they all began sharpening their knives. See, as far as Bowden was concerned, once Tony took the job, he'd exhausted his usefulness: here was a minority manager in Cincinnati. Hey, if you can't exploit minorities, what's the use of having them? Bowden can hire and fire as he pleases these days because Marge is on suspension for allegedly bad-mouthing minorities. She got dinged for being politically incorrect of speech; Bowden is too slick to get caught with his slurs showing. He only *acts* like the plantation overseer. Ironically, the real victim of Marge's suspension so far seems to be the Latino, Perez.

The Shadow used to whisper, "Who knows what evil lurks in the hearts of men?" This corner makes no claim to know much about evil lurkings, but from the sideline it looks very much like a general manager just out of swaddling clothes is in over his head and panicking. If he can steal a quick pennant—no matter the cost in PR or simple decency—before the boss gets back, his stock will boom high enough to cinch him a G.M. job with somebody. Hey, he's an '80s kind of guy!

Jim the Philosopher explains, "I think people will be able to separate things and say the decision was maybe not a good personal decision, but a good baseball decision." Look up *baseball decision* in your dictionary. If it says, "Alienate your fans by screwing one of your most popular, loyal, and respected employees," he's right.

But give Bowden credit. He's on the cutting edge. None of that old "sit-down-with-the-manager-and-discuss-the-options" stuff. No preamble of a phony vote of confidence. One telephone call and that was it. I can hear it now: "Collect call for the Reds' manager. Not you, Tony."

Perez is out. So is Coach Ron Oester, who proved himself a stand-up guy by resigning in protest. Good man to share a foxhole with, that Oester! Davey Johnson, who had the strongest team in the East for about six years and finished first twice, is in. He opened his new regime by saying the only way he'd get the players' respect "is by doing a lot of things right as a manager." Actually, he could have got a lot of respect from everyone by telling Bowden to take his job and shove it. Of course, that was as likely as Jaws passing on the Swimmer du Jour; in the last few years, Davey has campaigned for every managerial opening except the one at Denny's. He'd better get good results quick; McKeon and Valentine are still skulking in the wings. Meanwhile, Jim the Knife is hoping like hell the Reds' high-priced roster can turn it around so everyone will see what a genius he really is.

It's only May as I write this. The probabilities are the Reds will right themselves and climb to third whether the manager is Davey Johnson or Davey Crockett. Ron Dibble will be back shortly. Likewise Hal Morris. Surely John Smiley will remember he's not pitching batting practice. Of course, if Cincinnati were to come all the way back and win the division, Bowden will have the last laugh. The bet here is he won't be doing a whole lot of chuckling in October.

The Fastest Firings

Even before Perez had a chance to pull the knife out of his back, both ESPN and *USA TODAY* ran features on the fastest firings of managers in their first year. Including only those on the scene at a season's opening, they found four quicker cannings than Perez. We're all for an historical overview, but in this case we thought the rush-to-display ended up in giving a misleading picture. If you say, as *USA TODAY* did, that Tony's toppling was the fifth-fastest first-year firing, you give the impression that there have been four owners or G.M.'s in the past who were more grinch-like than Jim Bowden. And that's simply not true.

Let's look at the record:

Tony lasted 44 games into the 1993 season, and left with a 20–24 mark. The team was fifth.

According to *USA TODAY*, the Cubs fired Vedie Himsl after only 32 games in 1961 and replaced him with Harry Craft. What was forgotten was that 1961 was the year the Cubbies introduced their infamous "rotating coaches" system whereby eight different men were scheduled to handle the managerial reins, each for a previously determined period. Technically, Himsl wasn't a manager at all; he was a temporary head coach. Going in, G.M. John Holland said that no one would stay in charge for the full season, "no matter how well he's doing." If you were around then, you'll probably remember how everyone who wasn't Phil Wrigley or a Cubs coach giggled himself silly over the idea.

Actually, it had some merit (though not enough that anyone's tried it since). After a term in charge of the major league club, a coach would drop into the minor league system for a while so that instruction in the "Cub Way" of doing things could be maintained at all levels. The flaw in this thinking was that the "Cub Way" had been to finish out of the money for years.

So, when Himsl sat in the dugout in charge on opening day, he already knew when he would be replaced at the top and slip into a supporting role. When that time came after only 11 games, Himsl was not fired; he simply went on to his next stop. As a matter of fact, he came back for two more terms during the season for a *total* of 32 games and a 10–21 overall mark.

Others who took turns as king of Cub hill that summer were Harry Craft (7–9), El Tappe (42–53), and Lou Klein (6–7). The system was continued into the 1962 season before it was discarded as a brave experiment that presumably created more confusion than conquests. Himsl should not be listed as being fired earlier than Perez.

Hornsby Horns In

In 1928, Jack Slattery was out as Boston Braves headman after only thirty-one days. But, again, that's not the whole story.

Slattery had enjoyed a minor major league career and then gone on to better things, including a term as baseball coach at Tufts University. He was popular in Boston, and when the Braves needed a new manager for 1928, he received the backing of the Board of Directors. Judge Emil Fuchs, who did the day-to-day running of the club, wasn't enthralled with Slattery but didn't see anything better on the horizon. Wotthehell, Slats was hired.

But shortly thereafter, the Braves swung a deal that brought them Rogers Hornsby from the Giants. Rajah, still an adequate second baseman and the best right-handed hitter in captivity, was made available by New York because he wouldn't keep his big mouth shut about how much he deserved John McGraw's job as manager. He had won a pennant for the Cardinals in 1926, and don't you forget it! McGraw, who had ten pennants in his stack, weighed Hornsby's ego, ambition, and mouth against his bat and shipped him off to Boston.

Now Fuchs had a real, bona fide, major league manager playing second base and what's-his-name as a manager. Even before the season began, Hornsby was more than happy to explain to the press and the Judge all the things Slattery was doing wrong and how he, Hornsby, would have done them differently. His observations increased once the season opened. I forget how he advocated getting around the Braves' feeble hitting, shoddy defense, and laughable pitching, but he guaranteed he'd do wonders if given the chance.

Slattery was 11–20 when the team staggered back from a western road trip. He was so happy to see Boston again that he decided to stay there for the rest of the season. He sent his resignation to Judge Fuchs. The Judge only took time out to shout *Eureka* once before he accepted it. For what it's worth, the team did even worse under Hornsby (39–83) and the next year Rajah took his .387 batting average and .400 mouth to Chicago.

Again, for our purposes please note that Slattery wasn't fired faster than Perez. He wasn't fired at all; he quit.

Cy Exits

USA TODAY says Cy Young got the quickest heave-ho of any manager in this century when he went out after seven games as Red Sox skipper back in 1907. Once more they got it wrong.

That year, 1907, you'll recall was the first one in which the team that had been hiding out as the "Pilgrims" revealed itself as the "Red Sox." It was also the year that the team's manager, Chick Stahl, committed suicide during spring training. The two events were apparently unrelated.

Left with no one in the dugout to chew sunflower seeds and order a hit-and-run, owner John I. Taylor wired his aging ace pitcher Cy Young to take over. Old Young was forty and hoping for a comeback after an off year. "I . . . believe I do not have the ability to manage the team," Cy sighed to reporters. He agreed to manage the BoSox only until someone qualified could be found. In other words, he was an interim manager whose term just happened to coincide with the beginning of the season. The Red Sox heir apparent was apparently located seven games into the schedule when George Huff, the Athletic Director at the University of Illinois, was brought in. Young was allowed to return to pitching exclusively—hardly a firing as far as either he or owner Taylor were concerned. He won 20 games on the mound that year—17 more than he won as a manager.

Incidentally, although he didn't start the season with the club, Huff could be regarded as the quickest firing on record since he lasted only eight games and had not been hired with "interim" in mind. The reason for the quick trigger was that once Taylor and Huff met face-to-face, they discovered they couldn't stand each other. God only knows why Taylor hired Huff sight unseen in the first place. Officially, Taylor fired Huff, but it was as much mutual consent as anything else.

In a more recent instance, Buck Rodgers is listed by *USA TODAY* as having been fired by Milwaukee in 1980 after 47 games, just three more than Perez. Actually, Buck was a sort of long-term interim for George Bamberger, who'd had heart surgery over the winter. The team was 26–21 and in second place when Rodgers also took sick leave and was replaced by Bamberger. After 92 more games, Rodgers returned and stayed until 1982. Unless Jim Bowden steps out of a shower and pronounces it all a dream, you're not likely to see Tony Perez in a Reds uniform again for a while.

Aside from dozens of interims, there are some other quick midseason entrances and exits among managers, but they all seem to have been the products of hasty decisions arrived at after another manager was suddenly sacked or otherwise rendered unusable. Those aren't the same kind of thing as the Perez firing. Tony was chosen at calculated leisure, given the impression he was in charge from the start of spring training, and then axed as soon as the team failed to win the pennant in May.

The Nearest Thing

In the good ol' days, everybody liked to recite, "First in war, first in peace, and last in the American League" whenever the Washington Senators were brought up. In 1904, after finishing an awful 43–94 the year before, the Senators promoted manager Tom Loftus to team president (now, THERE's a switch!) and replaced him with a player-manager to save a salary. The lucky choice for double duty was regular catcher Malachi Kittredge. Seventeen games into the season, the Senators stood 1–16 and were in grave danger of becoming even greater laughingstocks than the real senators in D.C. When Malachi was ousted as skipper, no one complained—1–16 would get St. Francis fired at Assisi. Besides, Kittredge only relinquished the final say on strategy; he stayed on as the team catcher and hit .242, which was .002 better than Patsy Donovan, the poor patsy who succeeded him as manager. Apparently there were no hard feelings as far as Kittredge was concerned. How Donovan felt when the team lost 97 more games on his watch, I really can't say.

None of the four quicker "firings" or Rodgers' deal in 1980 resembles what happened to Perez. To get a perfect match for the Perez caper, we have to go outside baseball:

Over a hundred years ago, a man named Robert Ford called on another man who was using the name Mr. Howard but who was really Jesse James wearing a beard. Ford waited for Mr. Howard to climb on a chair to straighten a picture frame before he shot him in the back; Ford received a reward for doing that. Jim Bowden waited until the Reds went into a mini-spin before he did the same thing to Tony Perez. Let's hope he too gets his reward.

All right, class. Once more. And stay together on "shot Mr. Howard."

'Twas that dirty little coward
Who shot Mr. Howard . . .

⚾ 30 ⚾

Kill the Messenger!

Recently, on one of those ESPN programs where those-who-can't tell the world the skinny on those-who-can, a pride of sports reporters rendered their opinions on the low state of relations between athletes and the media. In that the renderers were all card-carrying media members and that none of them were athletes, it seemed likely a touch of bias might be present, but no one brought that up. Perhaps they were each too polite to suggest that the other fellows sitting at the table could let anything but pure reason color their views. But not surprisingly, all the Mensa candidates assembled agreed that today's athletes are much more difficult to deal with than those of yesteryear. Today's stars are often suspicious, resentful, uncooperative, and even surly. And—with the exception of one reporter who held out for tennis brats—the media reps listed baseball players as the worst.

One scribe related an incident. While in a team locker room recently, he approached a veteran ballplayer who was having a standout season. When the reporter indicated that the veteran was his *ballplayer du jour*, the player snapped, "Where have you been for the last ten years?"

"I should have asked him, 'Did he expect me to interview him the year he hit .223?' " cracked the reporter. That got a big laugh from his fellow writers.

Although this incident was offered as proof of the ballplayer's unco-operative attitude, the guy's question was never answered. Where *was* the reporter for the last ten years? Why hadn't he interviewed the player during one of his so-so seasons? Was the player any less interesting as a person then than now? And why should he suddenly grant access to his innermost thoughts to a reporter who ignored him for a decade? Why should the player open up to someone who viewed him not as a person but only as a story, the value of which is dependent on a batting average?

Times have changed.

Once, a long time ago, ballplayers and sports reporters existed if not in friendship at least with mutual trust. The reporters traveled with the teams on trains and they all got to know each other pretty well. Sometimes the reporters sat in on the players' card games. Sometimes they painted the town together.

At that time, the reporter's job was to report the game. For fans who couldn't be at the game itself, the next day's newspaper story was the only way to get the details. Any reporter who spent very long on the job soon learned a whole lot about baseball that he shared with his readers.

But there was a lot of other stuff they didn't share. In effect, they protected the players. If a player was a drunk or a chaser or didn't pay his bills, the reading public was not likely to learn about it on his local sports page. The reporter's blind eye stopped short of major crimes and scandals, but the lesser frailties of humankind were generally off-limits when discussing a ballplayer. Could he hit? Could he field? Those were the boundaries.

Even within those narrow limits, things could get prickly. Babe Herman, the great hitter-and-misser of the Dodgers' outfield in the 1920s, once waylaid a reporter in a hotel lobby and asked him to stop writing stories portraying him as a dunce. The reporter had been turning in humorous accounts of the Babe's encounters and near-encounters with fly balls, and Herman felt the constant harping on his defensive inadequacies reflected badly on his mental capacity.

"My family reads them things," quoth the Babe.

The writer allowed as how he might have been a bit harsh. He'd never really thought of Herman as an entity that might have feelings. He told Babe he'd go easier in the future.

"Thanks," said Herman, pulling a half-smoked cigar from his jacket pocket.

"Here's a match," fumbled the writer in a flood of good fellowship.

"Never mind," said Herman, as smoke billowed around his head. "It's still lit."

That's it, decided the writer. Anyone who walks around with a lit cigar in his pocket is fair game.

But in those days, even when a ballplayer was portrayed as a "character," he was a *lovable* character. Baseball, like every other profession, had its share of bottom-line jerks, but fans could only learn that by meeting them personally. The sports page harbored only nice guys.

Radio came on strong in the 1930s but it didn't change the situation much. The newspaper reporter's job was still primarily to rehash the game. The radio play-by-play guys, who were usually hired by the ballclub, thought of themselves as reporters and were not likely to delve deeply into a player's psyche or habits.

Following World War II, sports (as well as everything else) became fodder for the media explosion. Magazines, such as *Sport*, which debuted in 1946, and later *Sports Illustrated*, could not content themselves with stale retellings of games that had taken place months before the mags hit the newsstands. Instead, they probed deeper, telling their reader what his favorite third baseman was *really* like. The profiles, at first, were generally flattering, but occasionally a player was grilled on a part of his life he might rather not talk about.

And then television reared its intrusive head.

It's popular to blame television for all the shortcomings in our society, but that is like blaming a snake for having fangs. TV is neither good nor evil; it just *is*. Its nature is immediacy. And, because it not only tells the viewer the story but also shows him again and again in excruciating replay, it renders obsolete the long, discerning game descriptions that once filled newspaper columns. Today's game account in *The Daily Blah* need be nothing more than an introductory paragraph along with an intricately detailed box score. You don't need a reporter—just a CPA.

As television gained mastery, daily newspapers in major cities declined. Where once there may have been four or five papers, often only one or two survived. With their constant fight for readers, the papers' "most complete sports coverage" began to mean "most controversial sports coverage." The role of the baseball reporter changed from friendly describer of what happened on the field to judgmental snitch, looking for the story that hadn't already appeared on Channel Six. And, of course, after Watergate, everyone wanted to be the Woodward and Bernstein of baseball. Small suburban papers, many of them weeklies, also began beefing up their sports coverage, but in many cases they were staffed by young reporters just out of Journalism 102 who were not likely to know any constitutional amendments except the one that protected their right to blab.

Getting the story changed, too. Once upon a time the baseball reporter could pull a player aside, perhaps after dinner since all games were played in the daytime, and question him at leisure about a play in the third inning.

Now, a squadron of print and air media surround the player in the locker room right after the last out, shoving microphones and firing questions willy-nilly. Forget thoughtful analysis. The air guys want a juicy sound bite. The print guys have already written their stories and need only a quote or two to spice up their prose. And, because each reporter has his own agenda, one question seldom follows another in any logical pattern.

"How is it to try to hit Portnoy's curveball?"

"Was that your mother in the stands?"

"Do you think Mulligan should start you against lefties?"

"What's your favorite color?"

"What went through your mind when you threw wild to second in the sixth?"

The player, hot and sweaty and in the midst of an emotional high or low, must deal with each query, knowing that should he hesitate too long to think, the relentless television camera will make him look feeble-minded. If he's lucky, he'll be quoted correctly, but he can only pray his answer will be reported in context. When it's not, he edges toward paranoia. *They*, the media, are out to get him.

Some reporters have suggested that the huge salaries paid players have made them arrogant. Reporters tend to blame a lot of things on those salaries. Fortunately, no reporter has ever been jealous of a player's bank account. Never. Just ask them.

Ballplayers and reporters don't pal around anymore simply because the players don't trust the reporters. If a player hasn't been burned himself, he's seen it happen to a teammate. A dozen reporters can do their work fairly, honestly, and honorably for years; it only takes one shark to convince a player the waters aren't safe. And, although no one likes to come out looking stupid or venal in the first place, there's also a second place. A popular player can make more in ads and appearances than the ball club pays him. A reporter with a hatchet isn't just embarrassing the player; he's also taking caviar out of his babies' mouths.

Perhaps the worst thing a player can do is to make a joke. He may get away with it the first time. Even the second. But sooner or later, some reporter is going to quote even the most outrageous statement as gospel. "Hey, I was joking!" pipes the player. But the reporter always has the last word: "Apparently Clogschmidt finds humor in striking out with the bases loaded."

After a few bad sessions, even the most free-spirited become gun-shy. Steve Carlton finally stopped talking to reporters period. When you win 20 games every year, you can get away with that stuff.

Controversy is to a reporter as blood is to Dracula. An interesting situation developed when Barry Bonds left the Pittsburgh Pirates to become a rich man with the Giants. One reporter asked Bonds if he would miss having Andy Van Slyke playing alongside him in center field. The subtext seemed to be that Bonds, a Gold Glove left fielder, might be hard-pressed to maintain his reputation without Van Slyke's equally golden glove in the same outfield. Bonds, who has always been talented enough (and now is rich enough) to give less than a damn what anyone else thinks, shot back that Van Slyke might well miss having Bonds in left.

Aha, controversy! Reporters hustled to Van Slyke thirsting for a Bonds blast. But Andy plays the media game as well as anyone. He thoughtfully answered that, yes, with a rookie in left field this season, he would have to cover more ground until the youngster learned his way.

That might have ended it except for a less-than-flattering *Sports Illustrated* article that reported gleefully that when Bonds visited the Pirates' locker room on the Giants' first trip to Pittsburgh, Van Slyke didn't even bother to get up and walk across the room to greet him.

Oh boy! They really hate each other! It just so happened that a local TV channel filmed the titanic meeting. Van Slyke was sitting at a table playing cards when Bonds walked in. Andy didn't throw down his hand and rush over to embrace his former teammate, but he called out his hello along with others. Bonds walked over to Van Slyke and the two talked for several minutes. While there was no sound on the clip, it was clear from their smiles that the meeting was friendly. Of course, the clarifying clip aired only locally.

Most of the media tries to report fairly despite pressures from their editors to come up with something that will merit a headline. When a player ends up looking like a jerk, the odds favor his actually *being* a jerk. The world is not overflowing with saints, and just about all of us say or do stupid, selfish, and spiteful things that make us jerks from time to time. Fortunately, most of us don't see our faults revealed for all the world in the next day's newspaper. Nor should we.

For years we've heard about "the public's right to know." But wait. Where'd that right come from? Where is it written that the public has a right to know the intimate details of an athlete's life, mind, and personality? That's NOT in the Constitution. You can say athletes are public figures and if they can't stand the heat they should get out of the kitchen, but that doesn't wash. A politician or a film star sells his likability to the public. If his private persona is different from his public persona, maybe we should be told. After all, that's what we're paying for. But no one sets out to be a *likable* third baseman. We pay to watch him hit, run, and throw. If we feel better thinking he is also a nice person, fine. Finding out he's a closet Nazi will not add or subtract one point to his batting average. It certainly won't help us enjoy the game more. It will only sell newspapers.

◖ 31 ◖

Mr. Morgan and Baseball

Ted Morgan has written a book called *Wilderness at Dawn: The Settling of the North American Continent*. It's a fine book about how the continent got filled up with people, starting with the Asian immigrants we now call Native Americans and continuing right into the days when we actually began to pass for a country. If you've got a long train ride or a short stay in the hospital, you could do a lot worse than to take along *Wilderness at Dawn*. However, I would suggest you skip quickly over pages 14 and 15. That's where Mr. Morgan expounds a theory on baseball and football that might upset some fans and certainly isn't up to the rest of the book.

Mr. Morgan explains the difference between the "frontier," which was a place of "anarchy and insecurity," and the "hinterlands," which was an "ever-growing area that was no longer frontier" and that "had law and government, institutions and stability":

> Much of our national life can be defined according to frontier and hinterland attitudes. Take our two national pastimes, football and baseball. Football is a frontier game, because it has to do with the conquest of territory. The aim of the game is to invade the other team's land and settle there until you've crossed the goal line. As on the frontier, time of possession is everything.
>
> Football is a metaphor for land hunger, a ritualized reenactment of the westward movement, going back to colonial times.

Before we go too far with Mr. Morgan's metaphor, we should point out that it applies equally well to all sorts of games wherein one side moves into another's territory. We could say chess or even checkers also reenact the westward movement. As a matter of fact, the metaphor applies beautifully to soccer and rugby, the two English ancestors of American football. What is not clear is why the young English noblemen of the nineteenth century who first played those games should engage in any land-hunger metaphor when they already owned all the land worth having.

Look at the names of some of the teams in the NFL, the Patriots, the Redskins, the Cowboys, the Broncos, the Forty-Niners, the Chiefs, the Raiders, the Buffalo Bills, and the Oilers, all names connected with different stages of the frontier epic.

Well, yes and no. Patriots, Cowboys, Broncos, Forty-Niners, and Raiders were chosen because they had some connection with the histories of the cities where the teams were located, and, except for New England, the western frontier was part of those histories. "Buffalo Bills" is a pun hung over from an earlier Buffalo team. "Chief" just happened to be the nickname of the Kansas City mayor who negotiated the migration of a team called the "Texans" from Dallas.

The Washington team was founded in Boston in 1932 and played its first games in Braves Field, home of the National League baseball team. Naturally, the football team was called the "Braves" too. In 1933, they contracted to play in Fenway Park, home of the American League Red Sox. The Braves name was out, but the footballers still had a lot of equipment painted up to look Indian-ish, so they changed their name to "Redskins" as sort of a compromise between Braves and Red Sox. The name stayed when the team moved to Washington in 1937.

The point is it's not a good idea to draw too many inferences from the name of a sports team. You can look all over California for the lakes of the Los Angeles Lakers; you'll find them back in Minnesota where the team began.

Look at the way a first down is measured. Officials bring out the chains, which are a vestigial replica of the surveyors' chains and a reminder of the men who marked off the wilderness, dividing it into ranges and townships and sections.

Funny. I always figured they used chains to measure because they worked better than anything else. Like ropes stretch, solid bars get broken or bent and are awkward, and radar is a bit expensive. Do you suppose the football rulemakers actually sat around and said, "Look here, old man, we must do our measuring with a vestigial replica"?

On their hundred-yard-long turf-covered universe, football players act out the conquest of the frontier. And just as they fought the taking of the land on the real frontier, Native Americans today protest the appropriation of their past on the football field, in the use of team names like Redskins and Chiefs, and in the hoopla of fans painting their faces, wearing chicken-feather headdresses, and waving foam-rubber tomahawks. In the game itself there are emulations of Indian customs, such as the huddle, which is a stylized Indian powwow, and the gauntlet that each player must run upon entering the stadium.

Now just a cotton-pickin' minute, Mr. Morgan. Don't tell me the huddle (i.e., a group gets together to discuss what to do next) is an emulation of an Indian powwow any more than it's an imitation of what groups have been doing ever since there were groups. They gather around! How about: "The huddle is an emulation of the Last Supper"? It makes as much sense and the numbers are close to right.

And, while we're stopped, it appears to us that the team most criticized for foam-rubber tomahawks and fake Indian chops is the Atlanta Braves, a baseball team. The Redskins, who could solve their problem by keeping the name and changing their logo to a bright red apple, are a distant second in receiving criticism, with another baseball team—the one in Cleveland—coming in third.

Another difficulty I have with this Native American thing is that no one is absolutely certain whether the majority of American Indians are insulted or pleased. The protesters get the publicity, but do they truly represent the common will? Some argue that if ANYONE is upset, a practice should be changed. That's nonsense. You can always find someone who's upset with anything. If we were ruled by that, we'd all end up hiding in a closet afraid to speak. A reasonable test is whether a particular practice, say, calling your team the "Indians," does any real harm. Despite a lot of protesting, that hasn't yet been demonstrated. In fact, we can argue that employing such team names as Indians, Braves, and Redskins serves a good purpose. The perhaps frivolous protests against them buy space in the media and cause us to look for once to the very real problems of Native Americans in this country. If the names went away,

Native Americans would be left with nothing to protest except the true and often tragic circumstances of their existence. Truth seldom buys a sound bite on the network news. The best answer seems to be to keep the names. And keep protesting.

[In football] skill gets taken for granted, while there's a degree of physical punishment reminiscent of life in the wilderness.

We have to remember here that Mr. Morgan is talking about the way it used to be—the good old days—when you were actually safer on a city street than in the middle of a buffalo stampede. Once upon a time, it was considered foolhardy to cross the American West without a gun; today, a lot of Americans take the safety off their nine-millimeters before they walk to the mailbox.

There's no unnecessary roughness penalty in baseball, a game with a refined hinterland sensibility, which was gentrified from the start, when A. G. Spalding organized the Knickerbocker Base Ball Club in 1845 in Manhattan for "men of high taste."

Here Mr. Morgan has obviously confused Spalding with Alexander Cartwright. The organization of the Knickerbockers was one of the few nineteenth-century baseball events that Spalding didn't horn in on, mainly because he wasn't born until 1850. Personally, I have no trouble forgiving Mr. Morgan for getting Cartwright wrong. Later on in his book, he's able to keep DeSoto and Coronado straight, which was more than I ever could.

And he DOES make a good point when he says baseball was "gentrified" by the Knicks, who we know considered themselves to be on a more refined social plane than the working class. On the other hand, American football began among the pampered students at Princeton and Rutgers and then spread to Harvard and Yale. Very few dollar-a-day ditch diggers on those campuses!

Baseball teams seem to be named by bird-watchers (the Orioles, the Blue Jays, the Cardinals), zookeepers (the Cubs, the Tigers) and believers in the Supernatural (the Angels).

Not the name thing again! What about the Indians, Rangers, Pirates, Braves, and Rockies? And why are the Detroit Lions on the frontier while the Detroit Tigers are stuck in a zoo? And are the Phoenix football Cardinals a killer-bird mutation of the St. Louis baseball Cardinals? Mr. Morgan then makes his final plea:

> In baseball, there's no fighting over territory, since the convention has been established that the teams will take turns occupying the same field. In baseball, you play out an inning no matter how long it takes, and there's no time anxiety, but in football you're running against the clock, it's a game of seconds, just as life and death on the frontier were determined in seconds. In baseball, there's always a team sitting in the dugout, but in football, there are always two full teams on the field, man on man, and until the fifties, the same players played both offense and defense. Unlike baseball, in which games are called on account of rain, football is still mostly played in frontier weather conditions of rain, snow, and ice. Baseball players might work up a sweat running bases, but that's pretty much the extent of their discomfort, because there's comparatively little physical contact. Baseball is a game of the civilized hinterland, while football harks back to the epic qualities of the frontier, which continue to live in the American psyche.

Despite Mr. Morgan's words, I think more footballers will still try to win one for the Gipper rather than for Kit Carson. Taken as a whole, all he's really saying is that a game that depends on force and confrontation (i.e., sumo wrestling, tractor pulls, boxing, tug-of-war) hearkens back to the frontier, whereas any game that relies more on physical dexterity and skill (i.e., tennis, gymnastics, basketball, synchronized swimming) is of the civilized city. He's equating muscles with the frontier and brains with the hinterlands.

But isn't he missing some obvious baseball-frontier connections here?

The eternal duel between pitcher and batter is a vestigial reminder of Wyatt Earp versus the Clampetts at the O.K. Corral. Running the bases is a symbolic reenactment of the rounds of the Pony Express. The pickoff play is a modern version of the bushwhacking of Belle Starr. The stolen base is a legal way to commemorate the actions of the Hole-in-the-Wall Gang.

The outfield fences stand for the posts that once protected Fort Apache. The bases where runners are "safe" are made of stuff similar to what once covered Conestoga wagons. A base hit ventures into the outfield just as scouts once ventured into the outlands. When the bases are loaded, does not the modern pitcher find himself in a predicament similar to that once experienced by the late and lamented General Custer? Can't we see in a runner speeding across the plate a remnant of that glorious moment when the Wells Fargo stage arrived?

Is it only a coincidence that a pitcher's speed—his fast draw, if you will—is measured by a radar *gun*? And when the Dodgers left Brooklyn for California they surely saw themselves as participating in a new Gold Rush.

Enough! Mr. Morgan wrote a swell book. He knows more than enough about William Bradford and Samuel de Champlain to entertain and edify for nearly five hundred pages. But his thoughts on baseball (and football) can be taken with some salt. Like a carload.